EAMONN ASHE

31 YEARS OF HELL!

1914–1945

**After The Great War, They Said It Couldn't
Happen Again. It Did!**

Published by FlasheForward Communications

Publisher: FlasheForward Communications, Roschoill, Drogheda, Co. Louth.

Printer: SprintPrint, Unit K9, Greenogue Business Park, Rathcoole, Co. Dublin.

Biography of Author

The author, Eamonn Ashe, spent the first twenty-two years of his life growing up in Salthill, Galway. He received his secondary education from the Jesuits at St. Ignatius College, Galway, (popularly known as 'the Jes') before going on to graduate from the National University of Ireland Galway (NUIG) as a Civil Engineer. His professional career included spells in local authorities, in Roadstone and in Tobin Consulting Engineers. For more than thirty years, he ran his own companies specialising in the design and construction of swimming pools and synthetic sports surfaces (Astro-Turf pitches, Tartan athletic tracks and tennis courts).

Eamonn Ashe has been gripped by the World Wars for many years, sparked by the loss of his grandfather in World War I. An avid reader, he has studied dozens of books about the wars and the interwar years. He has deepened his insight through documentaries and visits to war sites, including:

- Battlefields at the Somme, Messines and Passchendaele
- War museums in Ypres and Albert
- Sites of the Normandy landings
- Allied war cemeteries at Tyne Cot (Passchendaele) and Normandy
- Checkpoint Charlie
- Brandenburg Gate
- Soviet War Memorial (Tiergarten)
- Battle of Berlin sites
- Seelow Heights museum
- Wannsee Conference building
- Cape Helles, Anzac Cove and Suvla Bay in Gallipoli
- Atatürk monument
- Francis Ledwidge's grave

31 Years of Hell! is Eamonn's first book.

To my mother, Phyllis Ashe, whose father and whose history inspired me to write this book.

Publisher: FlasheForward Communications,
Roschoill, Drogheda, Co. Louth.
communications@flasheforward.ie
www.flasheforward.ie

Paintings of book cover images: Olive Eustace

Book cover design: Caoimhe Mulroy, Once Upon Design
www.onceupondesign.ie

Cartographer: Dr Siubhán Comer, National University of Ireland Galway

ISBN 978-0-9956542-0-4

First published in 2016

Printed and bound by SprintPrint
Unit K9, Greenogue Business Park, Rathcoole, Co. Dublin.
www.sprintprint.ie

Contents

Illustrations

Jesse Owens at the start of a record-breaking 200-metre race during the Olympic Games in Berlin, 1936. Photographer unknown. Public domain image, Wikimedia Commons.   — Page 132

Polish revolutionary Józef Piłsudski, Chief of State 1918–22, Minister for Defence 1926–35. US Library of Congress, George Grantham Bain Collection, Image Ref ggbain 31084.   — Page 161

Adolf Hitler and Benito Mussolini in Munich, Germany, ca. June 1940. Series: Eva Braun's Photo Albums, ca. 1913–ca. 1944. US National Archives (540151)/Wikimedia Commons.   — Page 189

British troops line up on the beach at Dunkirk to await evacuation, 1940. © IWM (NYP 68075).   — Page 190

Londoners sleep on the platform and on the train tracks at Aldwych Underground station during heavy all night Nazi bombing raids during the Blitz, 8 October 1940. PA Archive/PA Images (3496546).
                    — Page 190

Near Algiers, Operation Torch troops hit the beaches behind a large American flag (left), 8 November 1942. US National Archives (195516)/Wikimedia Commons.   — Page 202

SS Chief Heinrich Himmler visiting a Prisoner of War camp during World War II. Public Domain image, Wikimedia Commons.
                    — Page 214

Japanese attack on Pearl Harbor, Hawaii, 7 December 1941. US National Archives (197288)/Wikimedia Commons.   — Page 222

General Bernard L. Montgomery watches his tanks move up, North Africa, 1942. US National Archives (535939).   — Page 231

Torpedoed Japanese destroyer *Yamakaze* sinking on 25 June 1942. US National Archives (520769)/Wikimedia Commons.   — Page 240

Japanese aircraft carrier *Hiryu* manoeuvring during a high-level bombing attack by USAAF B-17 bombers during the Battle of Midway, 4 June 1942. US Air Force photograph (3725 AC).
                    — Page 246

Suppression of Warsaw Ghetto Uprising 1943. US National Archives (540124)/Wikimedia Commons.   — Page 258

Crash landing of F6F on flight deck of USS *Enterprise*. US National Archives (520642)/Wikimedia Commons.   — Page 266

Maps

Acknowledgements

The writing of this book could not have been achieved without the help of various people.

Back in 2012, I had the pleasure of the company of Fr. Fergus O'Donoghue on one of my trips to the various battle sites and war cemeteries. Fr. Fergus is a Jesuit priest, a retired history teacher and as such has a huge interest in the two world wars. He is also a former editor of *Studies* magazine. He offered to proofread World War I for me, the first draft of which I had just completed. I was very happy for him to do so. I took on board his feedback and suggestions, and the book is the better for his input. I wish to thank him sincerely.

I also wish to thank the various proofreaders: my daughter Clodagh, my neighbour and friend Owen Meegan, and my brother-in-law Brian O'Connor. Brian is a retired Army Colonel with an excellent knowledge of both world wars. The proofreading of all three was invaluable.

A special thanks to cartographer Dr. Siubhán Comer from NUIG. Siubhán produced a first-class set of maps, which are a key element of the book. Regardless of the many changes I requested, she was always co-operative, good humoured and a pleasure to work with.

I am truly grateful to artist Olive Eustace for her excellent artwork on the book cover and to Caoimhe Mulroy of Once Upon Design for her superb book cover design. Both creative contributions far exceeded my expectations and enhance the book greatly!

I truly appreciate the valuable advice about publishing from PJ Cunningham of Ballpoint Press; Lilian Chambers and Rachael Kilgallon of Carysfort Press; Des Kenny, Tom Kenny and Karen Golden of Kennys Bookstore in Galway; Kitty Harrison; and Hugh Stancliffe.

Sincere thanks to Gerry Kelly of SprintPrint for his personal attention, for being so accommodating, and for his very swift printing service.

On a personal front, I received immense encouragement from relations and friends throughout the book-writing process. A special thanks to my wife Joan for whom history is not a strong interest, but who recorded and referred me to many television programmes on the wars, which she felt might be of interest to me. She also showed exceptional patience and tolerance during the six years it took to write the book.

Finally, this book would not have seen the light of day were it not for the dedication, patience and professionalism of my daughter Fiona, the Editor-in-Chief of the project. There were occasions when she had to prioritise this book over her own work — FlasheForward Films and FlasheForward Communications — and the fruits of her labour have made the book what it is today. I will be forever grateful!

Preface

My grandfather, Joseph Phillips, a Company Sergeant Major in the Connaught Rangers, died on the fields of France on 21 March, 1918 during Germany's Spring Offensive towards the end of World War I. He is buried at Ste. Emilie Cemetery, Villers-Faucon, close to St. Quentin.

I first visited his grave in the company of my mother (his daughter) and my sister in 1991. It was my mother's first and only time to visit her father's grave. The visit was not as emotional as I expected it to be, as my mother explained later: *"I never knew him — I was only 3 years of age when he died, and he was away fighting in the war for most of those three years."* I would describe my mother as a 'war orphan'. I wondered then and I still wonder: how many war orphans were there? Based on the horrific death toll for the two wars — ten million in World War I and fifty million in World War II — the number of war orphans must indeed be huge!

The visit to St. Emilie along with subsequent visits to the battlefields and war graves of both World War I and World War II, along with a visit to historical Berlin, intensified my interest in the wars, so when I retired I decided to write this book.

On the following pages is a letter from a comrade soldier to Joseph Phillips' wife (my grandmother) informing her of her husband's death.

25th July 1918

Dear Mrs. Phillips,

I beg to take the Leave of writing you a few words on the man named here enclosed. He was Company Sergent Major of my Coy and I am very sorry to announce his death in action. He was killed by a German bullet in front of me on the 21st March and I am proud that I can call him my late C.S.M. He was a brave and Gallant soldier and he laid down his Life in Leading us to a counter attack. He was liked by all in the Battalion. God rest his soul and may God help you to bear your burden.

I remain yours Truly J. Hughes

I am but a humble Irish soldier myself and I cannot find words to express my feelings towards you.

from a Conn. Ranger

My mother died in 2010 at the age of 95 and I have dedicated this book to her and to her father.

Ramann Asle

25th July 1918

Dear Mrs. Phillips,

I beg to take the leave of writing you a few words on the man named here enclosed. He was Company Sergeant Major of my boy. and I am very sorry to announce his death in action. He was killed by a German bullet in front of me on the 21st March and I am proud that I can call him my late C.S.M. He was a brave and gallant soldier and he laid down his life in leading us to a counter attack. He was liked by all in the Battalion. God rest his soul and may God help you to bear your burden

16745 S. Pte J. Hugh.
C.P. Hut G. Lines
No 5 Coy. 2nd Batt.
M.G.C.
Belton Park
Grantham.

I remain yours
Truly J. Hughes.

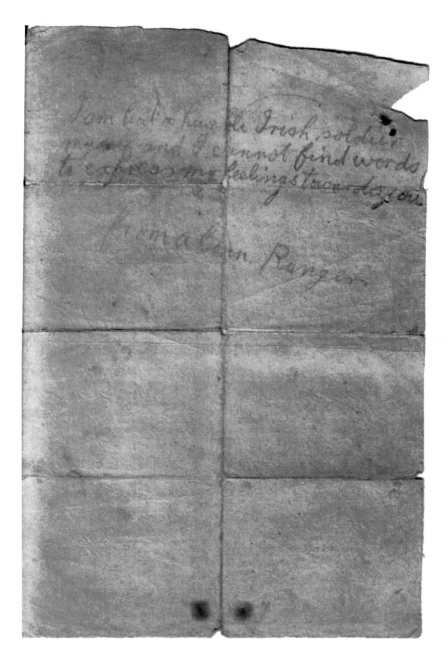

Introduction

As you will see from the preface, my interest initially was in World War I and was a personal interest — my grandfather died during the German Spring Offensive near the end of the Great War. The reader will see from the bibliography that my research was lengthy and varied, but the task I set myself quickly became a labour of love.

31 Years of Hell! is divided into three parts:

      Part 1 — World War I (1914–1918)
      Part 2 — Interwar Years (1919 –1938)
      Part 3 — World War II (1939–1945)

As I dug deeply into researching the world wars, I developed a huge interest in the interwar years, and I still think about the devastating impact on the world of those two ruthless dictators Hitler and Stalin reaching the height of their power at the same time.

Casualty figures in the book include the dead, seriously injured and missing in action. Exact figures are difficult to confirm for a variety of reasons, including doubts about the accuracy of figures provided by some countries. In the book, I have cross-checked the figures with several sources and included those which are in line with most experts' estimates.

The casualty figures in the two world wars are virtually beyond our comprehension. Just imagine every man, woman and child in Great Britain (population sixty million) being wiped out and you get some idea of the scale of the biggest disaster ever to befall this world.

This book is a concise history of the two world wars and the interwar years. The subject matter, while dark, is presented as a captivating, flowing narrative. The timelines and maps make the complex wartime situations easier to comprehend. The book is illustrated with photographs which evoke the emotions of the traumatic situations of war.

I hope you find it a compelling read!

Part One — World War I

(1914–1918)

CHAPTER 1

Build-Up To World War I

EMPIRES

At the beginning of the twentieth century, two empires — the Austro-Hungarian Empire and the Ottoman Empire — were coming to an end while the German Empire was newly-born, having been formed in 1871 after the Franco-Prussian War.

Austro-Hungarian Empire
The Austrian Empire (previously known as the Habsburg Empire or the Habsburg monarchy) was one of the powerhouses of Europe in the first half of the eighteenth century. However, by the middle of the century, the empire had lost much of her power. Within her boundaries lived numerous ethnicities and religions including Austrian Germans, the Magyars of Hungary, Poles, Czechs, Romanians, Serbs, Croats and others. Geographical boundaries were the only thing that kept these groups together and even then only for a limited period.

Things were brought to a head by Austria's crushing military defeats at the hands of the French and Piedmont (Italian) forces in 1859 and by the Prussians in the Seven Weeks' War in 1866.

Austria, meanwhile, was facing the dual threat of a rapidly-industrialising German state and a unified Italy; and it had little option but to court Hungary as a new political partner.

The two countries, Austria and Hungary, came to a compromise agreement in 1867 and the Austro-Hungarian Empire was born. It was described as a Dual Monarchy ruled by the Habsburg dynasty. Although this empire lasted until the end of World War I, it was weak from the outset with many of the minority groups such as the Croats and the Serbs seeking independence in their own right.

Ottoman Empire
The Islamic Ottoman Empire survived from 1299 to 1923. With Constantinople (Istanbul) as her capital, the empire was at the centre of interactions between the western and eastern worlds for six centuries. During the 15th and 16th centuries, the empire entered a long period of conquest and expansion, extending her borders deep into Asia and North Africa.

At the height of her power, the empire stretched over three continents, controlling much of south-eastern Europe, western Asia and North

Africa; and including almost all of the areas around the Mediterranean Sea and the Black Sea. At this time, the empire had a population of thirty million people. During her expansion, the empire had, of necessity, built herself up both militarily and on the high seas.

The empire remained a major expansionist power until the Battle of Vienna in 1683, which marked the end of Ottoman expansion into Europe. In the Battle of Vienna, the Ottoman forces (which had attacked Vienna) were swept aside by the combined allied forces of the Habsburgs, Germany and Poland. From this moment on, the Ottoman Empire began to shrink, with many constituent countries demanding independence.

At the height of the Ottoman Empire's power, Serbia, Montenegro, Bulgaria, Bosnia, Cyprus, Egypt, Sudan, Algeria, Tunisia and Libya were all part of it. However, the empire continued to wane down through the centuries: the Ottoman Empire which ruled vast territories during the 15th and 16th centuries entered World War I in 1914 as a significantly depleted empire, consisting only of Turkey, Mesopotamia, Syria and the west coast of Saudi Arabia.

It was at a low ebb in most respects, but it was still a formidable fighting force, as the Allies discovered to their cost at Gallipoli in 1915.

The Ottoman Empire came to an end as a regime under an imperial monarchy on 1 November 1922. It was succeeded by the Republic of Turkey, which was officially proclaimed on 29 October 1923.

The German Empire
When Otto von Bismarck (the 'Iron Chancellor') was appointed Prime Minister and Foreign Minister of Prussia by Kaiser Wilhelm I in 1862, his big ambition was the creation of a German Empire. His first step was to oust Austria (German-speaking at that time) from her influential position over many of the small German states. He achieved this by engineering war with Austria in 1866 over a territorial dispute. This Seven Weeks' War resulted in a humiliating defeat for Austria by an extremely efficient Prussian army. The removal of Austria's influence from many of the German states enabled Bismarck to unite the northern German states under the Prussian banner.

Bismarck then set about achieving the same success in the south. He managed this by goading France (he suggested that Kaiser Wilhelm I had insulted the French envoy) into declaring war on Prussia (the Franco-Prussian War) on 19 July 1870. However, once again the mighty Prussian army showed its superiority. To rub salt into the French wounds, the Prussian army laid siege to Paris between September 1870 and January 1871, starving the city into surrender.

The consequences of the war were far-reaching. Aside from the territorial gains, France ceded both of the coal-rich provinces of Alsace and Lorraine to Prussia and was forced to pay penal reparations for starting the war. The southern German states agreed to an alliance with their northern counterparts, resulting in the creation of Bismarck's cherished German Empire in 1871.

ALLIANCES

Bismarck's creation of a unified Germany was of direct relevance to the outbreak of war some forty-three years later, since it resulted in the assembly of the key alliances that later came into play in World War I.

Germany was well aware that France was intent on revenge at the earliest opportunity: the loss of Alsace and Lorraine would prove to be a lasting sore. Bismarck was aware that Germany needed an ally or two. His options were alliances with Russia or the newly-created Austria-Hungary or both. Bismarck began by negotiating the Three Emperors' League in 1873, which committed Germany, Austria-Hungary and Russia to each other's aid in time of war. This alliance only lasted until Russia's withdrawal five years later, leaving Bismarck in a new Dual Alliance with Austria-Hungary. This alliance, unlike others, endured into World War I.

Italian Alliances
Two years after Germany and Austria-Hungary concluded their dual agreement, Italy was brought into the fold with the signing of the Triple Alliance in 1881. One of the chief aims of the Alliance was to prevent Italy from declaring war on Austria-Hungary, with whom the Italians were in dispute over territory. In reality the Triple Alliance was meaningless for Italy, who subsequently negotiated a secret treaty with France, under which Italy would remain neutral should Germany attack France, which is exactly what happened. A year later, in 1915, Italy entered World War I not as an ally of her Alliance partners but as an ally of Britain, France and Russia.

Franco-Russian Agreement
A French Russian agreement — the Franco-Russian Military Convention — was signed in 1892 aimed specifically at counteracting the potential threat posed by the Triple Alliance of Germany, Austria-Hungary and Italy.

Britain
While all of this was happening, Britain chose to stay out of continental European politics in the 1870s by declaring a policy of 'splendid isolation' (a spin-off from Britain's imperial century 1815–

1914). After all, none of her extensive territories or colonies was under threat. However, Britain did get a wake-up call when she became aware that Bismarck's successor Kaiser Wilhelm II was determined to establish Germany as a great colonial power in the Pacific and, most notably, in Africa. The Kaiser embarked upon a massive shipbuilding exercise intended to produce a naval fleet the equal of Britain's — at that time the best in the world.

Britain's response (with Churchill in control at the Admiralty) was to commission a build-up in her own naval strength (including the development of the Dreadnought battleship) and by the time war was declared in 1914 Germany had built a fleet of twenty-nine battleships, while Britain's fleet had risen to forty-nine. The irony of Germany's build-up, however, was that her new fleet took little part in World War I. She deemed her battleships too valuable to risk in the war!

In 1902 Britain agreed a military alliance with Japan, aimed specifically at limiting German colonial gains in the east.

Britain was now being pulled into a war whether she liked it or not. In 1904 Britain signed the Entente Cordial with France. While this did not commit either country to the other's military aid in time of war, it did agree closer diplomatic cooperation and resolved numerous outstanding colonial squabbles.

Three years on, in 1907, Russia signed an agreement with Britain called the Anglo-Russian Entente. Together the two agreements formed the three-fold alliance known as the Triple Entente (Britain, France, and Russia), which lasted until 1917 when Russia withdrew from the war.

There were other smaller alliances too — such as Russia's pledge to protect Serbia and Britain's agreement to defend Belgian neutrality — and each served its part in drawing the other into the Great War.

Britain's Conflicts of Interest

Queen Victoria came to the throne in 1837 when she reached the age of 18 (her father died when she was only 1 year old). She reigned for sixty-three years until her death in 1901. In 1840 she married her cousin Prince Albert of Saxe-Coburg and Gotha. They had nine children — four sons and five daughters — before Albert's premature death from typhoid in 1861 when he was only 42 years of age.

The nine children and forty-two grandchildren were married to royalty across Europe, making Queen Victoria 'the grandmother of Europe'. The marriages resulted in certain conflicts of interest during the two world wars.

Victoria was succeeded to the throne by her son Edward VII. Her daughter Princess Victoria was the mother of German Emperor Kaiser Wilhelm II while her granddaughter Alexandra married Tsar Nicholas II, Emperor and last Tsar of Russia. The Kaiser's sister Princess Sophia of Prussia married King Constantine I of Greece. The three cousins King Edward, Kaiser Wilhelm and Tsar Nicholas never got along very well together (this was particularly true of the Kaiser). Communications were by letter only and once World War I started they were never to meet again.

Ireland
Ireland, which was part of the United Kingdom at that time, had for some considerable time been seeking Home Rule. Ireland was offered a form of Home Rule in 1912, but this was vetoed by the British House of Lords and by the Unionists in the north of Ireland. The problem was shelved pending the onset of World War I. Over 200,000 Irishmen fought with Britain in the war, many believing that this loyalty would be rewarded by Home Rule when the war was over. 40,000 of these men died in the war. *[See also Ireland's struggle for independence in Chapter 11, page 167].*

Russia
Japan offered an olive branch to Russia in 1903 asking that each recognise the other's interests in Korea and Manchuria. Russia declined, and over the next two years suffered several reversals at the hands of the Japanese, the most significant of which was the Battle of Tsushima in 1905 when the entire Russian fleet was wiped out. The western powers — Germany in particular — sat up and took notice!

Poland
Poland did not exist as an independent state during World War I. But when the war started, Polish territory — split between Austria-Hungary, Germany and Russia — became the scene of many of the operations on the Eastern Front of World War I.

The Balkans
The term Balkan Wars refers to the two wars that took place in south-eastern Europe in 1912 and 1913 over the last European territories of the Ottoman Empire.

In 1912 Bulgaria, Serbia, Greece and Montenegro (which collectively became known as the Balkan League) forced the Ottomans to give up Albania and Macedonia, leaving the area around Constantinople the only Ottoman territory in Europe. This became known as the First Balkan War.

Bulgaria was unhappy with the outcome of this war: she wanted Macedonia for herself. The following year, 1913, Bulgaria commenced military action against her former allies Serbia and Greece (located north and south of Macedonia) in the Second Balkan War. She was, however, unsuccessful in taking Macedonia.

Despite the re-establishment of peace in the Balkans, nothing had really been settled and tensions remained high. The numerous small nations that had found themselves under either Ottoman rule or Austro-Hungarian rule for many years developed a nationalistic fervour of their own. At the same time, they were united in identifying themselves as pan-Slavic people, with Russia as their chief ally. Russia was keen to encourage this identity as the Slav's natural protectors because — aside from a genuine emotional attachment — it was a means by which Russia could regain some of her lost pride.

On the home front, Russia had been struggling to hold back full-scale revolution ever since the Japanese naval disaster of 1905. In 1914 the Russian government saw war with Austria-Hungary as an opportunity to restore social order. In this they were successful, at least until they suffered a series of military setbacks (mainly at the hands of Germany) in the war. These setbacks — together with food shortages — brought about the long-threatened Russian Revolution, resulting in Russia's withdrawal from the war in 1917.

France did not need any encouragement to get involved in war, which she saw as the only way to recover the territories of Alsace and Lorraine. She was also very keen on avenging her defeat by Germany in the Franco-Prussian War of 1871.

As for **Germany**, she was unsettled both socially and militarily. The 1912 parliamentary elections had resulted in the election of no fewer than 110 socialist deputies. This made Chancellor Theobald von Bethmann Hollweg's task of liaising between the Reichstag (seat of parliament), the autocratic Kaiser Wilhelm II and the rigidly right-wing military high command next to impossible. Bethmann Hollweg came to believe that Germany's only hope of avoiding civil unrest lay in war; preferably a short, sharp war, although he did not rule out a European-wide conflict if it resolved Germany's social and political woes. Meanwhile, Germany continued to build her land and sea forces in an attempt to equal or better the forces of Britain and France.

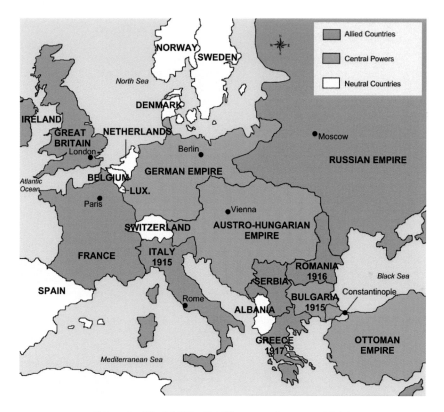

Map 1: World War I Alliances, January 1914

Archduke Franz Ferdinand with his wife Sophie, Duchess of Hohenberg, and their children.

Britain could see (as indeed could every other country) that war was looming. The British government spent the month of July 1914 trying to mediate, reserving at all times the right to remain inactive in the dispute. It was only when the war began that the British position hardened into support for Belgium and then France.

In summary, every country was gearing up for war: Austria-Hungary was determined to impose her will upon the Balkans; Germany wanted greater power and international influence; France was seeking revenge against Germany and the return of Alsace-Lorraine; Russia was desperately seeking the return of some semblance of national pride after her naval defeat by Japan; while Britain was intent on maintaining her position as a major world power.

There had not been a major war in Europe since the Franco-Prussian War of 1870–71 and it appears that people had actually forgotten how awful war could be. The imminent war was looked on by many as an adventure that would last for a few months: the general belief being that the war would be over by Christmas. How wrong they were! World War I was to last four years and would cost the lives of more than ten million people.

This then was the powder keg that was Europe at the beginning of the summer of 1914. All that was required was somebody to light the fuse, and that somebody turned out to be a member of a revolutionary Serbian nationalist secret society called Young Bosnia, which opposed being controlled by the Austro–Hungarians. The member's name was Gavrilo Princip. He was one of nine children in a poverty-stricken family. Six of the children died in childhood. The Young Bosnia society had no difficulty in recruiting Princip and on 28 June 1914, in the Bosnian capital Sarajevo, he assassinated Archduke Franz Ferdinand, heir to the Habsburg throne, and his wife, Duchess Sophie.

CHAPTER 2

1914
World War I Begins

World War I begins with declarations of war all around and the invasion of France by Germany through neutral Belgium. Major battles are fought at the Marne on the Western Front and at Tannenberg on the Eastern Front. The First Battle of Ypres takes place and trench warfare begins. War commences on the various fronts of the Balkans, the Middle East, the Far East and Africa. War at sea commences at Heligoland Bight in the North Sea.

WORLD WAR I — BELLIGERENTS

Allied Forces

France

Britain

Russia (1914–17)

Belgium

Balkan countries

Italy (1915–18)

Romania (1916–18)

Portugal (1916–18)

United States (1917–18)

Japan (1914–18)

British Empire, including:

- Australia
- Canada
- India
- Ireland
- New Zealand
- South Africa

Central Powers

Germany

Austro-Hungarian Empire

Ottoman Empire

Bulgaria (1915–18)

The assassination of Archduke Franz Ferdinand, heir to the Austro-Hungarian throne, on 28 June 1914 sparked off a chain of declarations of war which constituted the beginning of World War I.

Austria-Hungary

It took Austria-Hungary four weeks to react to the murder of her heir. The delay was due to the diplomatic efforts of other countries to dissuade Austria from declaring war, but the efforts proved in vain and Austria-Hungary declared war on Serbia on 28 July 1914. Germany encouraged Austria-Hungary by issuing them a so-called blank cheque. This was an assurance that whatever steps Vienna took, Germany would back them. It's very likely that this emboldened the Austrians.

Russia

Russia had been building herself up militarily for a number of years and, now bound by a treaty with Serbia, she proceeded to mobilise her vast army.

Germany

Germany — at this time the most powerful country in Europe and allied to Austria-Hungary by treaty — viewed Russia's mobilisation as an act of war and, with minimal delay, declared war on Russia on 1 August. She quickly followed up on 4 August by invading neutral Belgium to provide rapid access to northern France and Paris.

France

France was now at war with Germany and, by alliance, with Austria-Hungary. She was only too happy to avail of the opportunity of winning back Alsace and Lorraine with their rich deposits of coal and iron ore. She also welcomed the opportunity to get revenge for her defeat in the Franco-Prussian War in 1871.

Britain

Britain now had a twofold reason to enter the war: to defend both France and neutral Belgium. When Germany invaded Belgium on 4 August, Britain declared war on Germany later the same day. Like France, she was now by extension also at war with Austria-Hungary.

Italy

Italy, allied to both Germany and Austria-Hungary, was expected to join the war on their side. However, because of continuing hostility between Italy and Austria over territory, she declared a policy of neutrality. The following year, in May 1915, she joined the conflict by siding with the Allied forces against her two former allies.

Ottoman Empire

At the beginning of 1914 the once mighty Ottoman army was only a shadow of its former self. Germany, however, saw the Ottoman Empire as a useful ally (she could restrict Russia's use of the Dardanelles) and the empire became bound to Germany by a secret treaty on 3 August 1914.

Bulgaria

Bulgaria hedged her bets at the beginning of the war to see which side proved the stronger. In mid-1915, when the Central Powers (Germany, Austria-Hungary and the Ottoman Empire) gained control on the Russian and Turkish fronts, Bulgaria signed up to fight with them.

Romania

Romania remained neutral for the first two years of the war. Her big interest was to acquire neighbouring Transylvania (which was then part of Hungary). The only way she could succeed in this was to enter the war against the Central Powers, which she did in August 1916.

Portugal

Portugal remained neutral at the beginning of the war until German U-boats began to interfere with the sea trade between Portugal and Britain. Portugal responded by impounding German ships in Portuguese ports (at Britain's request). Germany, which also had an interest in the Portuguese colony of Angola in Africa, declared war on Portugal early in 1916.

Japan

Japan, honouring an agreement with Britain, declared war on Germany on 23 August 1914. Two days later, Austria-Hungary responded by declaring war on Japan.

United States

President Woodrow Wilson declared a United States policy of neutrality, an official stance that would last until 1917. However, in that year, Germany's policy of unrestricted submarine warfare began to seriously impact on America's commercial shipping. The last straw was the Zimmermann telegram on 19 January 1917 *[further details in Chapter 5, page 83]*, in which Germany offered US territory in Arizona and Texas to Mexico in return for joining the German cause. These two situations gave America the necessary push to declare war on Germany on 6 April 1917.

WORLD WAR I — THE VARIOUS FRONTS

World War I (the Great War) lasted four years from 1914 to 1918. It was spread over a number of different fronts all over Europe and Asia, but the principal theatre of war was the Western Front. More than ten million people died in the war.

WESTERN FRONT 1914

The first military action of World War I took place when Germany invaded neutral Belgium on 4 August 1914. This horrified the world because it was seen as Germany trampling on the rights of a small neutral country in contravention of international law.

Since the border between France and Germany was heavily fortified, Germany's plan was to use the flat plains of Belgium (Flanders) to access northern France and then Paris. This was part of Germany's 'Schlieffen Plan'. This plan was devised by Alfred von Schlieffen, a former German army Chief of Staff, who addressed the issue of how Germany could fight a war on two fronts.

Schlieffen's theory was that it would take Russia six weeks to mobilise her large army and, if France could be defeated in six weeks, this would leave Germany free to face Russia in the east. Germany was backed by an army of 1.7 million men against 1.1 million mobilised soldiers in France.

However, things did not go according to plan. The small Belgian army provided unexpected resistance, particularly at Liège where the Germans were delayed for eleven days. This gave France time to mobilise and it gave the British Expeditionary Force (BEF) time to cross the English Channel into Belgium and France. It also gave Russia time to mobilise her vast army (the main modes of transport in World War I were by railway and by horse) for war on the Eastern Front.

Belgian snipers gave the Germans a torrid time, but they paid dearly. For every German killed by snipers, the Germans executed ten Belgian civilians. They took their retribution a stage further by destroying the University of Louvain (Leuven) and burning the renowned Louvain Library to the ground. This was one of many examples of German thuggery and brutality in the war zone.

French Offensive

France's focus was on regaining the province of Alsace-Lorraine, which she had lost as a consequence of the defeat in the Franco-Prussian War of 1870. Her initial emphasis was on attacking Germany through her former provinces, rather than on the need to defend Paris. This oversight almost cost her dearly since the Germans advanced to within forty miles of Paris before they were stopped. Meanwhile, the French efforts to retake Alsace-Lorraine on 14 August proved unsuccessful. The German defences proved much too strong and France suffered substantial casualties.

Battle of the Frontiers

The Battle of the Frontiers comprised a series of battles at Mulhouse, Lorraine, the Ardennes, Charleroi and Mons in a war that took place in Belgium and France during the month of August 1914. Mons was the first battle in the war involving the British Expeditionary Force. The Allies spent the month retreating slowly down through north-eastern France and they eventually came to a halt south of the River Marne, which ran eastwards from Paris towards Alsace-Lorraine. At this stage, Paris was in imminent danger. However, France now used reconnaissance aircraft in the war for the first time: French airmen were able to inform their ground forces of German troop movements even though methods of communication between air and ground were still very primitive.

Battle of Le Cateau

This was essentially a rearguard action fought by the British in late August during the general Allied retreat along the Western Front in the face of sustained German successes at the various Battles of the Frontiers. The Germans attacked on 26 August; the British defended with rifle fire from hastily-dug shallow trenches (a tactic similarly employed at Mons). Casualties on both sides were heavy. Crucially, however, the battle succeeded in further delaying the German advance on Paris.

The Battle of the Marne

This was the first major battle of the war. France's unflappable Commander in Chief, Joseph Joffre, resolved on 4 September to launch a counteroffensive strike, assisted by the British under Sir John French. French only agreed to assist Joffre after being ordered to do so by the British War Minister Horatio Kitchener. On 6 September France and Britain launched their offensive opposed by the 1st and 2nd German armies, who were headed for Paris.

As they approached Paris, the two German armies separated leaving a gap of twenty miles between them. BEF forces arrived on the scene at an opportune moment to fill the gap. Even so, the Germans came very close to victory. The Allies' saviours were 6,000 French reserve infantry troops transported from Paris in a stream of taxis!

The German armies at this stage were stretched. Manpower losses were huge: France and Germany each suffered 250,000 casualties while Germany was finding it difficult to sustain the supply lines of armaments, foodstuffs and horses. On 9 September the German armies began a retreat ordered by the German Chief of Staff, Helmuth von Moltke. They retreated forty miles to a point north of the River Aisne, where they dug in.

At this crucial stage, the Allies committed what turned out in hindsight to be one the biggest blunders of World War I. Instead of concentrating on driving the Germans out of their trenches and back to Germany, they built a line of trenches parallel to their enemy all the way to the Belgian coast, thereby starting the trench warfare that would last until the end of the war.

Germany was not helped by a decision from higher up to transfer some of her forces to the Eastern Front to combat the increasing numbers of Russian forces arriving. This victory for the Allies in the Battle of the Marne ended any hopes the Germans had of bringing the war on the Western Front to an early close.

Trench Warfare
After the Battle of the Marne, both the Allies and the Germans began to dig a series of trenches in the so-called 'Race to the Sea'. Britain and France soon found themselves facing entrenched German forces from Lorraine to Belgium, a distance of 500 miles. The Allies sought to take the offensive, while Germany defended her occupied territories. The trenches with barbed wire surrounds were to prove a formidable obstacle for infantry (tanks had not been developed at this stage). The two lines of trenches were more or less parallel, but the gap between them — known as No Man's Land — varied from a hundred yards to several miles. The trenches were built in a zigzag fashion to make them more difficult to attack.

Life in the Trenches

Life in the trenches was appalling. Soldiers had to eat, sleep and toilet in rat- and lice-infested trenches, which in lowland areas such as Flanders were frequently waterlogged. Soldiers who stood in muddy and waterlogged trenches for long periods of time frequently developed 'trench foot'. As horrendous as life in the trenches was, it was the safest place to be. Once the order was given to attack — which meant 'going over the top' — the chances of survival were bleak!

First Battle of Ypres
Under strong pressure from the Anglo-French Allies, the Germans were driven from their trenches north of the River Aisne. The battles continued northwards towards Belgium, moving from one trench position to the next, until they eventually reached Ypres.

On the way there were battles at Albert and at Arras towards the end of September.

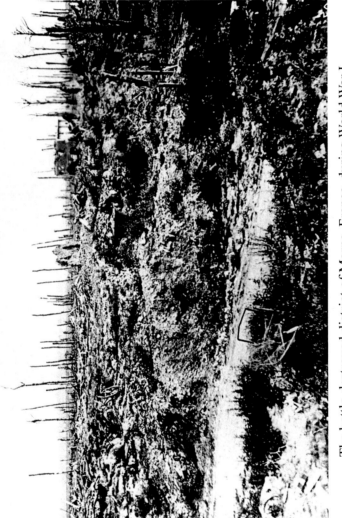

The battle-destroyed district of Marne, France, during World War I.

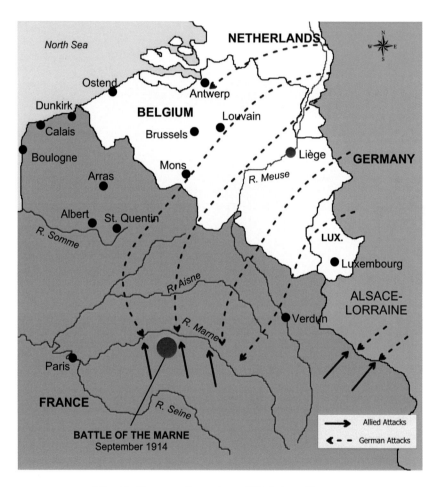

Map 2: German Invasion of Belgium/France
on the Western Front 1914

The First Battle of Ypres commenced on 14 October when Erich von Falkenhayn, the German Chief of Staff who had replaced Moltke after the defeat at Marne, sent his armies into Ypres. The battle began with a nine-day German offensive. This was only halted with the arrival of French reinforcements and the deliberate flooding of the Belgian front. Belgian troops opened the sluice gates of the dykes which were holding back the sea from the Low Countries: Belgium, the Netherlands and Luxembourg (so-called because they were located close to/below sea level and hence prone to flooding). With the onset of winter, this did nothing to enhance the condition of the trenches. It was, however, becoming clear that the nature of trench warfare favoured the defender rather than the attacker.

A series of battles took place between mid-October and mid-November, none of which had any real effect on the outcome. The Allies held Ypres, as they continued to do until the end of the war despite repeated German attacks. The Allies also held the Ypres salient, which extended six miles into German territory. The human cost, however, was huge: it's estimated that the casualties on each side exceeded 130,000 men.

Stalemate

The war on the Western Front reached stalemate. Each side remained in their trenches and this situation would continue for some time. As 1914 drew to a close, Germany controlled most of Belgium (except Ypres) and north-eastern France, including the cities of Antwerp and Lille. She also retained control over the valuable coal and iron ore deposits of Alsace and Lorraine between France and Germany.

Christmas 1914

On the first Christmas of the war on the Western Front near Messines, legend has it that British and German soldiers left the security of their trenches (100 yards apart), met in No Man's Land, exchanged cigarettes and greetings, and sang Christmas carols together before resuming their squalid existence in the trenches. Songs and stories abound regarding this event!

Occupied Territories

Belgium and north-east France were occupied by the Germans for the duration of the war. German troops controlled the territories with harsh repressive measures: confiscating houses and property for the use of occupying troops, and killing anybody who resisted. Mines, factories and farms were exploited and looted for whatever Germany needed.

EASTERN FRONT 1914

The Eastern Front was much longer than the Western Front. The 'theatre of war' extended from the Baltic Sea to the Black Sea, a distance of 1,000 miles. This drastically affected the nature of the warfare. While the war on the Western Front developed into trench warfare, the battle lines on the Eastern Front were more fluid. Breakthroughs occurred regularly since the huge distance was impossible to defend and when a line was breached it was equally impossible to get reinforcements to help due to the vast distances and poor communications.

The belligerents on the Eastern Front consisted of the Central Powers (Germany and Austria-Hungary) against Russia. Germany had promised to support the Austro-Hungarian invasion of Serbia, but various interpretations of what this meant emerged. Austro-Hungarian leaders believed that Germany would cover her northern flank against Russia. Germany, however, assumed that Austria-Hungary would send the majority of her soldiers to fight Russia while Germany dealt with France. This confusion forced the Austro-Hungarian army to divide its forces between the Russian and Serbian fronts. Germany, on the other hand, was taken unaware by the speed of mobilisation of the Russians and, as a result, had to move some of her forces from the Western to the Eastern Front.

Battle of Tannenberg

Initial Russian plans called for simultaneous invasions of German East Prussia and Austrian Galicia. Although Russia's initial advance into Galicia was largely successful, they were driven back from East Prussia by German Generals Paul von Hindenburg (brought out of retirement) and Erich Ludendorff, his Chief of Staff (the two were a formidable duo and played a major part throughout the war).

The Russians made it easy for them: none of their communications was in code and the Germans knew every move the Russians were planning. This was not the only weakness on Russia's side: she had a huge army, but it consisted mainly of raw recruits with little or no experience of combat, and she lacked military leadership — as indeed did the Allies!

The Battle of Tannenberg was the most comprehensive German victory of World War I; the encirclement and destruction of the Russian army in late August 1914 virtually ended Russia's invasion of East Prussia before it started. The victory at Tannenberg was facilitated in no small way by Germany's introduction of machine guns for the first time and by the use of reconnaissance aircraft to report on the movement of Russian troops. The Germans followed up in September with a further

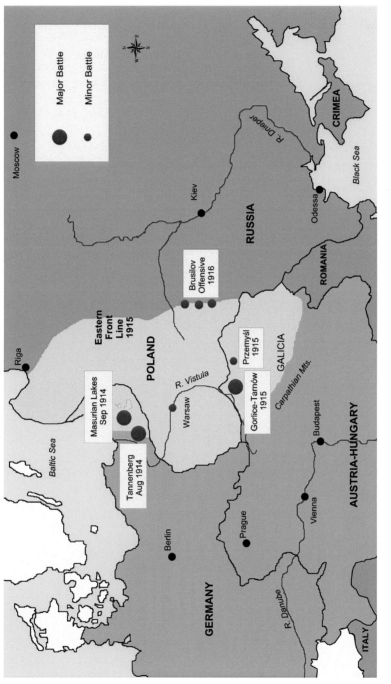

Map 3: Eastern Front 1914–16

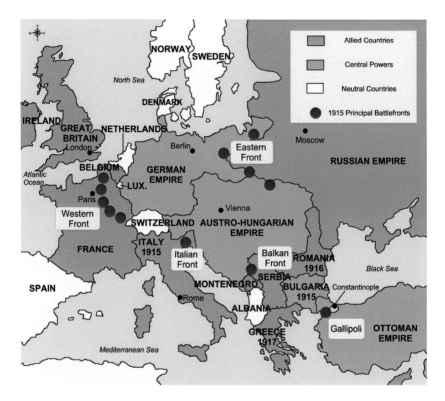

Map 4: Principal War Fronts in World War I

victory at the nearby Masurian Lakes. However, further south, sheer weight of numbers gave the Russians victory over the Austro-Hungarians in Galicia and they moved on from there to the Carpathian mountains.

Aircraft and Photography 1914

World War I saw huge developments in the fields of aircraft and photography. Both were in their infancy at the beginning of the war, but by the end of the war each made a considerable contribution in terms of observing troop movements and passing on this information to their ground troops.

While aircraft had mastered the art of synchronising machine-gun fire with the rotation of propeller blades, aircraft were not powerful enough at this stage to carry bombs.

BALKAN FRONT 1914

In the Balkans, Austro-Hungarian forces seriously underestimated the strength and fighting power of the Serbs. Austria-Hungary had declared war on Serbia on 28 July 1914 as a result of the assassination of Archduke Franz Ferdinand. The next day the Serbian capital, Belgrade, was bombed and on 13 August the first of a series of Austro-Hungarian invasions was launched. But for the rest of the year the Serbian army battled skilfully, culminating in the retreat of all Austro-Hungarian forces from Serbia in December 1914.

WAR AT SEA 1914

Naval warfare in World War I centred on the efforts of the Allies (mainly the British Royal Navy) — with their larger fleets and surrounding position — to blockade Germany by sea, the efforts of the Central Powers to break that blockade, and in turn the efforts of the Central Powers to disrupt sea traffic into both Britain and France. The main theatres of naval warfare were the North Sea and the Atlantic Ocean, but there was also action in the Pacific, the Mediterranean, the Black Sea, the Baltic Sea, the Indian Ocean and the South China Sea.

The first major naval action of the war was fought in the **Heligoland Bight** in the North Sea on 24 August 1914. A British force, including Vice Admiral Sir David Beatty's First Battlecruiser Squadron, caught the German fleet unaware, sinking three light cruisers and a destroyer, resulting in the deaths of more than 700 men. However, the Germans took their revenge on 16 December when a fleet of German battlecruisers under Rear Admiral Franz von Hipper raided the northeast coast of England. They bombarded Scarborough, Whitby and Hartlepool killing thirty-five people, wounding forty more and causing extensive damage. Overall, however, it was a substantial victory for the British navy.

A number of German ships stationed overseas at the start of the war engaged in raiding operations in poorly-defended oceans. The best known of these was the German East Asia Squadron, commanded by Admiral Graf Maximilian von Spee. When Japan entered the war on the side of the Allies, Spee's squadron moved from Far Eastern waters across the Pacific. Towards the end of 1914, Spee was preying on ships along the west coast of South America. In the meantime, one of Spee's squadrons the SMS *Emden* had broken away to concentrate her efforts on commercial shipping in the Indian Ocean. In this it was very successful: sinking or capturing more than thirty Allied merchant ships and warships before being seriously damaged by the Australian cruiser HMAS *Sydney*. The *Emden*'s captain, Karl von Müller, ran his ship aground to prevent her sinking. 133 of the 376 crew members drowned; the remainder were taken prisoner.

Battle of Coronel
Britain's Royal Navy (with Japan's assistance) had spent months searching for Spee and once news reached them of his whereabouts the West Indies Squadron, under the command of Sir Christopher Craddock who was patrolling South America at the time, was ordered by Churchill to confront Spee. Unfortunately for the Allies, Craddock's fleet was significantly inferior to Spee's and was comprehensively defeated; Craddock himself going down with his ship!

Battle of the Falkland Islands
When news of the scale of the British defeat and its consequent humiliation reached the British Admiralty, a huge naval force under Admiral Sir Frederick Sturdee was dispatched to engage with Spee's fleet. Spee was attempting to flee from South America when Sturdee's fleet engaged them off the Falkland Islands. The Royal Navy fleet was substantially superior on this occasion and scored a comprehensive victory. Spee was lost along with the majority of his crew when their ship, the *Gneisenau*, went down.

The German light cruiser *Dresden* escaped from the battle and made her way into the Pacific pursued by British cruisers. It took months to track her down, which they finally did at **Más a Tierra** in Chile. On 13 March 1915 they opened fire on her. She surrendered. While surrender talks were going on, the Germans scuttled the ship and abandoned her.

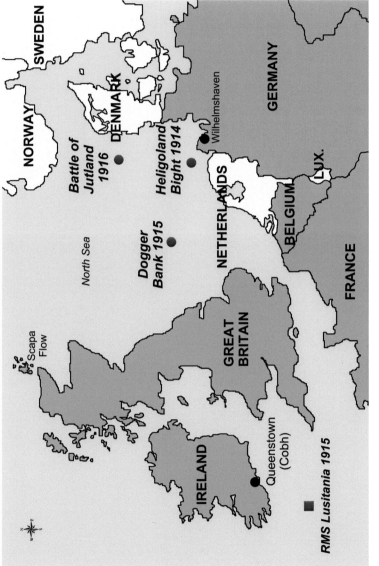

Map 5: Sea Battles 1914–16

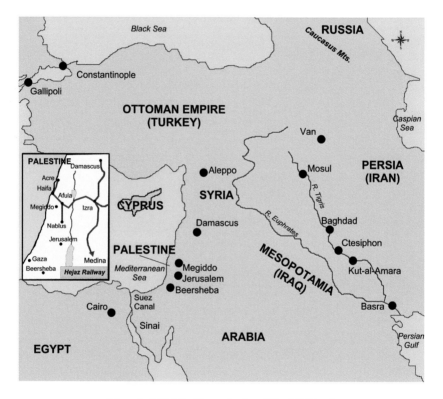

Map 6: Middle East during World War I

MIDDLE EAST 1914

The Middle Eastern front was the scene of action between 29 October 1914 and 30 October 1918. The combatants were the Ottoman Empire with some assistance from Germany against the British (supported by her colonies) and the Russians. Russia's big interest in the area was the oil in the Caucasus. However, she withdrew from the war in 1917 as a result of the Russian Revolution. Much of the activity in the Middle East concerned the oil resources in the area and, with the notable exception of Gallipoli, had little or no effect on the outcome of World War I.

There were five main campaigns:
1. Sinai and Palestine
2. Mesopotamia (modern-day Iraq)
3. Caucasus
4. Persia (modern-day Iran)
5. Gallipoli

1. Sinai and Palestine *[see Chapter 3 — 1915, page 68]*

2. Mesopotamia (modern-day Iraq)
The capture of Basra formed the opening action on the Middle Eastern front: it ran from 5 to 21 November 1914 with the belated entry of the Ottoman Empire into the war against the Allies. With hostilities between the Ottoman Empire and the Allies formally underway from 5 November, the Anglo-Indian force lost no time in taking Basra, which was weakly defended by the Turks. The battle ended on 21 November when the Turks retreated from Basra. Anglo-Indian forces lost 500 men in the battle, but the Turkish losses were in excess of 1,000 soldiers. Crucially, the British had secured a continuation of oil supplies from the Middle East, but it became necessary to keep a force of 500,000 men in Mesopotamia for the duration of the war.

3. Caucasus (mountainous region to the East of the Black Sea dividing Russia and Turkey; with Georgia, Armenia and Azerbaijan sandwiched in between)
A revolution in Turkey in 1908 saw the emergence of the 'Young Turks' — a group of modernisers whose aim was to make Turkey the power it once was. In January 1913 a group of soldiers led by 31-year-old Enver Pasha stormed into a cabinet meeting, shot dead the Minister of War and demanded that the Sultan form a coalition government. A year later, Pasha became Minister of War himself. Pasha did not lack ambition, but he clearly lacked experience! In November 1914 the Ottomans, led by Pasha, attacked Russia through the Caucasus. They were encouraged by Germany, as this would divert Russia's attention

away from the Eastern Front. However, the attack was a disaster. They were ill-equipped for the weather in the Caucasus and they lost up to 100,000 men, mainly due to the freezing conditions and disease. Armenia fought on the side of the Russians, which resulted in the Turks taking their revenge on Armenia in 1915, when they allegedly murdered more than one million Armenians *[see Chapter 3 — 1915, page 69]*. To this day, Turkey disputes this.

4. Persia (modern-day Iran)
The Persian campaign was a series of engagements in northern Persia, Azerbaijan and western Persia. These conflicts pitted British and Russian forces against the Ottomans from December 1914 until the Armistice of Mudros on 30 October 1918. The Russian operations were halted when they withdrew from the war in 1917 to be replaced by an Allied force from Britain, Canada, Australia and New Zealand under Lionel Dunsterville; the troops became known as Dunsterforce. The Allies were to be supplemented by locally-recruited Armenian forces. The military goal of the Allies was to reach the Caucasus via Persia. Operations ceased with the Treaty of Brest-Litovsk in March 1918, which imposed the reinstatement of the border between Russia and the Ottoman Empire to its pre-war position.

5. Gallipoli *[see Chapter 3 — 1915, page 57]*

FAR EAST 1914

Japan participated in World War I from 1914 to 1918 as one of the Allied powers and played a crucial role in securing the sea-lanes in the South Pacific and Indian Oceans against the German navy. Politically, Japan seized the opportunity to expand her sphere of influence in China.

On 7 August 1914, the Japanese government received an official request from the British government for assistance in repulsing German warships in Chinese waters. Japan sent an ultimatum to Germany on 14 August, which elicited no response. Japan then formally declared war on Germany on 23 August 1914. Japanese forces swiftly occupied German-leased territories in the Far East. On 2 September Japanese forces landed in China's Shandong Province and surrounded the German settlement at Tsingtao. During October, the Japanese navy seized several of Germany's island colonies in the Pacific without resistance. On November 7 the Siege of Tsingtao ended with the surrender of German colonial forces.

Ruins of the Cathedral in Ypres, Belgium, during World War I.

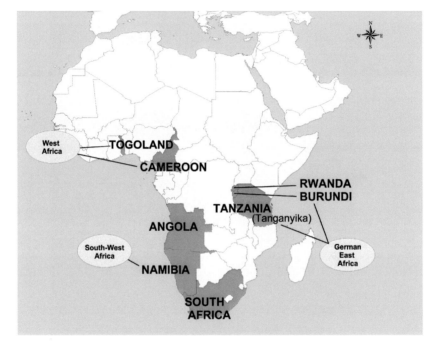

Map 7: Africa during World War I

AFRICA 1914–18

During the last quarter of the nineteenth century, Germany had acquired colonies in Africa and the Pacific. These colonies provided useful naval bases and sources for raw materials.

The British Empire, with near total command of the world's oceans, had the power and resources to conquer the German colonies when World War I started. Most German colonies in Africa had been recently acquired and were not well defended, with the notable exception of German East Africa. They were also surrounded on all land borders by African colonies belonging mostly to their enemies: Britain, France, Belgium and, later in the war, Portugal.

There were three main areas of conflict in Africa:
    (a)   West Africa
    (b)   South-West Africa
    (c)   German East Africa

(a) West Africa
Germany had two colonies in West Africa: Togoland and Cameroon. They posed a threat to the Allies because of their powerful wireless stations that were capable of communicating with Germany and America. The small colony of Togoland (modern-day Togo) surrendered to the British and French military forces on 26 August 1914 but not before blowing up their wireless station. The German troops in Cameroon fought fiercely against the invading British, French and Belgian forces; and it was not until March 1916 that the fighting ended with the surrender of the remaining German colonial armed forces.

(b) South-West Africa
German South-West Africa (modern-day Namibia) is a huge and arid territory. The only major German population there in 1914 was around the colonial capital of Windhoek, some 200 miles inland from the Atlantic Ocean. The Germans had 3,000 soldiers there and could count on the support of most of the 7,000 adult male German colonists. In addition, the Germans had very friendly relations with the Boers in South Africa, who had ended a bloody war with the British just twelve years previously.

The British began their attack by organising and arming their former enemies, the Boers. This was a calculated gamble, which initially did not pay off. Some of the Boers rebelled, but by the end of 1914 the rebellion had ended and the Boers were united under the leadership of Jan Smuts.

In January 1915 Smuts continued military operations into South-West Africa against the German colonists. The South African troops were battle-hardened and experienced at living in this type of terrain. They crossed the hundreds of miles of empty land on horseback. The Germans tried to delay this advance but without success. Windhoek was captured on 12 May 1915. Two months later, all of the German forces had surrendered. South Africa effectively ruled South-West Africa for the next seventy-five years.

Angola was a Portuguese colony in 1914 when the war started. It was located directly north of German South-West Africa and even before the declaration of war between Germany and Portugal in March 1915, the troops of the two colonies clashed several times on their common border. The Germans won these clashes, but they were defeated later in a British military campaign operating out of South Africa.

(c) German East Africa
In German East Africa (modern-day Tanzania, Burundi and Rwanda), the British were unable to fully subdue the defenders of the area despite four years of effort and tens of thousands of casualties. The German Commander Paul Emil von Lettow-Vorbeck fought a guerrilla campaign for the duration of the war. His forces operated throughout all of East Africa, living off the land and capturing military supplies from the British and Portuguese military.

In 1916 Britain entrusted the task of defeating the Germans to the Boer Commander Jan Smuts along with a very large force. Smuts was only moderately successful and in 1917 he was moved to the war cabinet in London. In fact, Lettow-Vorbeck's small army was never defeated. The soldiers fought on to the end of the war and only surrendered when they were informed that the war was over in November 1918. Lettow-Vorbeck's achievement became the stuff of legend and he was welcomed home to Germany as a hero.

Overall, the entire African campaign had little impact on the course of the war.

Zeppelin Airship

A Zeppelin airship, named after its German designer, is an elongated balloon-shaped structure comprising a fabric-covered, lightweight outer framework which contains a number of hydrogen-filled bags for buoyancy. It was powered by motor-driven propellers and was categorised as a 'dirigible' since it could be steered. Zeppelins were used in the First World War mainly for reconnaissance and for dropping bombs.

However, Zeppelins had major weaknesses: fire was the big danger since hydrogen is extremely flammable, they were difficult to steer in windy conditions and they were easily shot down by ground fire. They were used on and off by Germany during World War I but, when the war ended, their use was prohibited by the Treaty of Versailles.

1914 TIMELINE

28 Jun	Archduke Franz Ferdinand and his wife assassinated in Sarajevo.
28 Jul	Austria-Hungary declares war on Serbia.
30 Jul	Austrian warships bombard Belgrade, capital of Serbia.
31 Jul	Russia begins to mobilise her forces.
01 Aug	Germany declares war on Russia.
03 Aug	Germany declares war on France.
	Germany and the Ottoman Empire sign a secret treaty.
04 Aug	Germany invades neutral Belgium.
	Britain and her dominions declare war on Germany.
	The United States declares her neutrality.
06 Aug	Austria-Hungary declares war on Russia.
	French and British troops invade the German colony of Togoland in West Africa.
07 Aug	British Expeditionary Force (BEF) arrives in France.
12 Aug	France and Britain declare war on Austria-Hungary.
13 Aug	Austria-Hungary invades Serbia.
14 Aug	Battle of the Frontiers begins on the Western Front.
17 Aug	Russia invades Germany in East Prussia marking the start of war on the Eastern Front.
20 Aug	Germany occupies Brussels, capital of Belgium.
23 Aug	Japan declares war on Germany.
24 Aug	Naval action at Heligoland Bight in the North Sea, beginning the sea blockade on Germany, which lasted for the duration of the war.
26 Aug	Battle of Tannenberg begins on the Eastern Front.
	Battle of Le Cateau begins.
30 Aug	New Zealand troops occupy German Samoa in the Far East.
02 Sep	Japan attacks German naval base at Tsingtao in China.
06 Sep	Battle of the Marne begins.
12 Sep	Battle of the Aisne begins.
17 Sep	On the Eastern Front, Germany comes to the assistance of Austria-Hungary against Russia.
22 Sep	Britain bombs Zeppelin bases at Cologne and Düsseldorf.
18 Oct	First Battle of Ypres begins.
29 Oct	Ottoman Empire enters the war on Germany's side.

01 Nov   Major defeat for Britain in the naval battle at Coronel off
         South America.
         Austria invades Serbia for the third time. Again, she is defeated.
02 Nov   Russia declares war on the Ottoman Empire (modern-day
         Turkey).
03 Nov   Erich von Falkenhayn replaces Helmuth von Moltke as the
         German Chief of Staff.
05 Nov   Britain and France declare war on the Ottoman Empire.
06 Nov   British and Indian troops land in Mesopotamia.
07 Nov   German naval base at Tsingtao captured by the Japanese.
21 Nov   British and Indian troops capture Basra in Mesopotamia.
08 Dec   Major victory for Britain at the naval Battle of the Falkland
         Islands. German Admiral Graf von Spee killed along with
         most of his crew, including his two serving sons.
16 Dec   German navy bombards the British coastal towns of Whitby,
         Hartlepool and Scarborough, killing 35 people.
25 Dec   Christmas truce between British and German troops in the
         trenches in northern France.

CHAPTER 3

1915
Disaster at Gallipoli

1915 begins quietly. While trench warfare stalemates on the Western Front, the main events are the entry of both Italy and Bulgaria into the war on opposing sides, the disastrous campaign in Gallipoli/ Dardanelles by the Allies, and the use of poison gas by both sides. The year also features the beginning of the German U-boat campaign, the sinking of the Lusitania and the Second Battle of Ypres. War commences on the Italian Front.

GALLIPOLI

Early in 1915 Winston Churchill (First Lord of the Admiralty) came up with the idea of seizing control of Constantinople (Istanbul). This would give the Allies control of all sea traffic from Russia through the Black Sea and the Dardanelles Strait (called the Çanakkale Strait by the Ottomans) to the Mediterranean. If successful, this could certainly impact on the war. (The Dardanelles Strait is one of the busiest waterways in the world today.)

From Churchill's point of view, success in the Dardanelles could force Turkey to surrender, robbing Germany of one of her allies and opening the way for an Allied advance through the Balkans. A further benefit would be to link up with Russia on the Eastern Front. The Russians, in fact, encouraged the Allied attack at Gallipoli to take some pressure off the Russian army in the Caucasus.

Churchill believed that the Royal Navy, with minimum input from ground forces, would have little difficulty in defeating the Turks. He totally underestimated the Ottoman forces, who had built up a fearsome reputation as fighters down through the centuries. Shortly after the Ottomans entered the war, Germany dispatched one of her officers, Otto Liman von Sanders, to train the Turkish army. The Turks were resolute they would not be defeated in the Dardanelles since the Allies would then have a clear passage through to their precious Constantinople.

The British navy moved into position in the Aegean Sea in mid-February. This gave the Ottomans a full month's notice that they were about to be attacked. They occupied the time usefully by mining the Dardanelles Strait. Aware of the mines, the British used mine-sweepers to clear the strait. However, operating under fire from the surrounding hills, the mine-sweepers missed a complete line of mines and when the British attempted to rush the strait on 18 March, they met with disaster. Three British battleships — HMS *Irresistible*, HMS *Ocean*, and HMS *Inflexible* — were sunk or critically damaged by mines, while two French battleships were also damaged. What was left of the British fleet withdrew, handing a naval victory to the Turks. Churchill resigned as First Lord of the Admiralty.

The Allied forces now had to revise their strategy. Their revised plan was to take the Gallipoli peninsula, from where they could control the Dardanelles Strait. A Mediterranean Expeditionary Force (MEF) was assembled under General Sir Ian Hamilton (brought back from retirement) and preparations were made for a landing. One of Hamilton's first priorities was to send a supply ship back to Alexandria to be reloaded in accordance with his wishes! This took a month and during the month's delay the Turks had ample time to bring in troops and armaments for the battle ahead. The element of surprise had been lost.

The MEF forces included British, Irish, Indian and Anzac (Australian and New Zealand Army Corps) forces. On 25 April the British and the Irish landed at Cape Helles and Sedd el Bahr on the southern tip of the peninsula while the Anzac forces landed further north at a cove, later to be christened Anzac Cove. The Allied landings suffered a baptism of fire! The Turks, forewarned of the Allies arrival, were literally lying in wait in newly-built high-level defensive trenches. The Turks were under the command of the renowned Mustafa Kemal (later to become Atatürk, meaning 'Father of the Turks'), who rallied his troops with the words: *"I am not ordering you to attack; I am ordering you to die! In the time it takes us to die, other forces and commanders will come in our place."* Hamilton was no match for Kemal!

The British had no experience of amphibious landings on a hostile coast and once they came under attack, they proceeded to dig defensive trenches on the beaches, thus repeating the disastrous trench warfare of the Western Front. However, they were worse off than the troops on the Western Front: all they had behind them was the sea. This was how a young British officer described the attempted amphibious landing: *"The sight was indescribable — between the last barge and the shore was a pier formed by piles of dead soldiers. It was impossible to reach the shore without treading on the dead, and the sea around the cove was red with blood."*

On 27 April a large Turkish force under Kemal drove the Anzacs back onto the beach at Anzac Cove. As additional Ottoman forces arrived, the possibility of a swift Allied victory on the peninsula disappeared;

British battleship HMS *Irresistible* abandoned and sinking during the Gallipoli Campaign, 18 March 1915.

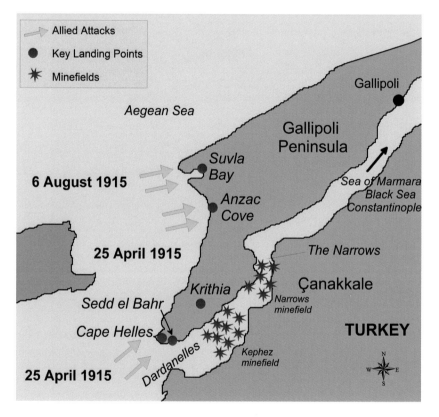

Map 8: Gallipoli 1915

and fighting at both Cape Helles and Anzac Cove became battles of attrition.

The three Battles of Krithia took place during the month of May. Krithia is located on high ground midway between Cape Helles and Anzac Cove; and Hamilton hoped to seize Krithia, thereby linking up the two landing zones. However, the Turks were well dug in and all attempts to move them ended in failure. On 19 May, the Ottomans attacked the Anzacs in an attempt to drive them back into the sea, but they were unsuccessful. Throughout the summer months, a number of battles took place without either side gaining any real advantage. Throughout the campaign in Gallipoli, thirst and dysentery were major problems due to the extreme heat.

On 6 August a landing at Suvla Bay was intended to take some of the pressure off the Allies at both Cape Helles and Anzac Cove. But the Turks were waiting and the Allies were now fighting even further away from the original target: the Dardanelles Strait. Four days later, the Turks responded with a major counter-attack by Kemal-led troops, during which they recovered ground taken earlier by the Allies.

As the autumn advanced and the weather deteriorated, Hamilton was replaced by Lieutenant General Charles Monro. Kitchener (British War Minister) paid a visit to Gallipoli and agreed with Monro that the situation had no future for the Allies and a decision was taken to evacuate the peninsula. Troops at Anzac Cove and Suvla Bay were evacuated in December, followed by those at Cape Helles in January 1916.

The Gallipoli campaign was a disaster. It lasted almost a year and achieved nothing. It cost the lives of 250,000 men on each side.

Anzac Day is commemorated every year in Australia and New Zealand on 25 April, the date of their landing at Anzac Cove.

WESTERN FRONT 1915

In Flanders fields the poppies blow
Between the crosses, row on row,
That mark our place; and in the sky
The larks, still bravely singing, fly,
Scarce heard amid the guns below.
— Lieutenant Colonel John McCrae,
Canadian Military Doctor.

There was little or no action on the Western Front in the early months of 1915 for a number of reasons. The various antagonists had really believed when the war started that it would be over by Christmas, but they had not bargained for the trench stalemate. It was, however, obvious to everyone at this stage that the trenches were effective in defence but no asset in attack. In fact, the attacking force invariably lost more men than those defending.

How then do you win a war when the development of aircraft and tanks is not yet sufficiently advanced? The only answer any of the participants had was to increase numbers and arms, and this was the priority in 1915. Recruitment became essential not just to replace troops killed in 1914 but also to strengthen the various armies. However, soldiers without weapons are not much use, with the result that production in industrial factories in the participating countries switched to munitions of all types and increased hugely. In the Allied countries, it was the women who manned the factories while their menfolk manned the battlefields!

One of the biggest problems the Allies had was the lack of a supreme commander. The lack of communication between the political leaders of the various countries did not help the situation. The generals on the various fronts were left to make their own decisions, but France did not inform Russia or Britain what her plans were and vice versa. Russia continued to battle against Germany and Austria-Hungary on the Eastern Front while the British involvement in various fronts around the world (apart from the Western Front) could only be described as empire consolidation. The problem of communications did not apply to one side only. On numerous occasions, Germany barely condescended to convey major plans to Austria-Hungary, whom she considered — with some justification — her junior partners. At this time, Erich von Falkenhayn was in command of the German forces, and communications between himself and the Austro-Hungarian Commander Franz Conrad were disastrous. They rarely spoke.

Battle of Neuve Chapelle
When Gallipoli took centre stage during spring 1915, Joffre was not happy on the Western Front. With some justification, he felt that the front was being neglected. To placate him, Sir John French staged an attack on the Germans at Neuve Chapelle on 10 March. After such a long period of inactivity, the Germans were initially taken by surprise. The British infantry punched a hole in the German defences but were unable to follow up due to a shortage of shells. German reinforcements quickly arrived and the gap was closed. The Battle of Neuve Chapelle lasted for three days and achieved little. The same could be said of a series of battles fought that year: at Champagne, St. Mihiel, Arras, Festubert and Aubers Ridge. In all cases, the Germans sat back on the

defensive while the Allies attacked. In doing so the Allies suffered almost 500,000 casualties in these battles but did not regain any territory.

Meanwhile, Falkenhayn was aware that sitting in trenches was not going to win the war and he attempted a further attack at Ypres on 22 April. This battle became known as the **Second Battle of Ypres** and it marked the entry of Canadian forces into the war. The Germans used poison gas for the first time — regardless of the fact that its use was banned by the Hague Convention. It was indeed a wicked weapon, causing blindness and lung damage to its victims. It could also be the ultimate folly though: if the wind was blowing in the wrong direction, its users could be on the receiving end of the damage. The German attack petered out because their forces were inadequate. They had, as it turned out, been concentrating their efforts on moving forces to the Eastern Front to counter the increasing threat from the Russians.

Joffre had only agreed to Gallipoli if the British agreed to resume action on the Western Front in the autumn (presumably after they mopped up the Turks in Gallipoli). Joffre decided that this resumption would take place at **Loos.** They attacked on 25 September, buoyed up by the knowledge that they were going to use gas. It was a disaster! The wind was blowing in the wrong direction and some of the gas blew back on the Allied forces. The outcome was a useless slaughter. Each side suffered casualties in the region of 100,000. This was a dreadful result for the Allies considering they outnumbered the Germans at the start of the battle. There was little or no change territorially on the Western Front in 1915, but there were many casualties. Two of the casualties at Loos were Rudyard Kipling's son John and Captain Fergus Bowes-Lyon, an older brother of Queen Elizabeth The Queen Mother. In December the British Commander Sir John French was recalled and Douglas Haig was appointed Commander in Chief of the British forces.

EASTERN FRONT 1915

Early in 1915, Germany decided to concentrate her efforts on the Eastern Front and accordingly transferred considerable forces there. The German Supreme Command moved east with Falkenhayn as Chief of Staff. This meant that Hindenburg and Ludendorff were now demoted to operate under Falkenhayn, a decision that was not received with much grace.

Russia, with her army of millions, was a major problem and more than Austria-Hungary could handle without help from Germany. To eliminate the Russian threat, the Central Powers began the 1915 campaign with the successful **Gorlice-Tarnów** offensive in Galicia in May. After the Second Battle of the Masurian Lakes, the German and Austro-Hungarian troops in the Eastern Front operated under a unified command. On 4 June the great fortress at **Przemyśl** was taken. The offensive soon turned into a general advance by the Axis forces followed by a strategic retreat by the Russian army. The cause of the about-turn by the Russian army was not so much due to errors in the tactical sphere but a shortage of artillery and ammunition. Only in 1916 did the Russian war industries increase production of weaponry.

By mid-1915, the Russians had been driven from Russian Poland and hence pushed hundreds of miles away from the borders of the Central Powers, removing the threat of a Russian invasion of Germany or Austria-Hungary. On 5 August Warsaw was taken by the Central Powers and on 5 September Tsar Nicholas II took personal command of the Russian army in an effort to rally his troops. At the end of 1915, the German/Austrian advance had forced the Russian line of defence three hundred miles eastwards and the general location of this front line would remain unchanged until the Russian collapse in 1917. This was a major and a humiliating defeat for Russia.

ITALIAN FRONT 1915

Italy was officially a member of the Triple Alliance with Germany and Austria-Hungary when the war started and as such should have entered the war on their side. However, she chose to remain neutral. At the same time, Italy knew she would never be recognised as a major European power by sitting on the sidelines, and both sides were doing their utmost to attract her in. The Germans offered Italy the Austrian territories of Tyrol and Trieste if she remained neutral which, of course, was not acceptable to the Austrians. The Allies, however, offered much more: Tyrol and Trieste as well as northern Dalmatia and a share of Asia Minor if Italy entered the war on the side of the Allies.

On 26 April 1915, Italy signed the London Pact with France and Britain, promising to enter the war within a month. Not many in Italy were in favour of the war, but on 23 May Italy declared war on Austria-Hungary. Strangely enough, she did not declare war on Germany for a further year!

The boundary between Italy and Austria-Hungary was vast and mountainous; in winter it was usually snow-covered and was basically very unsuitable territory for waging a war. When Italy entered the war, she had ample manpower, but her soldiers were poorly equipped, heavy artillery being particularly scarce. Although the Austrians were in rag order, they rallied to fight a foe who was once their ally and

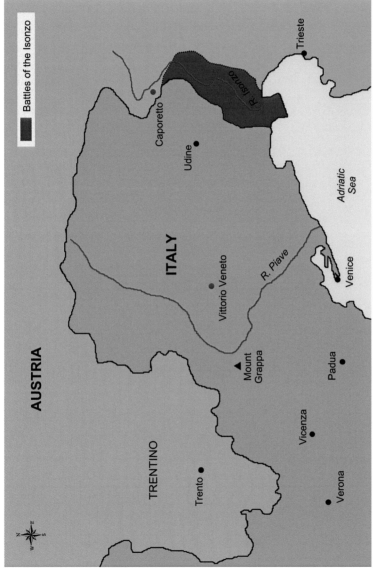

Map 9: Italian Front 1914–18

Sinking of the German armoured cruiser SMS *Blücher* in the naval engagement between German and British Dreadnoughts in the North Sea, 24 January 1915.

who they justifiably felt should be fighting on their side! Most of the fighting took place in the mountains of the Trentino region and along the River Isonzo, located on the border between the two protagonists near Trieste.

There were no less than eleven battles of Isonzo during the course of the war, the first four of them taking place in 1915. No appreciable territory was gained, but there were more than 200,000 casualties.

BALKAN FRONT 1915

Early in 1915, Germany tried to convince Austria-Hungary of the importance of conquering Serbia. If Serbia was taken, Germany would have a rail link through Austria-Hungary down to Constantinople. This would enable the Germans to send military supplies and troops to help the Ottoman Empire.

Bulgaria had remained neutral up to this stage in the war, but the German victory on the Eastern Front and the Ottoman success at Gallipoli helped Bulgaria to reach a decision. She joined the Central forces of Germany and Austria-Hungary and on 23 September 1915 Bulgaria began mobilising for war. At this stage the Allies woke up to the danger; and British and French forces, under the command of General Maurice Sarrail, landed at Salonika in neutral Greece. Criticism of Germany's invasion of neutral Belgium at the start of the war was conveniently forgotten!

Serbia was attacked by German and Austrian forces to the north and Bulgarian troops to the east. She was quickly overpowered by sheer weight of numbers. The Serbian forces retreated southwards into Greece.

On 11 October Bulgaria invaded Macedonia, which — as it turned out — was her main interest in entering the war.

Meanwhile, Britain wished to withdraw from Salonika, but France objected. Additional forces were sent to Salonika. Their only function was to keep an eye on Bulgarian troops, who were going nowhere. The Germans were quite happy to leave them in Salonika in what Germany called 'her largest internment camp' housing 500,000 men for the duration of the war.

WAR AT SEA 1915

There were two major events at sea in 1915: the Battle of Dogger Bank and the sinking of the Lusitania.

The **Battle of Dogger Bank** was a naval battle fought near the Dogger Bank in the North Sea on 24 January 1915 between squadrons of the British Grand Fleet and the German High Seas fleet. Britain had advance knowledge that a German squadron was heading for the Dogger Bank, so she dispatched her own naval forces to intercept it.

When the Germans were confronted by the British fleet, they took flight. The British pursued them and very quickly they had the Germans within range. Both sides engaged in long-range shelling, which resulted in heavy damage to ships on both sides. Believing they were being lured into a minefield, Britain broke off the chase and the Germans escaped.

Since the British lost no ships and suffered few casualties, while the Germans lost a ship and most of her crew, the action could be considered a British victory. However, in truth there was no winner and, shortly afterwards, the commanders on both sides were replaced.

The **RMS *Lusitania*** was a British ocean liner built in Scotland. The ship entered passenger service with the Cunard Line on 26 August 1907 and continued on the line's heavily-travelled passenger service between Liverpool and New York, which included a port of call at Queenstown (Cobh) in Ireland. The ship was named after the ancient province of Lusitania, which is part of present-day Portugal. In 1915, as Germany waged submarine warfare against Britain, the liner was recognised and torpedoed by a German U-boat (Undersea boat) on 7 May and sank in eighteen minutes. The vessel went down eleven miles off the Old Head of Kinsale near Cork in Ireland, killing 1,198 of the 1,959 people aboard. Around the world, the sinking gave rise to a storm of protest against Germany and contributed to America's entry into World War I. Argument over whether the ship was a legitimate military target has raged back and forth ever since as both sides made misleading claims about the ship. At the time she was sunk, it was claimed that she was carrying a large quantity of rifle ammunition and other war supplies as well as civilian passengers. The argument continues to this day. The sinking of the Lusitania resulted in the British Royal Family changing its name from the Germanic 'House of Saxe-Coburg and Gotha' to the 'House of Windsor'.

MIDDLE EAST 1915

Sinai and Palestine 1915–16

The major offensive in the Middle East in 1915 was at Gallipoli. However, on 26 January 1915 an Ottoman force invaded Egypt, at that time a British protectorate, and unsuccessfully attempted to interrupt the vital supply route running through the Suez Canal. The Suez Canal was of vital importance to the British. Instead of having to travel around the Cape of Good Hope, the Suez Canal cut the travelling time substantially from Britain to India, New Zealand and Australia. The canal had to be protected, which meant occupying the Sinai Desert and parts of Palestine. The bigger the area, the more men were needed to defend it. Britain had to retain a force of half a million men in Palestine for the duration of the war to protect the canal route.

Mesopotamia (Iraq) 1915–16

While the British were successful in Basra in 1914, their experience at Kut in 1915–16 was quite the opposite. Kut-al-Amara is a small town located 100 miles south of Baghdad where British and Indian troops, under Major General Charles Townshend, took a stand against the Ottomans. The British were retreating from Ctesiphon where they had suffered significant losses. General Townsend chose to stay and hold a position at Kut instead of continuing the march downriver towards Basra. The Ottomans had the British pinned down in Kut from 3 December 1915 until 29 April 1916, when they surrendered in a humiliating defeat for the Allies. Approximately 13,000 Allied soldiers were taken prisoner, many of whom died in captivity.

Armenian Genocide

The Armenian Genocide was a mini-Holocaust which took place in parallel with World War I in the same way as the Holocaust took place in parallel with World War II. The Muslim Ottoman Empire was on the wane and the Young Turks feared a takeover by the Christian Armenians. Armenia adopted Christianity in 301 A.D. — the first nation to do so. The Turks resolved to wipe out the Armenians completely. The slaughter commenced on 24 April 1915 and by 1923 it is estimated that 1.5 million Armenians had been murdered. Some were killed while many were placed on 'death marches' into the Syrian desert, where they died of starvation and exhaustion.

The Ottoman Empire ceased to exist in 1923 and was replaced by the Republic of Turkey. To this day the Turkish government denies that the genocide took place. The killings during the early years were obscured by World War I, but the written evidence is too strong to ignore. Pope Francis angered the Turkish government in 2015 when he called the massacres a genocide. In response Turkey recalled her ambassador to the Vatican.

FAR EAST 1915–16

In January 1915, with her European allies heavily involved in the war in Europe, Japan sought to consolidate her position in China. She presented China with the 'Twenty-One Demands', which would effectively have reduced China to a Japanese protectorate. Unsurprisingly, China refused to sign the agreement, which attracted international criticism particularly from America. Eventually, on 25 May, a much more reasonable treaty was signed between the two countries.

Throughout 1915 and 1916, German efforts to negotiate a separate peace with Japan failed. On 3 July 1916, Japan and Russia signed a treaty whereby each pledged not to make a separate peace with Germany, and agreed to consultation and common action should the territory or interests of either be threatened by an outside party.

1915 TIMELINE

17 Jan	Russia attacks Ottomans from Caucasus.
19 Jan	Germany begins an aerial bombing campaign against Britain using Zeppelins.
24 Jan	Naval Battle of Dogger Bank.
31 Jan	Germans use poison gas on Russia on the Eastern Front.
03 Feb	Ottoman troops' unsuccessful attack on Suez Canal.
07–20 Feb	Germans defeat Russians at Masurian Lakes in East Prussia.
16 Feb	French launch unsuccessful attack on Germans at Champagne.
18 Feb	Unrestricted U-boat campaign by Germany begins.
10 Mar	Battle of Neuve Chapelle begins.
18 Mar	Allied naval assault in the Dardanelles.
22 Mar	Russia defeats Austria-Hungary at Przemyśl in Galicia.
11 Apr	Major attack on British troops by Turks at Basra.
22 Apr	Second Battle of Ypres begins; Germans use gas.
24 Apr	Armenian genocide by Turkey begins.
25 Apr	British and Anzac troops land at Gallipoli.
02 May	Battle of Gorlice-Tarnów begins on the Eastern Front.
07 May	Lusitania sunk by German U-boat. 1,198 people were killed.
09 May	Britain attacks Germans in second battle at Neuve Chapelle.
15 May	Britain and Indian troops launch attack on German troops at Artois, near Neuve Chapelle.
23 May	Italy declares war on Austria-Hungary.
31 May	German Zeppelins kill twenty-eight people in London.

12 Jun	Austro-Germans resume offensive in Galicia and drive Russians eastwards.
16 Jun	Second attempt by French to take Vimy Ridge unsuccessful. Major casualties.
23 Jun	First Battle of Isonzo begins on the Italian Front.
01 Jul	Russia suffers major shortage of arms.
09 Jul	German South-West Africa (Namibia) taken by Allies.
13 Jul	Austro-German offensive against Russians begins in Northern Poland.
01 Aug	Germans achieve supremacy in the air with their Fokker aircraft which featured synchronised machine gun fire.
05 Aug	Warsaw taken by the Central Powers, ending a century of control of the city.
06 Aug	Allies renew offensive at Suvla Bay in Gallipoli.
05 Sep	Tsar Nicholas II takes personal command of the Russian army in an effort to rally his troops.
06 Sep	Bulgaria enters the war on Germany's side.
18 Sep	Germans shift their U-boat campaign from the Atlantic to the Mediterranean fearing reprisal from the United States.
25 Sep	Battle of Loos on Western Front; gas used by Allies.
26 Sep	Third attempt by French to take Vimy Ridge successful. British victory in the Battle of Kut-al-Amara in Middle East.
03 Oct	French and British forces land at Salonika in Greece.
06 Oct	Serbia invaded by Austria and Germany from the north and Bulgaria from the east.
11 Oct	Bulgaria invades Macedonia.
05 Dec	Siege of Kut-al-Amara by Turks begins in Mesopotamia.
14 Dec	Haig replaces French as Commander in Chief of BEF.
19 Dec	Britain begins orderly evacuation of Gallipoli.

CHAPTER 4

1916
Two Battles: 1.6 Million Lives Lost!

The major events in 1916 are the Battles of Verdun and the Somme on the Western Front, which together cost the lives of 1.6 million soldiers. At sea, British and German fleets fight the Battle of Jutland. Kitchener drowns when his ship strikes a mine and sinks. The Brusilov Offensive between Russians and Germans is the main event on the Eastern Front. Romania finally enters the war.

WESTERN FRONT 1916

A major problem in 1915 was a shortage of artillery shells; however, by early 1916 the armament factories of Europe had rectified this.

In December 1915 a conference was held between the French and the British at the French headquarters of Chantilly, presided over by General Joffre. The conference agreed that 1916 would see coordinated attacks by the Allies on the Western, Eastern and Italian fronts. However, nothing was agreed on the timing of the various offensives, which made coordination rather difficult.

Joffre decided that the attack on the Western Front would be along a 25-mile stretch of the River Somme in Picardy at a point where the French and the British armies met. There was no logic in this choice of battlefield. If anything, it favoured the Germans, who were located on higher ground.

Before the Somme, however, Britain had a problem to deal with in **Ireland**. In 1912 John Redmond's Irish Parliamentary Party at Westminster had been offered a form of Home Rule, but it was unacceptable to the Irish Parliamentary Party since it involved partitioning the country into north and south. Redmond believed that Home Rule would be granted when the war was over (at this stage, nobody realised that the war would continue for four years). On this premise, Redmond urged Ireland to support Britain in the war. However, a small number of Irish nationalists saw the war as an opportunity and on Easter Monday 1916 (in what became known as the Easter Rising) they rebelled against British rule. Germany saw this as an opportunity to unsettle Britain and she supplied some weaponry to the rebels. Britain had to divert forces from the Western Front to put down the Rising in Ireland, which they did in no uncertain manner.

[This issue is dealt with in more detail under Ireland's independence in Chapter 11, page 167].

Douglas Haig had just become Commander in Chief of the British forces in France, and Haig and Joffre together set out to plan the Somme offensive but not in any particular hurry. They decided to wait for the good weather of the summer to begin the offensive. Haig appointed Henry Rawlinson as army commander for the offensive even though Rawlinson had his doubts about the project. Meanwhile, the German commander Falkenhayn was alert to the danger, thanks to his reconnaissance aircraft. He believed that the French were at a low ebb and that a big defeat might destroy them completely. He decided to attack without delay and he chose Verdun as the battleground.

Battle of Verdun
Verdun and its fortress held a prominent place in French history and defeat here would be a grievous psychological blow to France. It was located at the head of a salient in the French line. It protruded into German-occupied territory — as is the case with a salient — and was surrounded on three sides by German forces.

The bombardment at Verdun began on 21 February when over 1,200 guns fired off two million shells in eight hours along an eight-mile front. At that time it was the heaviest bombardment ever carried out in any war, but the French were not easily defeated. General Pétain, who had been looking forward to his retirement, took charge of the French defences and — between himself and General Robert Nivelle — attacked the Germans on both sides of the River Meuse. The fighting was intense and continued from the end of February on and off until the end of the year when the fighting died away. Casualties were enormous on both sides: the French (310,000 soldiers) losing slightly more than the Germans (280,000 soldiers). The French spirit had been sorely dented. On the other hand, they held Verdun, which could be deemed a victory in itself. Pétain's reputation after Verdun stood him in good stead: he would subsequently become French head of state, while later in the year Nivelle was rewarded with the French Commander in Chief's job.

Amongst those fighting at Verdun were Charles de Gaulle and Friedrich Paulus, who would subsequently play prominent roles in World War II.

Battle of the Somme
The embers were still glowing at Verdun when the infamous Battle of the Somme began. The plan was that after an initial devastating bombardment, the British and French forces would go over the top into No Man's Land and attack the Germans on the other side. The Germans

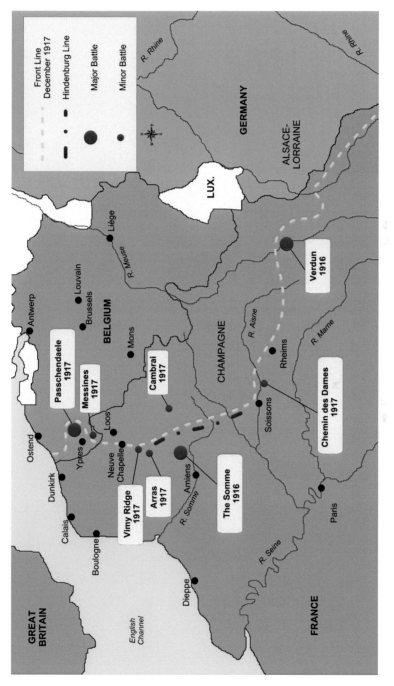

Map 10: Western Front 1916–17

British soldiers from 'A' Company, 11th Battalion, the Cheshire Regiment, in a captured German trench at Ovillers-la-Boisselle on the Somme, 1916. Photograph by Lt. J. W. Brooke. Painted by Olive Eustace (cover image).

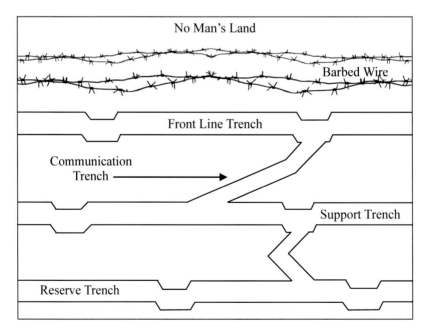

Trench Warfare

had several months notice of the impending battle and they spent their time deepening and reinforcing trenches, and building concrete bunkers as deep as forty feet. The British — with minimal support from the French (due to Verdun) — had little to offer but shells and enthusiasm.

Many of the British soldiers were raw recruits as a result of Kitchener's very effective *"Your Country Needs You"* campaign in 1915. More than two million men signed up. As an enticement, many groups of friends and neighbours were promised they would be stationed together. Groups came from all walks of life, from stockbrokers to football supporters. They became known as Pals Battalions. The sad outcome was that, while huge numbers of friends and neighbours fought together, they also died together. The practice was discontinued later in the war.

Although the Irish and British were at war with each other in Ireland in 1916, during the Battle of the Somme the 16th Irish Division fought shoulder-to-shoulder with the 36th Ulster Division in the British Army.

Towards the end of June, the planned ferocious bombardment began and lasted for five days. On 1 July the British advanced, assuming that the Germans had been obliterated or, at the very least, severely damaged. This was not the case: their deepened trenches and bunkers had saved them. Also, many of the shells failed to explode. As the British approached, the Germans climbed out of their bunkers and set up their machine guns on the edge of No Man's Land. What followed can only be described as slaughter. Wave after wave of British infantry were mown down. 20,000 British soldiers died on the first day, the heaviest loss in World War I on any one day. However, Haig would not admit defeat. Day after day, the attacks continued achieving nothing but dead soldiers. It remains incomprehensible to this day why Haig didn't call a halt to the insanity. Horse and man were no match for machine guns: the carnage was appalling. Haig had a huge number of cavalry troops ready to charge after the original bombardment, but they never got out of the stables! The battleground was churned up so badly by the bombardment that it was totally unsuitable for horses.

Equine Losses in World War I

A little known fact is that — between donkeys, mules and horses — eight million animals died in World War I.

The Battle of the Somme had the effect of dampening the enthusiasm and spirit of the ordinary soldier on both sides. It is estimated that total losses in the battle between British, French and Germans came to over a million men. The only Allied success at the Somme was achieved by the French, who broke through the German trenches over a small area near Mametz, before being driven back again by the Germans.

The battle dragged on into September when Haig decided to use the first tanks that became available in the war. However, the tanks were untried and very slow; they broke down easily and served no purpose in a battle that had already died. Only eighteen out of forty-eight tanks survived day one. The battle eventually petered out in November. It is estimated that a total of 1.6 million men died between Verdun and the Somme.

After the carnage of these two battles, during the winter of 1916 Hindenburg and Ludendorff devised a new defensive system on the Western Front. In what became known as the **Hindenburg Line,** they built a series of trenches superior to all previous efforts. The line was built across a German salient stretching from Arras to Laffaux near Soissons on the River Aisne. By withdrawing to this line, the Germans shortened the length of the front to be defended by thirty miles. The Germans learned a lesson from the Somme. The trenches were deeper with reinforced concrete walls and interconnecting tunnels, concrete bunkers and machine gun emplacements. As the work took place in German-held territory, it progressed without interruption. The Hindenburg Line left the Germans well prepared for 1917 on the Western Front.

Trench Warfare in World War I

As the war progressed, trench construction became more sophisticated: one trench became three trenches in parallel. Trench #1 was the front line, Trench #2 the support trench while Trench #3 was the reserve trench where soldiers rested and recovered. All three trenches were connected by a series of communication trenches running at right angles to the main trenches *[see Trench Warfare drawing, page 76]*. The trenches were built in a zigzag fashion. This made it more difficult for an enemy soldier to wipe out a large number of defenders at one time, or for a shell to inflict major damage.

EASTERN FRONT 1916

Russia had promised her Allies that she would launch an attack on the Eastern Front and, by diverting huge resources in terms of both arms and men to the war front, she was in a position to do so. However, the cost back in Russia was huge: severe food shortages (it was more important to feed the two million horses at the front), factories which produced nothing but armaments, and a railway system which did nothing else but ferry soldiers to and from the front. There was huge discontent throughout the country culminating in the Russian Revolution and Russia's withdrawal from the war the following year. Yet Tsar Nicholas II remained as absolute ruler, relying on the repressive power of his police to continue his rule!

A new Russian commander, General Aleksei Brusilov, had come to the fore. He had learned from past experience that the system of massive bombardment on a single target followed by a slow attack by the infantry was not successful. It gave defenders too much time to send for reinforcements. His plan was to attack twenty different positions on the Eastern Front at the same time. This became known as the **Brusilov Offensive**. These attacks took place in Galicia along the southern half of the Eastern Front, which was defended by Austro-Hungarian soldiers. Their defence quickly collapsed. Once more, Germany had to come to the rescue of her allies. Troops were moved from the Western Front and when Brusilov attempted a further advance, he was confronted by well-prepared German troops. The Russians were driven back eastwards suffering up to a million casualties, and these losses contributed in no small way to Russia's withdrawal from the war the following year.

Russia was not the only country to suffer. Austria-Hungary was now a spent force and for the remainder of the war, she fought on the coat-tails of Germany.

ITALIAN FRONT 1916

There were a further five Battles of the Isonzo during 1916. During one of them in May, a breakdown in communication between Falkenhayn (Germany) and Conrad (Austria), resulted in a lost opportunity to knock Italy out of the war. Austria had attacked the Italians from the Trentino, hoping to break out onto the Venetian plain and possibly cut off the Italian army at the Isonzo River. Austria, who had moved troops from the Eastern Front, had the upper hand but needed help from Germany to 'finish off' the Italians. No help arrived, however, due to the breakdown in communication so the opportunity was squandered!

BALKAN FRONT 1916

Romania finally entered the war on 27 August 1916 when she declared war on Austria-Hungary. She was persuaded to do so by the success of the Brusilov Offensive on the Eastern Front and by a promise of the territory of Transylvania by the Allies. Germany was taken by surprise. After the initial success of the Brusilov (Russian) campaign, the German general Falkenhayn was demoted and put in charge of the Romanian Front. Romania had little experience of war and by the end of the year Bucharest had fallen to Falkenhayn and the entire country was in German hands. Before this happened, British agents had managed to torch Romanian oil wells and thus deprive Germany of an important fuel supply.

WAR AT SEA 1916

Battle of Jutland
The Battle of Jutland took place in the North Sea close to Norway and Denmark on 31 May 1916. Both the British and the Germans had built up extensive navies (including Dreadnought battleships) at this stage of the war, but both were very wary of the dangers of mines and torpedoes.

A fleet of 100 German ships under newly-appointed Admiral Reinhard Scheer sailed forth from Wilhelmshaven, while the British fleet of 150 ships under the cautious Sir John Jellicoe sailed from Scapa Flow in the Orkneys. They met at Jutland, or to be more precise they stood off one another at Jutland and used their long-range guns to bombard each other. The battle lasted only a few hours with the British losing fourteen ships and the Germans eleven. Neither side was willing to lose a large number of ships (after all, battleships did not come cheap) and the battle ended when the German fleet headed for home, where they would stay for the remainder of the war. As was the case with many battles in World War I, both sides claimed victory. There was no clear victor, but Britain lost 6,000 sailors and the Germans almost 4,000.

The one positive outcome of Jutland was that Germany became aware that the war could not be won with surface ships (they were too expensive and the British fleet would always be superior in numbers). From that moment on, they would concentrate their efforts on their U-boats.

Blockade
The Allies had initiated a blockade on Germany from the start of the war in 1914: the British naval base at Scapa Flow in the Orkneys gave them control over the North Sea. By the end of 1916, the blockade was hurting. Germany was experiencing severe food shortages. A poor harvest in 1916 made matters worse. Turnips became a staple part of the German diet during the winter of 1916/17, which is often referred to in Germany as the 'turnip winter'.

However, as much of Britain's food supply was imported by sea, the British people were suffering at the hands of the German U-boats. Severe food rationing was implemented and a huge factor in their survival was the resourcefulness of the British women who ran the farms, the factories and the hospitals while their menfolk were away fighting the war.

German propaganda ensured that the true German casualty figures at Verdun and the Somme were not released to the German people. If the true facts were known, Germany would have found it very difficult to continue in the war. In the meantime, Kaiser Wilhelm II continued with his game shooting and fishing!

COMMAND CHANGES 1916

Austria
On 21 November Franz Joseph, Emperor of Austria, died at the age of 86. This marked the end of the Habsburg Empire and all the pomp and ceremony that went with it. It also began the spread of nationalism throughout Europe.

Britain
Horatio Kitchener met a violent end on 5 June 1916 when the HMS *Hampshire* was sunk by a mine off the Orkneys. Almost all of the crew were lost, along with Kitchener himself. David Lloyd George took command at the war office. On 7 December Lloyd George succeeded Herbert Henry Asquith as British Prime Minister and he would retain the position until World War I was over.

Germany
Falkenhayn paid for the German lack of success at Verdun and the Somme. He was removed as German Chief of Staff. On 29 August he was replaced by the pairing of Hindenburg and Ludendorff, who had been so successful in the Eastern Front in 1914–15. As Hindenburg had come out of retirement, the younger Ludendorff was the de facto leader for the remainder of the war.

France
The French had tired of Joffre and his apparent indifference to their losses. Nivelle became their hero after Verdun and on 12 December he was appointed French Commander in Chief.

1916 TIMELINE

09 Jan   Evacuation of Gallipoli completed.

18 Feb   In Africa, French and British take German Cameroon.

21 Feb   Battle of Verdun commences at the historic city of Verdun. Germans attack French. Continues throughout the year.

18 Mar   Germans score major victory over Russia on Eastern Front.

18 Apr   In response to threat from President Woodrow Wilson, new U-boat campaign by Germany around Britain called off.

24 Apr   Ireland revolts against British rule: Easter Rising in Dublin.

29 Apr   In Middle East, British and Indian troops suffer major defeat by Turkish forces at Kut-al-Amara in Mesopotamia.

14 May   Austrian offensive against Italy begins in the Trentino.

25 May   Compulsory conscription begins in Britain.

31 May   Battle of Jutland in North Sea between British and German navies. No decisive outcome.

04 Jun   Start of Brusilov Russian Offensive on Eastern Front.

05 Jun   Kitchener drowned.

22 Jun   War of attrition continues at Verdun.

24 Jun   Battle of the Somme begins with a week-long artillery bombardment.

01 Jul   Battle starts with disastrous British attack. 20,000 British soldiers killed on first day of Allied advance!

13 Jul   British try a night attack against Germans on Somme front.

27 Aug   Romania enters war by declaring war on Austria-Hungary.

28 Aug   Italy declares war on Germany.

29 Aug   Hindenburg succeeds Falkenhayn as German Chief of Staff.

01 Sep   Romania invaded by Central Powers of Germany, Ottoman and Bulgaria.

15 Sep   Tanks used for the first time in Battle of the Somme.

20 Sep   Brusilov Offensive on Eastern Front grinds to a halt.

25 Sep   British and French renew attacks on the Somme, capturing several villages, including Thiepval.

10 Oct   Romanian troops driven out of Hungary by Austrian and German troops, who then invade Romania and head for Bucharest.

24 Oct   French forces under Robert Nivelle have major success driving Germans back at Verdun.

13 Nov   British troops capture Beaumont Hamel and Beaucourt on the Somme.

18 Nov   Britain and France cease the disastrous Battle of the Somme.

21 Nov   Emperor Franz Josef of Austria dies, aged 86. Is succeeded by his great-nephew Karl, who tries to negotiate peace with Allies.

06 Dec   Bucharest (Romania) falls to the Central Powers.

07 Dec   Lloyd George succeeds Asquith as British Prime Minister.

12 Dec   Nivelle replaces Joffre as French Commander in Chief.

15 Dec   Germans finally withdraw from Verdun after almost a year.

CHAPTER 5

1917
America Enters The War

The main events in 1917 are Germany's unrestricted submarine campaign resulting in America's declaration of war, the Russian Revolution resulting in Russia's withdrawal from the war, and several battles on the Western Front including the notorious Battle of Passchendaele. War continues on the Italian Front with the Battle of Caporetto.

There had been several efforts to promote peace talks during the war, but the problem was always the same: Germany insisted on retaining the territories and colonies she had annexed and this, naturally, was not acceptable to the Allies. By the start of 1917 individuals in Russia, France, Austria and even Germany would have been quite happy to end the war, but on the other hand there were many who believed that the only way to end a war is with a victory. The United States was always reluctant to become involved in the war but, as events transpired, she was left with little option.

Zimmermann Telegram

Germany attempted to exploit Mexico's long-standing grievances against the US. Arthur Zimmermann, Germany's Foreign Secretary, sent a telegram to Mexico offering support for any action undertaken to reclaim territory lost to the US in the previous century (which included territory in Arizona and Texas) in return for joining the German cause. The telegram was intercepted by the Allies and its contents revealed. It had an immediate impact in the US, and many previously in favour of neutrality now favoured America entering the war.

WAR AT SEA 1917

On 31 January 1917 Germany declared a policy of unrestricted submarine warfare. This meant that all merchant shipping, including neutral shipping, would be sunk on sight in the Atlantic war zone. Germany had been preparing for this and throughout 1916 had doubled her fleet of U-boats from fifty to over a hundred. The results were dramatic. In the spring months, Allied losses at sea increased from 540,000 tons in February to 880,000 tons in April! These included substantial American losses.

America had been a huge financial contributor to the war up to this point (without her, Britain would have been broke), but now she had to become physically involved and this would take time. America had a very strong navy but no army to speak of. Recruitment and training started immediately and within a year she had two million soldiers ready for action. From the spring of 1918 onwards, American troops began to pour into France and would eventually prove to be the vital factor in ending the war.

In the meantime, the U-boat problem had to be resolved and it was resolved very simply. It was Lloyd George (who had been appointed British Prime Minister in December 1916) who came up with the solution: convoys! Merchant ships would cross the Atlantic in large groups protected by a few destroyers. Lloyd George did not have the support of his admirals who claimed the convoy system would not work. Lloyd George stuck to his guns and wearing his 'head of the admiralty' hat, insisted that the convoy system must be implemented. It was an immediate success.

The first convoy sailed on 10 May. Whereas shipping losses before the convoys started were as high as twenty-five per cent, losses afterwards dropped to one per cent. This one decision by Lloyd George changed the entire face of the war.

WESTERN FRONT 1917

There were problems with the leadership of the Allies at the Western Front. France and Britain were not pulling together (they had not done so since the beginning of the war). In France, Aristide Briand was now Prime Minister with Nivelle — living on his Verdun reputation — as his Commander in Chief. Lloyd George had become Prime Minister of Britain in December 1916, taking over from Asquith. The commander of the British forces Douglas Haig did not enjoy the confidence of Lloyd George, but he did have the support of King George V. Everybody was shouting for a 'knockout' battle on the Western Front to finish the war, and one of the most vocal was Nivelle who claimed to have the secret to victory!

In Germany, Ludendorff was now Commander in Chief with Bethmann Hollweg as his Chancellor.

An Anglo-French conference was held at Calais on 26 February. All agreed on the need for an offensive on the Western Front and a decision was taken that Nivelle would be in charge with Haig taking orders from the French general. This was not well received by the British officers, but they were not aware that this decision had been rubber-stamped earlier by Lloyd George and his five-man war cabinet.

The Germans moved to their newly-relocated Hindenburg Line in March 1917, leaving behind a desolate territory which in places was fifty miles wide. As they withdrew, the Germans systematically destroyed the area: demolishing houses, mining roads and poisoning water supplies. This meant that in order to advance through this area, the French and British had to make it safe and extend road, rail and water systems to the new Hindenburg Line.

Before the Hindenburg Line came to light, Nivelle had planned an attack on the Western Front. Ever the optimist, he now planned to continue his proposed offensive, but everybody else advised against it, particularly Haig. On top of this, Nivelle had lost his chief backer, Prime Minister Briand, who had been replaced by an octogenarian named Alexandre Ribot. He appointed Paul Painleve, a distinguished mathematician as his Minister of War. Both did their best to dissuade Nivelle, but he threatened to resign and was allowed to proceed with his promised miracle.

Meanwhile, on 9 April, the Canadians launched a surprise attack on the Germans at **Vimy Ridge**, one of the few hills in Flanders. Initially they drove the Germans back. However the old failings quickly manifested themselves. The offensive dragged on, the Germans brought up reinforcements and the territory was retaken. There was no change in territory, but again there were substantial casualties on both sides. The Canadians were led by General Julian Byng, who went on to become Governor-General of Canada. The Canadian National Vimy Memorial stands on the site today.

This offensive was meant to be a diversion to Nivelle's main plan of attack in an area known as the **Chemin des Dames** located between the Rivers Aisne and Ailette. The Germans had advance knowledge of the plan: a captured French officer had full details of the proposal on his person so when the attack came on 16 April, the Germans were dug in and waiting. Having apparently learned nothing from the Battle of the Somme, the French attack followed a major artillery bombardment. The results were the same: another 270,000 French casualties! This became known as the **Second Battle of the Aisne**.

The French army had had enough. They rebelled. Fifty divisions refused to obey orders; thousands deserted! Deserters were harshly treated. Thousands were jailed and sentenced to hard labour. As many as forty-three deserters were executed.

On 15 May Philippe Pétain, fresh from his victory at Verdun, replaced Nivelle. He promised his troops longer periods of leave and that there would be no more 'suicidal' offensives. The French army would become a defensive army instead of an offensive one. These changes enabled Pétain to win back the confidence of the French troops!

Through bitter experience, the Allies realised that the method of attack had to change and so the 'creeping barrage' system came into being. Shells were no longer in short supply and a barrage of shells up to 1,000 yards wide ahead of advancing troops was proving to be very effective.

It did, however, leave the terrain very difficult for the advancing troops as the soldiers found to their cost at the **Battle of Passchendaele**, also known as the Third Battle of Ypres.

Haig always had in mind an attack from the Ypres salient and when Nivelle was moved, Haig emerged from his shadow as belligerent and stubborn as ever. He was still convinced after three years of failure that he could defeat the Germans and he believed that Ypres was the place to do it. He chose to ignore the lessons learned previously in Flanders and the fact that Flanders was called a 'low country' for good reason. It had an extremely high water table and when it rained, the territory turned into a sea of mud and became impassable.

Haig had many critics of the proposed offensive, including Lloyd George, but the British Prime Minister was not in any position to speak out as his support for Nivelle at the Chemin des Dames had proved to be poor judgment!

However, before the battle commenced, the British had a remarkable success at **Messines Ridge**. The ridge, which was a great observation post from which to view Ypres and the surrounding countryside, had been in the hands of the Germans since 1914. For two years, the British under Herbert Plumer had been constructing a series of tunnels more than 100-foot deep under the ridge and filling them with one million tonnes of explosives. At 3:00 a.m. on the morning of 7 June 1917, the explosives were detonated. Thousands of German soldiers were simply vaporised! The explosion was clearly heard in London. The German defences were shattered and the British took over the ridge. But now, as on many occasions during the war, the Allies failed to take advantage of their success. Preparations and talks (mostly trying to dissuade Haig from his plan for Ypres) went on for seven weeks resulting in the element of surprise and the good weather of June and July being squandered.

The Battle of Passchendaele (Third Battle of Ypres) commenced on 31 July. The British and the Canadians had some success on the first day, but then the rain started and it rained continuously for seven days. The lowlands were swamped. The 'creeping barrage' churned the ground into a sea of mud. As was the case at the Somme, the ground was totally unsuitable for cavalry. Soldiers and horses were drowned in shell holes filled with water. Artillery and tanks proved useless in the quagmire. It proved impossible to move the wounded out. Haig (as obstinate as ever) ordered his men to continue. They fought on into the autumn, eventually crawling through the mud to take the village of Passchendaele. This was one of the most notorious battles of any war. Allied casualties were in excess of 300,000 while German losses were almost 200,000. The territorial gains were minimal. AJP Taylor in his book *'The First World War: An Illustrated History'* described Passchendaele as *"the blindest slaughter of a blind war"*.

Amongst the many casualties at Passchendaele was the Irish poet Francis Ledwidge. One of a military road repair team, he was blown to pieces by a German shell on 31 July 1917.

However, there was one good news story on the Western Front before the end of 1917. The **Battle of Cambrai** took place fifty miles south of Passchendaele. The rain had stopped and the ground dried up. It became possible to use newly-produced tanks. Aerial reconnaissance had also improved. On 20 November, 380 tanks moved forward in formation with artillery support. They quickly punched a hole in the German defences. Unfortunately, there was no infantry backup: there was none available after Passchendaele. The Germans brought up their reserves and quickly won back the territory lost. However, Cambrai showed the value of tanks in future warfare.

Tank Potential

It was Churchill, in his position as First Lord of the Admiralty, who saw the potential of tanks. They were called tanks (meaning water tanks) to confuse the enemy, and the name stuck. The French quickly saw their potential and proceeded to manufacture them in their thousands. The Germans initially saw them as a waste of time but during the interwar years realised their huge potential.

As 1917 drew to a close, the Allies looked forward to the arrival of American troops in the spring.

EASTERN FRONT 1917

There were two separate revolts in Russia in 1917 (jointly referred to as the **Russian Revolution**), which destroyed the Tsarist autocracy and led to the creation of the Soviet Union. In the first revolt in March, Tsar Nicholas II was deposed and replaced by a Provisional Government. In the second revolt in November, the Provisional Government was replaced by a Bolshevik (Russian word for majority) communist government.

The winter of 1916/17 was particularly harsh in Russia. Food shortages were widespread. Inflation was rampant. The army had suffered severe setbacks on the Eastern Front, which left them in mutinous form. At the beginning of March, there were food riots in Petrograd (St. Petersburg) organised mainly by the wives of soldiers. Members of the Imperial parliament, the Duma, took control of the country forming the Russian Provisional Government. The word Soviet (council) was created, and representatives of factories and soldiers were appointed to the various Soviets. There was agreement on one item: Tsar Nicholas II had to go! The generals urged him to step down and on 15 March 1917 he abdicated. The Russian monarchy had ended. Later, on 16 July 1918, the Tsar, his wife Alexandra and their five children were executed by Vladimir Lenin's revolutionaries.

Romanov Dynasty

The Romanov dynasty ruled Russia for 304 years from 1613 until 1917, when Tsar Nicholas II abdicated at the behest of the new Provisional Government.

1917 was a calamitous year for Russia. She had suffered major defeats by the Germans in 1916 in World War I, while at home after a long harsh winter; she endured food riots in Petrograd (St. Petersburg). It was easy for the populace at large to blame the Romanov monarchy for their troubles. The Romanovs consisted of Tsar Nicholas, his wife Alexandra and their five children. They had one son Alexei and four daughters Olga, Tatiana, Maria, and Anastasia. Alexei was 13 years of age in 1917, while his sisters were aged between 16 and 21.

After the abdication of the Tsar in March, the governance of the country was taken over by the new Provisional Government led by Alexander Kerensky, but governments in Russia in 1917 were fragile affairs. The Romanov family was moved to Siberia "for their own safety" in July. In October 1917 the Bolsheviks, led by Vladimir Lenin, seized power. However, in March 1918 Lenin's Bolsheviks (the Reds) came under pressure once more from Kerensky's Provisional Government

---

Russian Imperial Romanov family. *Seated:* Grand Duchess Olga, Tsar Nicholas II, Grand Duchess Anatasia, Tsarevich Alexei, Grand Duchess Tataiana. *Standing:* Grand Duchess Maria, the Tsarina Alexandra.

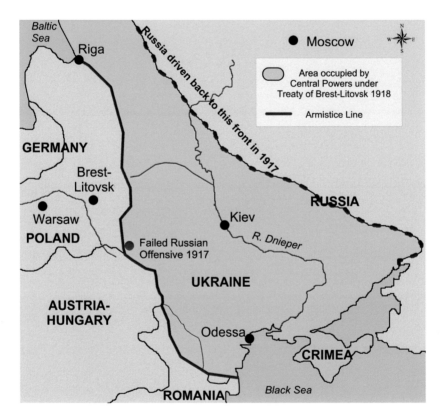

Map 11: Eastern Front — Russia driven back to a new front 1917

(the Whites). Lenin ordered that the Romanov family be exterminated: he feared that the Romanov dynasty might rise again with the help of one or more European countries.

Without trial, the assassinations took place on 17 July 1918. The Romanov family, their physician and some of their servants were led into a cellar in the early hours of the morning. The executions were a botched affair with many of the victims surviving the initial barrage of gunfire and being subjected to vicious bayonet stabbings and further shootings. Their bodies were dumped down a disused mine shaft. Some of the bodies were only recovered and identified by DNA as recently as 1991. A demeaning end to a powerful dynasty!

After the Tsar's abdication, no obvious leader emerged from either the Duma or the Soviets — that is, until Vladimir Lenin stepped up to fill the gap. Lenin was a very powerful character. He preached international socialism: *"Bread for the people, land to the peasant, peace to all peoples."* He returned home from exile in Zurich to lead his followers — the Bolsheviks — one of whom was named Joseph Stalin! Lenin's return to Russia was facilitated by Germany, who was quite happy to stir things up amongst the enemy. She had done so previously in 1916 by sending arms to Ireland to assist her in her revolt against British rule. Now, Germany could see that the revolt in Russia might lead to Russia's withdrawal from the war. In a matter of weeks, Lenin was joined by Leon Trotsky. Trotsky was a superb orator and was soon to prove his worth as a political organiser also. Leon Trotsky joined the Bolshevik Party alongside Lenin and Stalin. Trotsky never got on with Stalin and was removed from power by him in 1927.

When the Provisional Government chose to continue the war with Germany, the Bolsheviks campaigned for the abandonment of the war effort. They formed workers' militias under their control into the Red Guards (later the Red Army) over which they exerted substantial control.

Meanwhile, Alexander Kerensky became head of the Provisional Government. Another eloquent speaker, he succeeded in rousing the Russian army for one final effort against Germany. In early July 1917, Russia attacked the Germans. They had a few days of success before the Germans counter-attacked and quickly drove them back. When the Germans reached Riga in Latvia, the Russian effort collapsed completely. This was Russia's dying kick: she would take no further part in World War I. War on the Eastern Front had ended and Germany was now free to move her troops elsewhere.

In November a second revolt took place. In Petrograd, the Provisional Government under Kerensky was overthrown by the Bolsheviks under Lenin. The Bolsheviks took over the most important government positions: Lenin became Chairman and Trotsky became Commissar for Foreign Affairs. However, this marked the beginning of the Russian Civil War between the 'Red' (Bolshevik) and 'White' (anti-Bolshevik) factions, a war that would continue until 1921.

ITALIAN FRONT 1917

On the Italian Front, the last two battles on the Isonzo River took place in 1917. As before, there was no definitive outcome.

As a result of the Russian withdrawal on the Eastern Front, Germany now had spare forces to send elsewhere. Ludendorff, prompted by Hindenburg, sent troops to the Italian Front to keep Austria-Hungary in the war and hopefully deliver a knockout blow to the Italians.

Territorial gains on the Italian Front from 1915 to 1917 were minimal, but casualties were enormous. Italy suffered 1.5 million casualties compared to the Austrian's 600,000. The Italian Front was of no significance in the overall outcome of World War I, but it kept two 'bit players' — Italy and Austria-Hungary — occupied for two years.

The elderly Italian General Luigi Cadorna was an extremely brutal man. He believed that the best way to train his troops was to terrorise them. Cadorna resorted to the Roman practice of decimation — the killing of every tenth man — from units that failed to perform in battle. In Italy, deserters who were caught were shot. Several hundred men were executed for desertion. Cadorna banned the Italian press from the front lest the truth become known.

Up to 1917, the Italians had held their own against the Austrians but at a cost. However, when the German troops from the Eastern Front arrived in 1917, the situation changed. On 24 October nine Austrian and five German divisions attacked the Italians at **Caporetto**. Erwin Rommel, who would later become famous in World War II, commanded one of the German units. The Italians were routed and fell back a distance of seventy miles from the River Isonzo to the River Piave. The use of poison gas by the Germans played a key role in the rout of the Italians. However, the Germans were geared neither for the territory (they couldn't get supplies) nor for the weather and were unable to press home their advantage.

The Italian commander, Cadorna, was replaced by General Armando Diaz on the instructions of the Italian Prime Minister Vittorio Orlando.

The Italians took the opportunity to regroup under the much more reasonable Diaz and they now received long-promised support from Britain and France, who set up defensive positions at the River Piave and at Mount Grappa. As the year drew to a close, the Germans were moved to the Western Front, where a more important offensive awaited them.

BALKAN FRONT 1917

Greece
When the war commenced in 1914, the Greek Prime Minister Eleutherios Venizelos was in favour of Greece joining the Allies. However, King Constantine I had a very good reason to disagree: he was married to Sophia of Prussia, a sister of Kaiser Wilhelm II of Germany. This conflict of interests resulted in Greece remaining neutral for the early years of the war. However, Allied forces used Greece as an operational base. The relationship between Greece and Russia was further complicated by the royal relationship between King Constantine and the Russian Tsar: they were cousins. In June 1917 King Constantine abdicated in favour of his son Alexander. Prime Minister Venizelos took control of the country, and Greece declared war on Germany and the Central Powers on 30 June 1917.

Before Greece entered the war, Bulgaria occupied Thrace in northern Greece, which she would hold until the war ended the following year.

MIDDLE EAST 1917

Mesopotamia (Iraq)
In February 1917 British forces under Sir Frederick Stanley Maude recaptured Kut-al-Amara, which they had lost so ignominiously in 1916. Maude then set his eyes on the much more important prize of Baghdad, defended by the Turks under Khalil Pasha. The Turks were outnumbered and, once the Anglo-Indian forces overcame initial difficulties in crossing the River Tigris, they entered Baghdad unopposed on 11 March.

This was a decisive propaganda victory for the Allies and the fall of Baghdad brought an end to Ottoman activity in the area.

Sinai and Palestine
Gaza is the capital city (population 500,000) of the Gaza Strip. At the beginning of World War I, the Ottomans — supported by Germany — controlled Gaza, but the British War Office resolved to change this in 1917.

Turkish forces under the command of German General Kress von Kressenstein were in commanding positions on a series of ridges between Gaza and Beersheba, controlling the only practical entry into Palestine.

British forces under Sir Archibald Murray made their first attack on 26 March (**First Battle of Gaza**) but were defeated by a smaller army of Turks. British losses outnumbered the Turkish losses two to one, but Murray's report to London gave a more positive report of the battle. As his reward, he was instructed to try again. The **Second Battle of Gaza** began on 17 April and lasted for three days. The outcome was no different: defeat for the British! They suffered over 6,000 casualties in comparison with 2,000 for the Turks.

Murray was recalled to London and was replaced by Sir Edmund Allenby. With the assistance of colonial troops from Australia, Allenby reorganised his forces and on 31 October the **Third Battle of Gaza** began. Allenby's plan was to attack Beersheba and surround the Turkish forces defending Gaza. The plan succeeded and by 7 November Beersheba and Gaza had both fallen to the Allies. In the fighting, 18,000 British troops were killed, wounded or went missing while the Turkish casualties numbered 25,000.

The victories at Beersheba and Gaza opened the way to Jerusalem and on 9 December Allenby entered the Holy City on foot out of respect. The religious Lloyd George was delighted!

FAR EAST 1917

On 18 December 1916 the British again requested naval assistance from Japan. During 1917 two Japanese cruisers were sent to Cape Town while four destroyers were sent to the Mediterranean to be based in Malta. Their function was to carry out escort duties for troop transports and anti-submarine operations. The Japanese escorted almost 800 ships from Malta carrying 700,000 soldiers, thus making a substantial contribution to the war effort. In return for this assistance, Britain recognised Japan's territorial gains in Shantung and in the Pacific islands north of the Equator.

When America entered the war on 6 April 1918, the Americans and the Japanese found themselves on the same side, despite their increasingly acrimonious relations over China and competition between them in the Pacific.

1917 TIMELINE

19 Jan   Zimmermann telegram intercepted by British.

01 Feb   Germany begins unrestricted U-boat campaign.

03 Feb   US severs diplomatic relations with Germany over U-boat warfare.

25 Feb   Britain retakes Kut-al-Amara in Middle East.

11 Mar   British forces follow up by taking Baghdad.

08 Mar   Russian civilians revolt against Tsar Nicholas II and the war.

15 Mar   The Tsar abdicates. New democratic Provisional Government established in Russia.

16 Mar   Germany begins orderly withdrawal to the Hindenburg Line (called the Siegfried Line by Germany).

26 Mar   First Battle of Gaza in Middle East.

06 Apr   The United States finally declares war on Germany.

Apr   Bad month for the Allies in the air: Germans shoot down 150 Allied aircraft.

09 Apr   Battle of Arras begins. Canadians capture Vimy Ridge.

16 Apr   Unsuccessful French offensive at the Chemin des Dames. Lenin returns to Russia after twelve years exile in Zurich. Joins up with the Bolsheviks, including Joseph Stalin.

17 Apr   Second Battle of Gaza.

15 May   French Commander in Chief Robert Nivelle replaced by General Philippe Pétain.

18 May   Selective Service Act passed in America authorising increase in US army to four million men.

19 May   Provisional Government in Russia to remain in war against the wishes of Lenin's Bolsheviks.

27 May   Major discord in French army: soldiers refuse to obey orders. Pétain takes control and promises no more 'suicide battles'.

07 Jun   Battle of Messines Ridge, south of Ypres. Major underground explosion kills 10,000 Germans.

13 Jun   Germans bomb London killing 160 and wounding 400.

21 Jun   First American troops land in France.

01 Jul   Russia attempts to retake Lvov on the Eastern Front but is routed by the Germans.

02 Jul   Greece joins Allies and declares war on Central Powers. Pro-German King Constantine abdicates. Control of the country is assumed by pro-Allies Prime Minister Venizelos.

31 Jul   Third Battle of Ypres (Passchendaele) begins. Continues until 6 November when Canadians capture the village of Passchendaele. A 'disaster in the mud' led by British Commander Douglas Haig.

01 Sep   Final battle between Germany and Russia on Eastern Front near Riga. Russia, unable to cope with Germany's new storm troop tactics, abandons Riga and retreats.

20 Sep   Revised British strategy at Ypres. Features narrowly-focused artillery and troop attacks. The first such attack along the Menin Road toward Gheluvelt produces a gain of 1,000 yards but results in 22,000 British and Australian casualties.

12 Oct   The Ypres offensive peaks around the village of Passchendaele. Many thousands of Allied troops die in a liquid mud battlefield.

24 Oct   Germany helps Austria to rout the Italians at Caporetto.

31 Oct   Third Battle of Gaza: Britain with the help of Lawrence of Arabia's Arabs capture Beersheba from the Turks.

06 Nov   Bolshevik coup d'état (October Revolution) led by Lenin and Trotsky in Petrograd. Lenin withdraws Russia from the war.

26 Oct   Another unsuccessful attempt to take Passchendaele, this time with the Canadians involved.

06 Nov   Passchendaele eventually taken by the Canadians, bringing the Third Battle of Ypres to a close. Passchendaele was a complete disaster with the Allies suffering 300,000 casualties and the Germans 200,000.

11 Nov   German High Command meets at Mons in Belgium to agree strategy to end the war before the Americans arrive.

15 Nov   Georges Clemenceau elected Prime Minister of France at the age of 76.

20 Nov   Battle of Cambrai begins. First all-tank battle in the war. Initial Allied gains taken back by Germans, demonstrating the potential of tanks for the future.

07 Dec   Romania concludes an armistice with the Central Powers due to the demise of her former ally, Imperial Russia.

09 Dec   Jerusalem surrenders to British forces. Ends four centuries of control by Turks.

15 Dec   Russia signs armistice with Germany.

CHAPTER 6

1918
World War I Ends

1918 begins with President Woodrow Wilson presenting his Fourteen Points plan to Congress. Germany makes a Herculean effort to finish off the war on the Western Front before the Americans arrive: generally referred to as Germany's Spring Offensive. In mid-1918 Europe is hit by the Spanish flu, which results in the deaths of twenty-five million people. In late spring, the Americans begin arriving. Under the pressure of these additional troops and the development of Allied tanks, the war ends in November with Germany seeking an armistice.

Woodrow Wilson's Fourteen Points

The President presented his Fourteen Points to the joint Houses of Congress on 8 January 1918. This was his plan for the end of World War I.

1. The abolition of secret treaties.
2. Freedom of the seas.
3. Free trade.
4. Disarmament.
5. Adjustment of colonial claims. Colonies to be given a say in their own future.
6. Russia to be assured of independent development in Russian territory.
7. Restoration of Belgium's pre-war status.
8. Alsace-Lorraine to be returned to France.
9. Italian borders to be redrawn on lines of nationality.
10. Autonomous development of Austria-Hungary as a nation.
11. Balkan states to be granted autonomy. Serbia to be given access to the Adriatic Sea.
12. Ottoman Empire to be dissolved. Turkey and all nations in the Ottoman Empire to be granted independence.
13. Establishment of an independent Poland with access to the sea.
14. The League of Nations to be formed to enforce peace.

Had the Allies at last got the supreme commander they lacked throughout the war? Here, at least, was a target for all to aim at, although it would take more than a line on a piece of paper to sort out most of the problems. The Allies (in particular the British) did not react to Wilson's plan with any great enthusiasm. Analysts have since speculated that this may have been because they hadn't come up with a plan themselves. Clemenceau's comment on the plan was: *"The good Lord needed only ten!"*

EASTERN FRONT 1918

As a direct result of Russia's withdrawal from the war, the Treaty of Brest-Litovsk was signed between Germany and Russia (Bolsheviks) on 3 March 1918. Brest-Litovsk, a town destroyed in the Russian retreat in 1915 was the headquarters of the German army in the east and the Bolsheviks had no option but to sign the treaty. The treaty turned much of Tsarist Russia into a huge German protectorate. The Baltic states, Poland and Ukraine became independent, in theory at least. The treaty gave the Allies some idea of how difficult Germany would be to deal with if she won the war, which was about to be decided on the Western Front. However, the Russian withdrawal left Romania surrounded by Central forces and on 7 May Romania surrendered in the Treaty of Bucharest peace agreement. Land along the coast of the Black Sea was surrendered to Bulgaria and the Central Powers took control of the mouth of the Danube. However, the Treaty of Versailles at the end of the war redressed the situation and gave Transylvania to Romania, which had been her sole objective from the beginning.

Then came an unexpected intervention in the war. Czechoslovakia asked to be recognised as one of the Allies. Her aim was to be recognised as an independent nation, thus expediting the demise of the Habsburg Empire. The Czechs proved themselves by taking control of the Siberian railway thus controlling the movement of the Bolsheviks in Russia.

WESTERN FRONT 1918

Ludendorff and Germany now had a situation they had craved right from the start: a war on one front only. Fifty divisions were moved from the Eastern to the Western Front and Germany was in a hurry. She realised that if she was to win the war, she had to triumph before the Americans arrived. Also, her position at home was critical. The output of agricultural machinery and industrial plant had more or less ground to a halt because war materials were prioritised in the factories. In addition, there were major food shortages due to the embargo. Germany was on the cusp of an internal revolution! On the battle front, Germany's ally Austria-Hungary was in poor shape and would have willingly agreed to peace talks. At home, many Austrians were close to starvation.

Meanwhile, the Allies were divided in their defensive priorities. The French concentration under Pétain was to defend Paris while the British priority under Haig was to defend Flanders and prevent the Germans taking control of the Channel ports. However, the Germans now changed tactics. The emphasis for the remainder of the war would be on fast-moving squads of elite storm troopers, armed with automatic rifles, light machine guns and flame-throwers, and supported by a creeping barrage of artillery fire. Trench warfare would be a thing of the past!

From the beginning of the year, it became obvious that the Germans were planning an offensive in the Somme region, but neither Haig nor Pétain was willing to move their respective armies initially. When the attack did come, Pétain did send in reserves but it was a case of too little, too late. Haig, meanwhile, stayed put in Flanders. Troop movements along the Somme and aerial reconnaissance indicated that an attack was imminent in the area of St. Quentin/Arras. The use of aircraft, however, was a double-edged sword: the Germans could pinpoint exactly the location of the Allies' heavy artillery and knew where to direct their firepower.

Operation Michael, the first of the German Spring Offensives (Kaiserschlacht), began on 21 March; as it turned out, a very foggy day. British forces under Sir Hubert Gough were at the receiving end. Because of the fog, the British did not see the Germans approaching until they were literally upon them. They were driven out of their trenches and forced to retreat over the old Somme battlefield as far as Amiens. The fighting had now changed to open warfare: a totally new experience and one that only the Germans were geared for. The Germans advanced rapidly over a three-day period and the Allies were forced back a distance of some forty miles. Casualties totalled 300,000 men in what was Germany's greatest victory since 1914. However, Ludendorff was getting carried away with his own success: Amiens was well beyond the Hindenburg Line (into enemy territory) and German troops were far ahead of their food and artillery supplies. They failed to take either Arras or Amiens.

Author's Grandfather — Casualty of World War I

One of the casualties on 21 March 1918 was Joseph Phillips, grandfather of the author of this book. Phillips was a Sergeant Major with the Connaught Rangers and was one of 40,000 Irish soldiers who died in World War I.

The Allies regrouped at Amiens with reserve troops arriving by rail, by lorry and even by red London bus! The Germans, however, called off the offensive on 4 April to concentrate their efforts in Flanders.

Haig was correct in assuming that Ludendorff would target the Channel ports, which were essential to give British and newly-arriving American troops a foothold in France. Back again on the old battleground, the Ypres salient, the British were in a very vulnerable position, being open to attack on three sides. British, French and Portuguese troops were rushed to the area and on 9 April the Germans began their second Spring Offensive, Operation Georgette. Also known as the **Battle of the Lys,** the Germans used similar tactics to their 21 March offensive. Again they were successful, initially at any rate, but the Germans were running short of troops. The only viable way to get them to the front was by rail and the British had control over the rail lines in the area. In the meantime, British reserve troops arrived from across the Channel, French troops arrived by rail, and — finally — American troops began to arrive in substantial numbers. The writing was on the wall for the Germans!

Earlier in the year, even Haig had agreed on the need for an Allied commander and on 26 March General Ferdinand Foch was given the title of 'Commander in Chief of the Allied Forces in France'. It did not make a great deal of difference. Haig, Pétain and the new American Commander John Pershing had only one meeting with Foch to discuss strategy. Pershing was extremely arrogant (a quality that many war generals possessed in abundance). He insisted that the Americans would do things their own way: *"After all, you guys haven't had much success in four years."* They did it their own way and made the same mistakes as the Allies did in 1914. There was no Allied headquarters. The three Allied armies would continue to fight independently.

WAR AT SEA 1918

During 1917 the German fleet had hardly put to sea, much to the frustration of German sailors. In April 1918, to justify its existence, Admiral Scheer decided to attack one of the naval convoys coming from Norway. His timing was bad: he decided to attack on 23 April, a day when no convoy sailed. The British fleet was more successful. Rear-Admiral Roger Keyes attacked Zeebrugge and Ostend in an effort to make them unusable for German submarines. They sank three ships at Zeebrugge, partially blocking the Channel. However, since German submarines rarely used the two harbours, this operation was simply a waste of three ships.

The British fleet spent some of her idle time laying mines in the North Sea and the English Channel, an operation that was only moderately successful in curtailing the German fleet.

WAR IN THE AIR 1918

Aircraft were now making an entry into the war. Up to this point, the only aircraft available were lightweight biplanes capable of reconnaissance. Single-wing aircraft capable of carrying light bombs were now being produced on both sides but too late for World War I.

On the Allies' side, April 1 saw the formation of the Royal Air Force (RAF), which would see much action in World War II. While it did have the capability of launching a restricted bombing campaign, its primary function was to assist the British Army in France through surveillance.

BALKAN FRONT 1918

In June 1918, when Paris was once again in danger of attack by the Germans, French General Adolphe Guillaumat was summoned home from Salonika in Greece. He was replaced by Franchet d'Esperey. When the danger to Paris had receded, Guillaumat persuaded Clemenceau and Lloyd George to launch an offensive from Salonika, where 500,000 troops were stationed for the duration of the war. D'Esperey was instructed to attack Bulgaria and he did so on 15 September.

The Bulgarians were in rag order and surrendered without any real attempt at fighting. On 29 September Bulgaria requested an armistice and withdrew from the war. The withdrawal of Bulgaria left a large gap in the Balkans and d'Esperey found he was able to advance northwards as far as the Danube unopposed.

ITALIAN FRONT 1918

The two armies involved on the Italian Front — namely the Italians and the Austrians — both at the end of their tether, managed to continue their private battle into 1918. However, after the Battle of Caporetto in 1917, the Germans moved to the Western Front leaving their allies, the Austro-Hungarians, to fight alone once more. At the same time, the Italians under Generals Diaz and Badoglio completely reorganised their troops, resolving not to get dragged into battle again until they were properly prepared. In June the Austrians launched an offensive on the Italian Piave defensive line, which was not successful and resulted in major casualties on both sides.

The Italians now received long-promised support from their British and French allies and on 24 October (the anniversary of the Battle of Caporetto) the **Battle of Vittorio Veneto** commenced on the Piave. It wasn't much of a battle!

The Austria-Hungary alliance, which had been set up to fight the war, had ceased to exist. When this news reached the front, the Austro-Hungarian Army — not unexpectedly — refused to fight and as many as 250,000 of them were taken prisoner. This defeat marked the end of the Habsburg Empire.

On 31 October revolutions broke out in Vienna and Budapest. Austria agreed an armistice on 3 November; Hungary did likewise ten days later.

MIDDLE EAST 1918

The war-weary Ottoman Empire could have been quickly defeated with campaigns in Palestine and Mesopotamia, but the German Spring Offensive on the Western Front tied up any available British troops. The war in the Middle East at this stage had boiled down to a war between Britain (with some French and Arab support) and the Ottomans. To compound the problem, the Turks moved their best troops to the Caucasus to confront the Armenians, who had taken up the running after the Russian withdrawal in 1917. When activities resumed, the **Battle of Megiddo*** took place on 19 September. This was the climactic battle of the British invasion of Palestine. The British, under General Allenby, completely outnumbered the Turks, who had no option but to retreat.

The retreat continued throughout October as the British took control at Damascus, Beirut and Tripoli; and on 30 October — with Palestine, Syria and Mesopotamia lost — the Turks requested an armistice. The Armistice of Mudros was signed on 30 October between the British (much to the annoyance of the French) and the Ottoman Empire, and all Ottoman activities in the Middle East ceased on this date.

On 13 November Constantinople (Istanbul) was occupied by the French, followed a day later by the British. This marked the end of the Ottoman Empire.

Armageddon

* The word 'Armageddon' comes from Hebrew meaning 'Mountain of Megiddo'. According to pre-millennial Christian teaching, the Messiah will return to Earth and defeat Satan, the devil, in the Battle of Armageddon. The term is now used in a generic sense to refer to any 'end of the world' scenario.

Lawrence of Arabia

A history of the Middle East during World War I without a mention of Lawrence of Arabia would be incomplete. T.E. Lawrence was British, studied history at Oxford University and spent the early years of his career working as an archaeologist in the Middle East. This gave him an intimate knowledge of the districts and its peoples.

He enlisted in the British Army in October 1914. At this stage, the British were looking at the Middle East countries not as candidates for the British Empire but as an extension of the range of British imperial influences and oil supplies, and the weakening and destruction of a German ally: the Ottoman Empire.

During the war, Lawrence fought with Arab troops under the command of Emir Faisal, a son of Sharif Hussein bin Ali. Lawrence proved to be a shrewd operator. He persuaded the Arabs to concentrate on guerrilla tactics rather than a full frontal offensive with the Ottomans. They concentrated their attention on sabotaging the Hejaz railway *[see Map 6, page 48]*, which ran from Damascus to Medina through the Hejaz region of Saudi Arabia and which supplied the Ottoman garrison at Medina. This tied up a considerable number of Ottoman troops protecting and repairing the railway line.

As the war progressed, Lawrence and his Arabs became more adventurous. On 6 July 1917 they attacked and seized the port town of Aqaba. Lawrence now had two admirers in the area: British Commander Sir Edmund Allenby and Emir Faisal. In 1918 Lawrence was involved in the build-up to the capture of Damascus in the final weeks of the war. However, the Australians who arrived a few days before Lawrence and accepted the surrender of the city stole his thunder!

Lawrence liked the Arabs and kept a very good relationship with them by adopting local customs and traditions: he is best remembered dressed in Arab clothing riding a camel in the desert. He was not, however, enamoured with the way British officers treated the Arabs. Having said that, he was no angel himself in his treatment of the Turks.

After the war, he returned to Britain where he worked for the Foreign Office before joining the RAF. When awarded a knighthood after the war, he declined the award in protest at Britain's poor treatment of the Arabs. He was killed in a motorcycle accident at the age of 46.

FAR EAST 1918

In 1918 Japan continued to extend her influence in China. Following the Bolshevik Revolution in Russia, Japan and the US (uneasy bedfellows) sent forces to Siberia to bolster the armies of the White Movement against the Bolshevik Red Army. When Japan planned to move through Siberia as far as Lake Baykal, she was restrained by the Americans.

Towards the end of the war, Japan increasingly supplied war materials to her Allies and gave herself a huge trade boost. However, this led to inflation at home, and in August 1918 'rice riots' caused by inflation erupted in towns and cities throughout Japan.

WESTERN FRONT 1918 (CONT.)

Throughout the month of May, the Germans were moving troops southwards in preparation for an offensive near Paris. They were planning an attack at the Chemin des Dames near the River Aisne. The attack came on 27 May: the Third Battle of the Aisne and Germany's third Spring Offensive (Operation Blücher-Yorck). A huge German force broke through and on the first day alone advanced ten miles. The advance continued and by 3 June the Germans had reached the Marne and were within sixty miles of Paris. The French were now seriously concerned for the safety of their capital, as they had been in 1914, and there was good reason for their concern. Huge numbers of German troops had gathered in the area of Rheims in preparation for an attack on Paris. However, the French had regrouped and when the attack came they were prepared. The offensive came on 15 July. Foch's French army retaliated with a mass attack using tanks and the Germans were forced to retreat.

On 24 July a meeting of the Allied commanders was held at Foch's headquarters. The meeting was attended by Haig, Pétain and Pershing. Foch set down the plan for a major offensive: Britain (and her colonies) would attack from Flanders in the north, the Americans would attack at Verdun in the south while the French would be

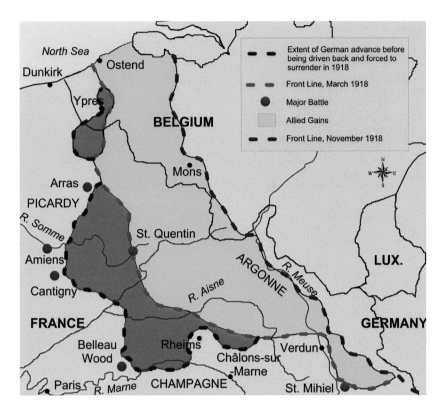

Map 12: Western Front 1918

Troops ready to hold the railway line, Merville, France, Ypres Salient and area, 11 April 1918.

responsible for the entire central area. Here at last was a plan to confront the Germans along the entire Western Front!

On 8 August at Amiens, the British forces attacked with tanks as their main weapon, and over the next month there was a series of Allied victories, culminating in an American victory on the St. Mihiel salient south of Verdun on 12 September. The month of August marked the turning point in the war, and was marked by the arrival of both increasing numbers of Americans and of tanks. Ludendorff referred to 8 August as *"the black day of the German army"*. The Germans had suffered a million casualties since March.

The Americans had a further success at the Argonne Forest while the British achieved a major success along a section of the Hindenburg Line. This included the canal at St. Quentin, which was notoriously difficult to cross because of its steeply sloping sides. Specially-equipped tanks solved the problem. On 26 September the Allies (mainly Americans) commenced their attack in the Meuse-Argonne Offensive in the Verdun region. 250,000 US soldiers went over the top. This was a new experience for the Americans and they suffered major casualties. However, sheer weight of numbers ensured that all objectives were realised. Meanwhile, French units broke through in Champagne and closed on the Belgian frontier. The Germans were forced to retreat to the Dutch border. Germany was now faced with total annihilation or an armistice.

At this moment, news had just reached Ludendorff of events at Salonika: Germany's ally Bulgaria had withdrawn from the war. On 29 September Ludendorff recommended to a summit of senior German officials that they seek an armistice. The dust was removed from President Wilson's Fourteen Points. The Germans tried to negotiate directly with Wilson in the hope of better terms, but the American President refused to deal with them directly. The arrogant General Pershing expressed his opinion that the only way to deal with the Germans was to drive them all the way to Berlin and make them surrender on their knees: *"Otherwise, they will come back to haunt us."* Prophetic words indeed!

On 30 September a new chancellor was appointed in Germany: Prince Max von Baden, a liberal-minded south German. His cabinet consisted mainly of centre and left-wing parties. Throughout the month of October, discussions continued between Germany and the Allies regarding a possible armistice. While the talking continued, the fighting and the killing continued.

On 12 October a German U-boat sank a British passenger liner, the RMS *Leinster,* traveling between Britain and Ireland. 450 people, including women and children, died. It was a senseless action which would not help the Germans in the upcoming negotiations.

Then came another unbelievable moment in the war: Ludendorff and Admiral Scheer decided to launch a last attempt to restore the valour of the German navy, which had lain defunct for the majority of the war. They resolved to send the High Seas Fleet into action against the British Royal Navy. Word spread and the crews, who were not enamoured with the idea of a watery grave, mutinied. On 29 October the German navy went ashore and on 3 November they took over Kiel. The German Revolution had begun!

One of Kaiser Wilhelm II's final acts was to dismiss Ludendorff, which he did on 26 October. On 9 November the Kaiser abdicated and fled to the neutral Netherlands, never to set foot on German soil again. Germany declared itself a republic. A new Germany was born: the Weimar Republic (named after the town of Weimar).

The German army arrived home to big celebrations. Their country was structurally undamaged in the war and German propaganda had the country believing that they had not been defeated. The German army blamed their politicians for the armistice (the so-called 'stab in the back' theory). They conveniently ignored the fact that it was their own Commander in Chief, Erich Ludendorff, who requested the armistice.

The armistice between the Allies and Germany was signed in a railway carriage in the forest of Compiègne in France on 11 November. At the eleventh hour of the eleventh day of the eleventh month, the guns fell silent! The end of World War I is commemorated on 11 November to this day. Bulgaria (29 September), Turkey (30 October) and Austria-Hungary (3 November) had already signed separate truces. A formal state of war between the two sides persisted for another seven months until the signing of the Treaty of Versailles on 28 June 1919.

World War I — the Great War — was over. Little did the protagonists realise that it would be followed twenty years later by an even greater war.

More than ten million people died in World War I. Four empires (German, Russian, Habsburg, and Ottoman) had collapsed. Large parts of Belgium, France, Russia and Poland were devastated. If there was an irony in the war, perhaps it was that Germany suffered little territorial damage.

1918 TIMELINE

08 Jan	President Woodrow Wilson's Fourteen Points presented to the joint Houses of Congress.
03 Mar	Peace treaty between Russia and Germany signed at Brest-Litovsk. Terms very punitive on Russia.
21 Mar	Germany begins Operation Michael, the first in a series of Spring Offensives, in an attempt to finish the war before US troops arrive.
26 Mar	Chief of Staff of French forces, Ferdinand Foch, appointed Allied Supreme Commander on the Western Front.
01 Apr	Royal Flying Corps and Royal Naval Air Service merged to form Britain's Royal Air Force (RAF).
09 Apr	Germany begins second Spring Offensive: the Georgette Offensive.
21 Apr	Germany's Red Baron (Manfred von Richthofen) shot down by the British. He achieved fame by shooting down eighty Allied aircraft.
23 Apr	British navy sinks redundant ships at the entrances to Zeebrugge and Ostend harbours in an effort to make them unusable by German U-boats.
07 May	Romania surrenders. Treaty of Bucharest peace agreement.
27 May	Germany begin their third Spring Offensive, the Blücher-Yorck Offensive, which runs out of steam after a few days due to the exhaustion of their troops.
29 May	American troops under General John Pershing begin to arrive at the rate of 100,000 per week.
06 Jun	Americans taste defeat for the first time in the Battle of Belleau Wood where they lose 5,000 soldiers.
09 Jun	Germany's fourth Spring Offensive, the Gneisenau Offensive, is stopped by French and American counter-attack.
15 Jun	Austrian forces urged by the Germans to attack Italy along the Piave River but are driven back by a revitalised Italian army.
15–17 Jul	Start of last big German offensive at Marne-Rheims. Successful counter-attack by French-American forces.
17 Jul	Tsar Nicholas and his family murdered by Bolsheviks, sparking off the Russian Civil War.
18 Jul	With the Allies now strengthened by the arrival of the Americans, the counteroffensives begin. Germans driven back from the Marne.
08 Aug	British troops defeat Germans east of Amiens. General Ludendorff describes this date as the *"black day of the German army"*.
21 Aug	British drive Germans back along ten-mile front at Arras.

12 Sep	Major victory by Americans supported by Allied aircraft at St. Mihiel.
15 Sep	Bulgarians driven out of Serbia by Allied forces.
19 Sep	Battle of Megiddo in Middle East. Turkish forces driven out of Palestine by British, Australian and Indian forces.
26 Sep	Start of Franco-American offensive at Meuse-Argonne. Germans defend fiercely in the battle between the Meuse River and the Argonne Forest. Americans suffer 75,000 casualties.
27 Sep	British and American troops break through Hindenburg Line between Cambrai and St. Quentin.
28 Sep	Belgian and British take Messines. Ludendorff requests Hindenburg and Kaiser Wilhelm II to seek an armistice.
30 Sep	Bulgaria signs armistice with the Allies.
01 Oct	Damascus falls to Australian and Arab troops.
04 Oct	General retreat by Germans. Germany requests discussion with US regarding terms for ending the war. President Woodrow Wilson rejects this 'back door approach'.
23 Oct	Ludendorff forced to resign by the Kaiser.
24 Oct	Battle of Vittorio Veneto on Italian Front. Austro-Hungarians driven out of Italy in the final battle of the war.
30 Oct	Turkey signs armistice with the Allies. Belgians and British advance toward Ghent and Mons in Belgium.
03 Nov	Austria-Hungary signs armistice with the Allies.
09 Nov	Kaiser Wilhelm II of Germany abdicates.
11 Nov	The armistice between the Allies and Germany is signed in a railway carriage at Compiègne, France, formally ending World War I.

The Influenza Pandemic of 1918 (also known as the Spanish flu)

In 1918 World War I was coming to an end when the entire world was hit by an epidemic of the 'flu'. However, this was no ordinary flu: it became known as 'The Influenza Pandemic of 1918'. It was much more severe than the common flu and in very many cases it proved fatal. While the normal flu hit the very old and the very young, the 1918 flu mainly affected persons in the 20 to 40 age group. It killed twenty-five million people: more than twice the death toll in World War I. Soldiers who were carrying the flu virus brought it home with them to all corners of the globe. It had such a swift effect that people were struck down in the street and died there. It was estimated that there were 675,000 deaths in America alone. One story relates that of four ladies playing bridge together one night, three of them died during the night. 1918 was a year which would not be forgotten.

WORLD WAR I — ESTIMATED DEATH TOLL

[Note: figures do not include deaths from famine or disease]

Allied Forces		**Central Powers**	
Russia	1,700,000	German Empire	2,037,720
France	1,357,000	Ottoman Empire	1,325,000
Great Britain	744,000	Austria-Hungary	1,320,000
Italy	463,400	Bulgaria	87,500
Romania	380,000		4,770,220
Serbia	300,000		
United States	117,465		
India	64,449		
Belgium	61,870		
Australia	59,330		
Canada	58,602		
Ireland	40,000		
New Zealand	16,711		
Portugal	7,235		
South Africa	7,121		
Greece	5,000		
Montenegro	3,000		
	5,385,183		

TOTAL   10,155,403

Part Two — Interwar Years

(1919–1938)

CHAPTER 7

The Challenges in the Interwar Years

The end of World War I saw the participating nations exhausted, an entire generation of young men dead on the battlefield and major political changes. The German, Austrian and Russian monarchies had been driven from power and replaced with democratic or revolutionary governments, and many European ethnic groups who had been subject to these three States seized the opportunity to seek independence. In addition, several British colonies renewed their quest for independence.

The formation of the League of Nations was one of the most important agreements in the Treaty of Versailles. Although this was the proposal of President Wilson, the American Senate failed to ratify it with the result that America did not become a member at that time. Neither did Russia or Germany.

By the end of the war, many European economies were in ruins and consumer spending fell to virtually zero. France and Belgium suffered major territorial damage while Germany suffered hardly any. The Treaty of Versailles was intended to compensate.

CHAPTER 8

The Treaty of Versailles

The **Treaty of Versailles** was the major peace treaty signed at the end of World War I. It was signed on 28 June 1919 after six months of negotiations.

Russia had withdrawn from the war in 1917 and in March 1918 signed a peace treaty with Germany at Brest-Litovsk. The terms of the treaty were harsh on Russia with Germany seizing a large portion of Russia's land and resources. However, Germany would pay for this later in the Treaty of Versailles. The other Central Power countries were also obliged to sign punishing treaties. The Treaty of Neuilly (November 1919) reduced Bulgaria's territory and army. The Treaty of Trianon (June 1920) redefined Hungary's borders, taking away more than two-thirds of its territory. The Treaty of Sèvres (August 1920) abolished the Ottoman Empire.

The final negotiations for the Treaty of Versailles were determined by the leaders of the 'Big Three' nations: British Prime Minister David Lloyd George, French Prime Minister Georges Clemenceau, and American President Woodrow Wilson.

The Italian Prime Minister Vittorio Orlando was included at the start of the negotiations, but after his claim to Fiume (now Rijeka: a port on the Adriatic coast of Croatia) was rejected, he left the negotiations, returning only in June to sign the treaty. Germany, together with the other defeated Central Powers, was not invited to participate. Neither was Russia. Perhaps, in hindsight, all of the participants in the war should have been included. Could World War II have been averted if they had been?

All of the negotiations for the treaty, which were long and arduous, took place in Paris, but the signing of the Treaty took place in the more opulent surroundings of the Palace of Versailles. The palace had previously been used in 1871 for a similar purpose at the conclusion of the Franco-Prussian War.

Attitudes of the Big Three
The victors of World War I were not inclined to be magnanimous, and Germany was held responsible for the war and its consequences.

Georges Clemenceau of France was single-minded: he believed that the war was Germany's fault, and she must be so severely punished that she would never again be in a position to start a war. When the war was over, the north-east of France (and the whole of Belgium) lay in ruins and Germany would have to pay for the rebuilding of both. Taking into account that France had lost 1.5 million soldiers and 400,000 thousand civilians, Clemenceau's attitude was understandable. Territorially, Clemenceau demanded the return of the rich industrial land of Alsace-Lorraine, which had been annexed by Germany in the Franco-Prussian War of 1871.

David Lloyd George of Great Britain had conflicting views on how Germany should be treated. His first view was that Germany must be punished and he knew that if he himself was going to be re-elected, she must be seen to be punished. A more balanced view, however, was that Germany was Britain's primary European trading partner and to leave her destitute would not benefit Britain. An added concern was the spread of communism. The western world had an inordinate fear of the 'red tide' that was threatening to sweep across Europe from Russia, and Lloyd George rightly believed that Germany was the only European power strong enough to hold back that tide.

President Woodrow Wilson of America had produced his Fourteen Points plan at the beginning of 1918 for the ending of the war and this was to be the basis for the Treaty of Versailles. One of the points was the formation of the League of Nations to which all future disputes would be referred. In America itself, the predominant feeling was that they should get out and leave Europe to sort herself out. Wilson, however, was a sensible politician and agreed that Germany must be punished but not to the extent of destroying her as a trading partner.

The Treaty of Versailles was divided into a number of sections under the headings General, Territorial, Military, and Economic Reparations.

GENERAL

There were three vital clauses:
1. Germany had to admit full responsibility for starting the war.
2. Germany was responsible for all war damage.
3. The League of Nations was set up to deal with all future disputes.

TERRITORIAL

Germany had to forfeit the following lands:
- Alsace and Lorraine were to be returned to France.
- The Polish Corridor, which provided access to the port of Danzig (Gdansk) and the Baltic Sea, was to be given to Poland. This involved separating East Prussia from Germany.

- West Prussia, Posen (Poznan) and parts of Upper Silesia were to be ceded to Poland.
- Eupen-Malmedy was to be transferred to Belgium.
- Northern Schleswig was to be returned to Denmark.
- The Memel part of East Prussia was placed under the control of France and was later annexed by Lithuania.
- The Saar was to be controlled by the League of Nations.
- Land taken by Germany from Russia in the Treaty of Brest-Litovsk was to be returned. This resulted in the formation of new Baltic states: Latvia, Lithuania and Estonia.
- The League of Nations took control of Germany's colonies in Africa and the Pacific, and these were divided amongst the Allies.
- Germany was forbidden to enter an alliance with Austria.

MILITARY

- The Rhineland (all territory west of the Rhine plus a 30-mile-wide strip east of the river, including Cologne, Düsseldorf and Bonn) was to become a demilitarised zone administered jointly by France and Great Britain.
- Germany's army was to be restricted to 100,000 men.
- Germany was not permitted to build any tanks.
- Germany was not permitted an air force.
- Germany's navy was to be restricted to six battleships, six cruisers and six destroyers. No submarines permitted.

ECONOMIC REPARATIONS

Making the belligerent party pay war reparations to cover the damage they had done was common practice going back many centuries. The Treaty of Versailles set reparations against Germany at 132 billion gold marks (£6.6 billion sterling) — a vast sum of money — which economists estimated would take in excess of eighty years to pay! However, these reparations could be made in a variety of forms including coal, steel and agricultural products, in no small way because currency reparations of that magnitude could lead to hyperinflation (which it did). Up to 1930, Germany was to provide France, Belgium and Italy with millions of tons of coal while France was given full possession of Germany's coal-bearing Saar basin for a period.

Judging from the treaty, it would appear that Clemenceau dominated proceedings. He further humiliated Germany by insisting that the treaty be signed in the Hall of Mirrors at the Palace of Versailles, scene of the Treaty of Frankfurt, which was signed at the end of the Franco-Prussian war in 1871 when the boot was on the other foot!

Germany's Reaction

There was huge anger in Germany when the terms of the treaty were made known. When she signed the armistice in November 1918, Germany assumed she would be consulted on the terms of the treaty, but this did not happen. Germany's first democratically-elected Chancellor, Philipp Scheidemann, refused to sign the treaty and immediately resigned. A new coalition government was formed under Gustav Bauer. Germany was given the option: sign or be invaded. She was in no position to argue. The Treaty of Versailles was signed on 28 June 1919 and ratified by the National Assembly on 9 July.

Outcome

Wilson's Fourteen Points plan, on which the treaty was to be based, was considered democratic, liberal and enlightened: in sharp contrast to the treaty that emerged. It was harsh, brutal and punitive, mainly due to France's vengeful but understandable attitude. President Wilson did not have a greater say because he was caught in a dilemma: both Britain and France owed vast sums of money to the United States as a result of the war and their only hope of repaying in the near future was with reparations from Germany.

In his book *'The Economic Consequences of the Peace',* the British economist John Maynard Keynes states: *"I believe that the campaign for securing from Germany the general costs of the war was one of the most serious acts of political unwisdom for which our statesmen have ever been responsible."*

Talks to negotiate a peace treaty following World War I commence at the Palace of Versailles, France, 18 January 1919.

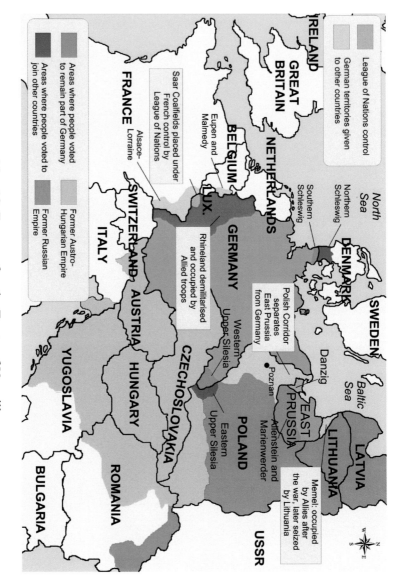

Map 13: Europe after the Treaty of Versailles

CHAPTER 9

Economic Hardship and the Rise of Dictators

Great Britain

France

United States of America

Russia (Soviet Union)

Germany

Italy

Japan

BRITAIN 1919–39

Britain's economy had been in decline since the end of the nineteenth century and this decline was exacerbated by World War I. Britain's big challenge after the war was to get its economy moving again, but it was facing an economic climate that could hardly have been worse. Furthermore, the one major asset that Britain needed but did not have in the 1920s and 1930s was an outstanding political leader! David Lloyd George, the Liberal Prime Minister, had returned from Versailles to general approval (having been seen to punish Germany). He retained his office for a number of years, although now dependent on Conservative support, but he resigned in 1922 having failed to make any real progress.

Between 1922 and 1940, there were eight changes of government in Britain. It was difficult, if not impossible, for the country to progress in the face of such political instability. Government policy swayed from the capitalist policies of the Conservative Party to the socialist policies of the Labour Party. The centrist Liberal Party got swallowed up between the two. The Labour Party can take credit for one major achievement during this period: it initiated Britain's new welfare state, creating the old age pension, medical care, public housing and unemployment relief. The welfare state was further progressed by the Beveridge Report of 1942, which recommended a national, compulsory, flat-rate insurance scheme which would combine health care, unemployment and retirement benefits. It was not until after the postwar Labour Government of 1945 took office that the various Acts of the welfare state eventually became law in 1948.

Throughout the twenties, Britain was hit by a series of strikes, the most notable being the miners' strike in 1926. The miners' strike was badly timed from its own point of view since it coincided with a major change in world energy use from coal to oil. The Conservative government did not yield to the strikers, who eventually returned to work in 1929.

During the early 1930s, Britain's economy — like most countries — suffered acute depression. Prime Minister Ramsay MacDonald of the Labour Party aspired to the policies of Keynesian economics, authored by John Maynard Keynes, which advocated increased government spending during a depression in order to get the economy moving again. However, Britain did not have money to spend and did not have the courage to borrow as Roosevelt did in America.

The 1931 election was a marked success for the Conservatives, who were elected with a substantial majority under the leadership of Stanley Baldwin. However, the depression continued and, if anything, the situation got worse. The problem was the same as occurs in every depression: people stop spending which merely exacerbates the problem. Traditional heavy industries such as shipbuilding were left to work out their own salvation, resulting in unemployment figures as high as seventy per cent in the north-east of England.

In 1931 the Statute of Westminster created the Commonwealth of Nations consisting of Canada, New Zealand, Australia and South Africa. These nations were given autonomy but continued to be linked to Britain through trade. The big issue towards the end of the 1930s was the resurgence of German aggression in Europe and how to deal with it. In 1935 Britain signed the Anglo-German Naval Agreement, agreeing to increase the permitted size of the German navy as set down in the Treaty of Versailles.

Essentially Britain appeased Germany, knowing it was in no position to enforce any limitations. Later, in 1939, Hitler would renounce the agreement as war loomed.

Stanley Baldwin, leader of the Conservatives for fifteen years, resigned in 1937 and was replaced by Neville Chamberlain. Chamberlain's method of dealing with Hitler was to continue the policy of appeasement: he signed the Munich Agreement giving the Sudetenland to Germany, which — as events were to prove — was disastrous. However, the basic fact was that Britain was in no way prepared to fight a war. Appeasement was also the policy of the American Ambassador to Great Britain, Joseph P. Kennedy, father of the future US President John F. Kennedy. Chamberlain clung to power, presiding over Britain's declaration of war on 3 September 1939. However, the pressures of war took their toll. He died on 9 November 1940 and was replaced by Winston Churchill.

Royalty

On 10 December 1936 King George V died. He was succeeded by his son Edward VIII, who shortly afterwards abdicated to marry Mrs. Wallis Simpson, an American divorcee. His brother, who took on his father's name and became King George VI, succeeded him.

Armed Forces: Britain 1919–39

After the horrors of World War I, Britain had no desire to don her military cap for a long number of years. During the early part of the interwar years she was more concerned with servicing her vast empire and dominions. It was not until the mid-30s — when Churchill brought the German build-up to war to everyone's attention — that any action was taken. Even then, any British build-up was to be seen as a deterrent to opposing forces rather than an effective fighting force. The expansion of her superb Royal Navy and the expansion of the Royal Air Force were intended as a deterrent to the Axis forces of Germany, Italy and Japan. Spitfires and Hurricanes (which served Britain so well in the Battle of Britain) were being produced but only in small numbers. A general weakness in both political and military leadership at this time meant that little was done to improve the British Army.

The development of tanks, which proved so effective towards the end of World War I, was seriously neglected. Due to her neglect of the army and her lack of tank development, Britain was seriously unprepared for World War II when it began. Conscription was not introduced until the spring of 1939 and, as a result, at the start of World War II in the autumn of 1939 she was only in a position to send four divisions (80,000 soldiers) and fifty tanks to help France.

She had, however, a huge backup with her Commonwealth and her empire, but again they needed time to prepare. Her main policy was appeasement: a policy that continued right up to the commencement of the war and a policy that proved fruitless at the end of the day.

On the positive side, the numbers involved in civil defence increased to almost a million and a half at the end of 1938, while major improvements in the fields of radar and radio communications were achieved. In addition, peacetime planning for war was well advanced. As soon as the war started, gas masks were issued, air raid shelters dug and evacuations arranged.

FRANCE 1919–39

France suffered grievously in World War I. She lost 1.5 million men, with another 3.5 million wounded. The complete north-east of the country was destroyed. What France really needed after the war was another 'Belle Époque'.

La Belle Époque

La Belle Époque was a period of peace and prosperity in France from 1890 to the start of World War I in 1914. The period was characterised by optimism, new technology and scientific discoveries; a period during which the arts flourished and many masterpieces of literature, music, theatre and visual art gained recognition. The Eiffel Tower was built as the grand entrance to the 1889 World's Fair in Paris. La Belle Époque was named in retrospect, when it was considered a golden age in contrast to the horrors of World War I.

When faced with the rebuilding of the north-east of the country, France expected Germany's war reparations to pay for the damage, but Germany began to default from an early stage. She had further problems when both industry and agriculture fell into decline after the war.

Raymond Poincaré became Prime Minister in 1922 and under his leadership France demanded full payment of reparations by Germany. When Germany asked for a moratorium on payments and subsequently defaulted, Poincaré sent 40,000 troops to occupy the industrial Ruhr in Germany. If Germany would not pay the reparations due, France would take them! This move proved to be a costly failure, merely resulting in the drafting of the Dawes Plan under which the annual payment of reparations was reduced. This resulted in Poincaré's loss of office to a socialist government in 1924. The socialists made no progress with the French economy and in 1926 Poincaré was invited back as Prime Minister.

In 1928 Poincaré decided to devalue the franc, a move that proved relatively successful in the short term only. Apart from his blunder at the Ruhr, Poincaré proved a capable politician in his two periods as Prime Minister of France (1922–24) and (1926–29). He had a passion for his country and this, coupled with his persistence, brought a stability to the country that other European countries envied. Unfortunately, Poincaré was forced to resign from political life due to ill health in 1929 and France became a rudderless ship for a number of years without any clear direction.

The worldwide economic depression hit France in the early 1930s and with it came support for extremist groups such as fascists and communists. Political turmoil was the only way to describe French politics in the early 1930s, culminating in street riots in Paris in 1934. Edouard Daladier, a French Radical politician, became Prime Minister on three different occasions in the 1930s: January–October 1933, January–February 1934 and April 1938–March 1940. Known as the Bull of Vaucluse, Daladier was under no illusion about Hitler's intention to dominate Europe.

1936 saw the emergence of a radical left Popular Front movement under Léon Blum. Many disliked Blum because he was a Jew. Anti-Jewish feeling was spreading throughout Europe at this time. The Popular Front, supported by the Communist Party in France, felt strongly that France should take a stand against Hitler and Mussolini. However, memories of World War I were still very vivid and no action was taken. Within a year, the Popular Front government had collapsed, to be replaced once more by Daladier's Radical Party, which continued in office through the commencement of World War II.

When it became obvious that Hitler was about to invade Czechoslovakia in 1938 (he had already occupied the Sudetenland), Daladier in his bullish way wanted to confront Hitler (France was seen as an ally of Czechoslovakia). However, he was dissuaded by both Chamberlain and members of his own government.

Armed Forces: France 1919–39
When Germany invaded France at the start of World War II, the collapse of the French army was a big surprise. On the surface, the army appeared to be a large, well-prepared fighting force: they were able to move eighty divisions to the front at the start of the war, and in 1938 Winston Churchill described the French army as, *"the most perfectly-trained and faithful mobile force in Europe"*. Appearances were deceptive! In truth, France had not moved on from 1918. The level of her artillery was still the same, her infantry was not motorised, and her tank design (while she had plenty of them) had not improved since 1918: her tanks still moved at the same speed as the infantry. They had virtually no anti-aircraft facility. Her navy was formidable though and had she combined with Britain's Royal Navy, between them they certainly would have had the capability to make life difficult for Germany on the high seas.

France had emerged from World War I as a world leader in aviation, but Britain and the United States quickly pulled ahead of them in terms of aircraft development. Daladier tried to compensate for their lack of productivity in the 1930s by placing a large order for planes with the US in 1938. However, the French were unable to pay for the order and the Americans supplied the planes to Britain instead.

France spent several of the interwar years and considerable finance constructing the Maginot Line along the border between France and Germany. This defensive system was initiated by Marshal Pétain (who had emerged from World War I with much credit) and it was named after war veteran Andre Maginot. The line was a defensive system consisting of concrete trenches and pillboxes, gun emplacements, barbed wire and rail linkups. The big flaw in the Maginot Line was that it stopped at the Ardennes Forest (to the north of France) due to Belgium's intransigence. Nothing was built between the border of Luxembourg and the Channel coast, leaving the whole northern sector open to any attack on France through Belgium. It appeared that France had already forgotten how easily Germany invaded their country in World War I.

France believed that the Ardennes Forest was not navigable, but they had not done their homework. Furthermore, the Germans had made huge strides in tank development.

While the French were building the Maginot Line, the Germans were developing their *blitzkrieg* (lightning war) system, which they had initially produced in the spring of 1918 towards the end of World War I. When the attack came, it came not through Belgium but at speed through the Ardennes Forest into France.

In truth, both Britain and France were poorly equipped for World War II. Both had placed inordinate faith in the League of Nations, a body which had no army of its own and consequently had no means of enforcing any of its recommendations. A further weakness in both countries was a lack of quality leadership. Bearing in mind that Hitler's intentions were obvious to both Chamberlain and Daladier, there was a complete lack of co-ordination between the two. A series of aggressive invasions by Germany in the late 1930s — the Rhineland (1936), Austria (1938), the Sudetenland (1938) and Czechoslovakia itself (1939) — brought no response (apart from verbal threats) from Britain and France.

UNITED STATES OF AMERICA 1919–39

When President Woodrow Wilson returned home after signing the Treaty of Versailles, his first task was to persuade the American Senate to accept the treaty and, more importantly, the League of Nations charter. This was easier said than done as the Republicans now held the balance of power in the Senate (Woodrow Wilson was a Democrat). When Wilson presented the treaty, his words were: *"Dare we reject it and break the heart of the world?"* They did reject it — by a mere seven votes — and in doing so literally broke Wilson's heart. He suffered a stroke, which incapacitated him permanently and forced his retirement from politics. Warren Harding, a Republican, replaced him as President. Woodrow Wilson died in 1924 having served America admirably during World War I.

The next two decades in America could not be more of a contrast: the Roaring Twenties and the Great Depression of the 1930s. The 1920s got off to a bad start with an epidemic of Spanish flu brought home by the American army from Europe and resulting in the deaths of over half a million people in the US. The decade will be remembered for huge developments in radio and film; the jazz age; organised crime; prohibition; great writers such as Hemingway and Fitzgerald; great sportsmen such as Bobby Jones and Babe Ruth; the development of aircraft (Charles Lindberg's Atlantic crossing); and, above all, rampant consumerism! Is it any wonder that the 1920s in America are frequently referred to as the 'fabulous twenties' or the Roaring Twenties? This was America's Belle Époque!

The boom in consumerism meant that people splashed out on newly-invented items such as radio, telephones, television and, of course, a Ford car! Men and particularly women sported new clothes and hairstyles, while smoking and drinking became the norm — amongst the middle and upper classes, that is! Apart from spending money on the aforementioned items, America found a new way of using (and they thought of making) money: investing in the Stock Market.

The Wall Street Crash and The Great Depression
The euphoria came to an end with the stock market crash on Wall Street which began on 24 October 1929, thereafter known as Black Thursday, and reached its peak five days later. The value of shares fell to near zero and many investors were left penniless.

The banks, who had thrown money at their customers in the good times to buy consumer goods, to invest in the stock market or — in the case of farmers — to buy farms, now foreclosed and so began the Great Depression, which would last until the mid-1930s. Banks and businesses went bust and millions ended up homeless. 1932 marked the peak of the Great Depression with unemployment rising to thirty per cent. A further blow to American farmers occurred in 1933–34 when severe drought hit the Midwest in what became known as the Dust Bowl. Fertile topsoil weakened by over-farming and hedge removal was blown away, leaving desert conditions.

There were two contributory causes of the Great Depression in America: (a) war debts owed by the Allied countries to the US as a result of World War I and (b) the failure of Germany to repay a substantial loan made to her by America in 1924. Calling in the debts, however, was a double-edged sword. It meant a huge fall in America's exports as the purchasing power of the countries concerned was drastically reduced.

Republican Herbert Hoover became President in 1929 but was resoundingly defeated in the Presidential election of 1932 by Democrat

Franklin Delano Roosevelt. Roosevelt was the breath of fresh air that America needed. He went on to serve an unprecedented twelve years in office as President and is generally acknowledged to be one of the greatest American Presidents of all time.

He contracted polio in 1921, which left him paralysed from the waist down and confined to a wheelchair for the rest of his life. However, he never let his disability affect his performance. Roosevelt was an advocate of Keynesian economics, which recommended government spending (by borrowing if necessary) in times of depression.

New Deal
Roosevelt immediately set to work promising the American people the New Deal — a variety of programmes designed to produce the three 'R's: relief (government jobs for the unemployed), recovery (economic growth) and reform (through regulation of Wall Street, banks and transportation). His first speech to the American people is remembered for the famous words: *"We have nothing to fear but fear itself."*

Roosevelt pushed through a series of reform programmes including: Civil Works Administration, Farm Credit Administration, The Public Works Administration and the National Industrial Recovery Act. All of these contributed to the fall in unemployment from thirty per cent in 1932 to a much more acceptable twelve per cent in 1937. Employment was provided in developing national forests and parks; a huge programme of railroad improvements and the building of a series of dams on various major rivers to provide electricity and to control land irrigation. The Tennessee Valley Authority was set up to develop the Tennessee River basin to provide one of the world's greatest irrigation and hydroelectric power systems. Construction of the famous Hoover Dam (initiated by President Hoover) on the Colorado River commenced in 1931 was completed in 1936. The renowned Golden Gate Bridge in San Francisco was opened on 27 May 1937.

The Great Depression came to an end in 1939 with the opening of World's Fairs in New York and San Francisco indicating to the American people that after a decade of depression there were good times ahead. Unfortunately, World War II was just around the corner!

Armed Forces: United States of America 1919–39
When the United States agreed to enter World War I on the side of the Allies in 1917, it took a year to recruit and train an army. It was spring 1918 before they made their very effective arrival on the battlefields of France and Belgium. When the war ended, the US armed forces were considerably downsized. When the Senate refused to join the League of Nations in 1919, America effectively said *"no"* to any form of world

32-year-old Florence Owens Thompson, mother of seven children, suffering during the Great Depression, Nipomo, California, 1936. Photograph entitled 'Migrant Mother' by Dorothea Lange, who later wrote, *"The hungry and desperate mother ... said that they had been living on frozen vegetables from the surrounding fields, and birds that the children killed. She had just sold the tires from her car to buy food."*

Crowd of depositors gather in the rain outside the
Bank of United States in New York after its failure in 1931.

Jesse Owens at the
start of a record-
breaking 200-
metre race during
the Olympic
Games in Berlin,
1936. He won four
gold medals in
athletics: a big
blow to the
Führer's
Aryan race theory!

security. President Hoover stated: *"We shall enter into no agreements committing us to any future course of action or which call for the use of force to preserve peace."* This gave Congress the excuse to severely restrict the budget of the combined armed forces. Throughout the 1920s and the 1930s, the strength of the army rarely exceeded 135,000; bear in mind that the US sent over a million troops to Europe towards the end of World War I!

At the end of the war, America had a Tank Corps, but it was abolished in 1920 and tanks were assigned exclusively to the infantry. This meant that tanks were regarded simply as a support for ground troops.

The navy was similarly restricted. At the Washington Conference of 1922, the US, Great Britain and Japan agreed to restrict the size of their navies in line with one another in the ratio 5:5:3. At a further disarmament agreement in London in 1930, the three naval powers agreed to limit the number of cruisers each would build. Germany was not considered a major naval power and was ignored.

The US also agreed not to construct any bases in the Pacific. American naval officers were very unhappy with the outcome of both conferences. The lack of a base in the Pacific, the navy believed, meant it would not be possible to carry out a successful war against Japan (it was Japan, not Germany, that the US feared at this time). As a result of the various agreements, no new battleships were commissioned in the US until 1937.

The financial constraints of the Great Depression years meant that very little finance was available for the research and development of new weaponry. Despite this, developments in aircraft, radar and sonar were kept up-to-date. Resources were made available to the Air Corps for the development of aircraft. In this regard, the Americans got a wake up call in 1937 during the Sino-Japanese War when an American gunboat USS *Panay* was attacked and sunk by Japan on the Yangtze River outside Nanking. America responded immediately by resuming the building of battleships. However, she was adamant she would not get involved in a war either in Europe or in the Pacific. Isolationism was a major factor in the US at this time. As far as many were concerned, a war in Europe was of no concern to them.

However, towards the end of the 1930s, American views were beginning to harden against dictatorships; in particular, the large Jewish community in America had become very concerned at the treatment of Jews in Europe by Germany. By 1938 America became more sympathetic towards France and Britain and proceeded to supply them with armaments. Roosevelt had sufficient foresight to see that the time might come when America might be dragged into another global war whether she liked it or not. He began the difficult task of persuading his own country to resume rearmament!

In 1939 cash-and-carry legislation was passed in the US Senate, permitting arms to be sold to Britain and France provided that they were paid for up front and that the arms would be transported by the Allies. When the Allies' money ran out in 1941, the cash-and-carry policy was replaced by the Lend-Lease Bill, which allowed Britain to purchase arms on credit. At that stage, France had fallen to the Nazis!

Roosevelt's second term of office ended in 1940 and he was persuaded to run for a third term, which was unheard of. While he had huge support from the American people, who acknowledged his great achievements in the US in the 1930s, there were many who saw him as a warmonger who would lead America into World War II. His opponent, Republican Wendell Willkie, ran on the ticket of isolationism. On 5 November 1940 Roosevelt was re-elected President for the third time, outpolling Wilkie fifty-five to forty-five per cent.

It took the Japanese attack on the American base at Pearl Harbor in December 1941 to finally bring the US into the war.

RUSSIA 1919–39

The history of Soviet Russia and the Soviet Union reflects a period of great change not only for Russia but also for the world *[see also the Russian Revolution in Chapter 5, page 88]*. 'Soviet Russia' refers to the years between the abdication of Tsar Nicholas II in 1917 and the creation of the Soviet Union in 1922.

The Bolsheviks (communists) came to power after the October revolution in 1917. Vladimir Lenin became Chairman and Leon Trotsky the Commissar for Foreign Affairs. This marked the start of the civil war between the 'Red' (Bolshevik) and 'White' (anti-Bolshevik) factions, a war that continued up to 1921. In that year, Lenin produced his New Economic Policy (NEP), in which the state permitted a limited market to exist. Small private businesses were allowed and restrictions on political activity were eased. However, the key shift involved the status of agricultural surpluses. Farmers were now permitted to sell their surpluses on the open market. Meanwhile, the state still maintained ownership of what Lenin deemed the "*commanding heights*" of the economy: heavy industry such as coal, iron and mineral sectors along with the banking and financial components of the economy.

Thanks to the NEP, agricultural yields improved greatly during the 1920s and Russia became a major world grain producer. At the same time, its industry (in state ownership) was very much in the doldrums.

On 30 December 1922 the Bolsheviks proclaimed the Union of Soviet Socialist Republics (USSR).

Joseph Stalin
Joseph Stalin, who was involved in the Bolshevik revolution of 1917, first came to prominence on 3 April 1922 when Lenin appointed him General Secretary of the Communist Party. He would hold this position until his death in 1953. The history of Russia between 1922 and 1953 was determined by Joseph Stalin.

He was born Josef Djugashvili (his mother's name) in Georgia in 1879, and during a difficult childhood he answered to the name 'Soso'. In 1899 he joined the Russian Social Democratic Workers Party and adopted the nom de revolution 'Koba'. In 1913 he wrote an article using the nom de plume 'Stalin': this time the name stuck! The meaning of the word Stalin is 'steel' and how apt the name proved to be. The name would become permanently infamous throughout the world.

Lenin's health was very poor and he died on 21 January 1924 after a third stroke. A troika led by Stalin emerged to take over day-to-day leadership of the party and to block leftist Leon Trotsky and his socialist followers from taking power. Stalin intensified the campaign against Trotsky and succeeded in having him removed from the position of Commissar of War towards the end of 1924. He was dropped from the Politburo entirely in 1926 and was sent into exile in February 1929. He finally settled in Mexico where he was assassinated on Stalin's instruction on 20 August 1940.

There were three distinct phases in the Soviet Union during the interwar years: Industrial Development, Collectivisation of Farms and The Purges. In all three phases, Stalin proved to be a ruthless, tyrannical dictator. The remark, *"One death is a tragedy, a million deaths a statistic!"* is attributed to Stalin.

1. INDUSTRIAL DEVELOPMENT
In 1928, Stalin abandoned Lenin's New Economic Policy in favour of his own five-year plans. His first five-year plan focused on the harvesting of the Soviet Union's natural resources of coal and iron ore, later to be converted into steel. During the years 1928–32, the output of coal doubled while the production of iron ore more than tripled. These increases, however, were achieved at a cost. Workers had to work long hard hours for very poor wages. Working conditions were primitive and unsafe. It is estimated that up to one million workers died during

these five years. On the plus side, however, the plan achieved long-term industrial growth more rapidly than any country in history. With the benefit of huge increases in coal and iron ore, Stalin's second five-year plan (1933–37) got off to a flying start and heavy industry expanded extremely rapidly. A major side-benefit was rapid developments in the armaments industry.

2. COLLECTIVISATION OF FARMS

In 1928, Stalin decided that all farms would be taken into state ownership. The Soviet Union had substantial supplies of grain, which Stalin planned to use to feed the rapidly-growing urban areas. Grain was also exported: a source of foreign currency needed to fund the import and operation of technologies necessary for heavy industrialisation.

The collective farms were known as kolkhozes, and the kolkhoz produce was sold to the state at a low price set by the state itself. However, the speed of collectivisation was too slow for Stalin so forced collectivisation was implemented from 1929 onwards. Ukraine was the major sufferer. Stalin took her food; he also took the seed for the following year's grain crop and allowed millions of people starve to death. Kulaks (prosperous farmers) and Chechens were forcibly resettled in Kazakhstan, Siberia and the Russian Far North. Very quickly, however, anybody who opposed collectivisation was deemed a Kulak and Stalin's policy was to liquidate all Kulaks. It is estimated that his collectivisation policy resulted in the deaths of at least five million people.

3. THE PURGES

Stalin believed that many people were out to overthrow him. His solution was simple: exterminate anyone whom he considered a threat! From 1934 onwards, he instigated a series of purges against his suspected political and idealogical opponents — many his old comrades! Measures used against suspects included imprisonment in Gulags (work camps), executions and assassinations. A series of show trials were held in Moscow between 1936 and 1938, at which the accused were charged with counter-revolution, sabotage, spying, and conspiring with Germany and Japan to invade the Soviet Union. The defendants (who were always 'guilty') were executed or sent to Gulags.

The Great Purge occurred in 1937. The secret police was renamed the NKVD under the control of Nikolai Yezhov. The purge was known as the Yezhovshchina, the Reign of Yezhov. The rate of murders was staggering. In the armed forces alone, three of the five marshals of the Soviet Union, ninety per cent of the generals and all of the regional commanders — a total of 30,000 officers — were exterminated. The entire Politburo and most of the Central Committee were purged together with numerous intellectuals and bureaucrats. The number of people executed or imprisoned during the 'Great Purge' numbered about two million. It did not seem to dawn on Stalin that the purges weakened Russia to the extent that it would be very difficult for her to participate in any war. An army without generals is not much use!

Yezhov was relieved of all powers in 1939, and he was tried and executed in 1940. As was invariably the case with Stalin, he used people to do his 'dirty work' and once they outlived their usefulness, he had them executed. Stalin now had a major problem. As a result of the purges, he was extremely short of experienced, trained officers in the army and training would take time. He was given breathing space by the German-Soviet non-aggression pact (also called the Molotov-Ribbentrop Pact) he signed with Hitler in August 1939. Even then, he declared in January 1941 that Russia would not be ready for war for eighteen months to two years.

Collectivisation and the Purges together were comparable to the Holocaust but are seldom spoken about. The difference was that Stalin was murdering his own people!

Armed Forces: Soviet Union 1919–39

There was little development in the Russian army in the 1920s, but this changed in 1931 when Mikhail Tukhachevsky, who had been Chief of the Red Army Staff in the civil war, was appointed Deputy Defence Commissar. A huge increase in armaments production had begun during Stalin's first five-year plan (1928–32). Tukhachevsky's task was to incorporate the new armaments into the military organisations. To achieve this, he had to vastly increase the numbers in the various forces and more importantly to organise the training of these forces.

In several respects the Soviet Union had an advantage not enjoyed by any other country in the 1930s and during World War II. She was not short of manpower and she was not short of weaponry! What she lacked was technological expertise and training; and these deficiencies remained with the USSR into the first few years of World War II.

Stalin had been watching Hitler's emergence in Germany and in 1934 he informed the Seventeenth Party Congress: *"We are heading for a new war."*

By the mid-1930s, Tukhachevsky had become much too powerful for Stalin's liking and he disappeared in the Great Purge of 1937.

Throughout the 1930s, Soviet production plants continued to churn out armaments, but in 1938 it became obvious that much of what had been produced was now obsolete. However, in 1939 the USSR launched the T-34 tank, which would become the outstanding tank in World War II.

In the same period, her factories were producing 5,000 aircraft annually. The poor relation in the armed forces was the navy, which had been neglected for many years. In 1939 Stalin belatedly gave the navy equal status to the army and air force. However, you cannot build a battleship overnight and building a navy would take considerable time.

The big question at the commencement of World War II was why Russia did not form a 'triple entente' with Britain and France as she had in World War I. The Triple Entente was successful in World War I in forming two fronts against Germany, with Britain and France facing them in the west and Russia in the east. The big difference now was lack of trust in Stalin. However, Hitler outwitted everybody by persuading Stalin to sign a non-aggression pact between Russia and Germany in August 1939. The pact suited Stalin as he needed time to rebuild the 'officer core' of his army. Neither Hitler nor Stalin had any difficulty signing pacts or agreements as neither had any compunction about breaking an agreement when the occasion arose. On this occasion, the pact left Hitler free to devote his attention to Poland and the West.

GERMANY 1919–39

After the Treaty of Versailles, Germany was a broken country. The Kaiser had abdicated to be replaced by the Weimar Republic and the country was faced with massive reparation debts. The humiliating terms of the Treaty of Versailles provoked bitter indignation throughout Germany and seriously weakened the incoming Weimar Government. In 1919 Adolf Hitler first came to the fore as the leader of the new National Socialist German Workers' Party (NSDAP): the Nazis.

Apart from the emergence of Hitler, the other major happening in Germany in the early 1920s was hyperinflation, which dominated everything else between June 1921 and January 1924. The payment of reparations proved to be a formidable problem for Germany. She met her obligations initially but in 1923 was unable to do so. France reacted by occupying the Ruhr Valley (part of the Rhineland) and seizing the goods produced in lieu of reparations. The Ruhr Valley was Germany's industrial heartland, accounting for a huge percentage of the country's iron and steel production and more than eighty per cent of its coal. The occupation continued from January 1923 to July 1925, at which point the German workers refused to work for the occupying French forces any longer. France's answer was to occupy the area and produce the goods themselves. This left Germany poverty-stricken and with little or no coal. A rather spartan German army entered the Ruhr Valley and the French withdrew.

Inflation in Germany became so severe at this time that it was defined as hyperinflation. By 1 July 1923 the rate of exchange with the dollar had risen to 160,000 marks (German currency), by 1 August to a million, and by 1 November to 130,000 million marks. In other words, the mark was completely worthless.

The solution was twofold. In November Germany's Chancellor Gustav Stresemann decided to devalue. A new currency — the Rentenmark (later to become the Reichsmark) — was born, while the US came to Germany's assistance with major financial loans. During the remainder of the 1920s, Germany's economic situation recovered considerably.

However, the collapse of the mark impacted severely on the people of Germany: many of them lost their life savings. They blamed the Weimar Government for their woes. They were on their knees and what was needed more than anything else was a saviour to help them climb back up again. That perceived 'saviour' was waiting in the wings. His name was Adolf Hitler!

On the international front, Germany re-established diplomatic relations with the new Soviet Union in 1922 when they signed the Treaty of Rapallo, whereby the two signatories mutually cancelled all pre-war debts and renounced war claims. In 1925 the Pact of Locarno was signed by Germany, France, Belgium, Britain and Italy. The treaty recognised Germany's borders with France and Belgium; while Britain, Italy and Belgium agreed to come to France's assistance if German troops marched into the demilitarised Rhineland.

In 1926 Germany was admitted into the League of Nations.

Adolf Hitler (1889–1945)
Hitler was born in Austria in 1889 into a Catholic family. A demonic oddity, he was to become one of the most powerful leaders/dictators the world has ever known. His major talent was his public speaking ability, and one of his greatest pleasures in life was the adulation he received after one of his orations.

Hitler: Relationship With Geli

Hitler's father, Alois, married three times. His first marriage was childless. His second marriage produced two children: (a) a son Alois Jr., who married Irishwoman Bridget Dowling: their son William Patrick went on to serve in the US Medical Corps in World War II, and (b) a daughter Angela, who gave birth to a daughter whom she named Geli.

Alois' third marriage was to Klara Pölzl and they produced six offspring, one of whom was Adolf Hitler. Adolf had two brothers and a

---

sister, all three of whom died in infancy; another brother Edmund who died from measles in 1900; and a sister Paula who lived until 1960.

Adolf Hitler's father, Alois, who was a very brutal man, died in 1903. His mother, who had protected Adolf from his father and to whom he was very attached, died in 1907 from breast cancer leaving Adolf, who was very much a loner, to fend for himself.

From the late 1920s, a very deep and controversial relationship developed between Adolf Hitler and his niece Geli. In 1931 she was found shot dead in Hitler's Munich apartment (in his absence) with a bullet wound in her chest and his revolver by her side. Hitler was devastated. Her death was declared a suicide, but there has been much speculation since then about whether that was what really happened.

When World War I broke out, Hitler was adjudged to be too puny to be a soldier. He was given the job of 'regimental runner' instead, which required him to carry messages between the trenches. From 1916 onwards, however, he saw some action and was injured twice — first near the Somme when a shell hit the roof of a tunnel in which he was sitting and later in Ypres during the final month of the war when he was injured in a gas attack, which blinded him temporarily.

When the war ended in 1918, Hitler was one of the soldiers who faulted the politicians for seeking an armistice (the 'stab-in-the-back' theory). Germany had not been beaten on the battlefield and consequently there were many like Hitler who believed that an armistice was premature. However, they conveniently ignored the fact that it was German army chief Erich Ludendorff himself who requested the armistice. While Hitler formally renounced his Austrian citizenship in 1925, he did not become a citizen of Germany until 1932.

The Jews
In the early part of the twentieth century, there was a considerable anti-Jewish feeling throughout Europe, much of it based on jealousy since Jews held many of the top business positions such as doctors, dentists, bankers and business people. However, they dressed in long black coats and wore long beards, which made them an easily identifiable target. When things went badly for Russia in World War I, they targeted the large Jewish populations in Poland and in Russia itself. On the other hand, many Jews fought in the German army in World War I. When hyperinflation decimated the country from 1921 to 1923, Hitler, amongst others, conveniently scapegoated the Jews.

At this time Hitler was making a name for himself with his vitriolic beer hall speeches (targeting Jews, communists and the Treaty of Versailles). Meanwhile, the Nazi Party was rapidly increasing in popularity. Early followers included Rudolf Hess and Hermann Göring. It was, however, attracting a very violent element, led by Ernst Röhm, consisting of unemployed young men and malcontented ex-soldiers who paraded the streets in their brown shirts waving the Swastika flag. Anybody who opposed them was met with violence by Röhm's SA paramilitary 'storm troopers'.

Two men who had made a big impact in World War I on Germany's behalf now re-emerged in different guises. General Erich Ludendorff agreed to join Hitler in what became known as the Beer Hall Putsch in Munich in 1923. Hitler and the SA stormed a public meeting of 3,000 people which had been organised by Gustav von Kahr, the de facto ruler of Bavaria (a state in the south of Germany). They announced that the national revolution had begun, declaring the formation of a new government under Ludendorff and Hitler. They were not well received. The following day, Hitler and his followers marched on the Bavarian War Ministry, where they met with violent resistance: sixteen members of the Nazi movement and four police officers were killed in the failed coup. Hitler was arrested and sentenced to five years in jail for high treason. However, the Bavarian Supreme Court pardoned him after one year.

During his time in prison, Hitler wrote the book *Mein Kampf,* or to be more accurate, he dictated it to Rudolf Hess who edited much of it. The book could be described as part autobiography, part idealogy. In it Hitler refers to his hatred of what he considered the world's twin evils: communism and Judaism.

It was in *Mein Kampf* that Hitler first expounded his idea of Lebensraum (living space): new territory required for German settlement in Eastern Europe. In 1925 Field Marshal Paul von Hindenburg (Ludendorff's associate through most of World War I) was elected President of Germany, a position he would hold until his death in 1934.

Building the Nazi Party
As a result of the Beer Hall Putsch, the Nazi Party was banned in Bavaria and after his release from prison Hitler was banned from public speaking. The party ban was lifted in 1925 when Hitler agreed that he would only seek political power through the democratic process, but the speaking ban remained in place until 1927.

Politics were stable in Germany between 1924 and 1929. Germany's economic position improved with the help of financial assistance from the US and much improved industrial productivity. However, the Wall Street Crash in 1929 had a disastrous effect on world economies. In Germany millions became unemployed and several major banks collapsed. In addition, she had to repay loans to the US, who was also in dire straits.

The Nazi Party rose from obscurity to win eighteen per cent of the vote in the 1930 election, becoming the second largest party in parliament. In March 1930 President Hindenburg appointed Heinrich Brüning as Chancellor. Brüning introduced a package of austerity measures, which were extremely unpopular and brought little economic improvement.

Nazi Germany

The rise of the Nazi Party continued during the next two years. In the 1932 election, its share of the vote rose to thirty-three per cent, making it the largest party in the Reichstag. On 30 January 1933, under pressure from former Chancellor Franz von Papen along with other politicians and business people, President Hindenburg appointed Hitler Chancellor. When Hitler became Chancellor, Ludendorff — who had the experience of collaborating with Hitler in the 'Beer Hall Putsch' (attempted coup d'état) — wrote to his President: *"I solemnly prophesy to you that this damnable man will plunge our Reich into the abyss and bring inconceivable misery down upon our nation. Coming generations will curse you in your grave because of this action."*

1933 was a turbulent year. On 27 February the Reichstag was set on fire. Hitler quickly blamed a communist uprising (there was a suspicion that the Nazis themselves were to blame) and persuaded President Hindenburg to sign the Reichstag Fire Decree. This decree, which would remain in force until 1945, repealed important political and human rights of the Weimar constitution. As a result, 11,000 communists and socialists were arrested and brought into hastily-constructed concentration camps, where many of them were executed by Hitler's newly-formed secret police force: the Gestapo. Hitler, fully conscious of the dangers to himself personally, formed a 'personal protection squad' called the Schutzstaffel (SS).

On 23 March 1933, in order to achieve full political control despite not having an overall majority, Hitler forced through the Enabling Act, which gave his cabinet full legislative powers for a period of four years. The Enabling Act — together with the Reichstag Fire Decree — transformed Hitler's government into a de facto legal dictatorship. On 14 July 1933 Hitler's Nazi Party was declared the only legal political party in Germany.

Book Burning

On 10 May 1933 the German Pro-Nazi Student Association organised the burning of 25,000 'un-German' books, many by renowned authors such as Karl Marx, Thomas Mann, Hermann Hesse, H. G. Wells, and 'corrupting' American influences such as Ernest Hemingway. Many of the books destroyed had Jewish authors. The books were gathered from school and university libraries throughout Germany. The reasoning behind the burning was that Hitler deemed his own words to be more important than all of the great authors of the time. The burning was an act of sheer wanton vandalism. One of the authors whose books were burned was the nineteenth century German-Jewish poet Heinrich Heine who wrote in one of his plays: *"Where they burn books, they will in the end also burn people."* These words were written a century earlier. What remarkable prescience!

Röhm and his SA troops were now seeking more and more political and military power, causing much anxiety among military, industrial and political leaders. Hitler responded by purging the entire SA leadership in what later became known as the Night of the Long Knives, which took place from 30 June to 2 July 1934. Hitler used the purge to eliminate anybody who might be a problem to him in the future. Up to 200 people were executed in the purge. Hitler had ensured its success in April by coming to an arrangement with War Minister Blomberg and the army. They had agreed to support Hitler as President as well as Chancellor upon Hindenburg's death in return for the elimination of Röhm and his troops.

When Hindenburg died on 2 August 1934, Hitler became head of state as well as head of government. He was to be known henceforth only as the Führer (leader). His Nazi regime became known as the Third Reich.

In early 1938 Hitler forced Blomberg to resign due to a sex scandal involving Blomberg's wife. Hitler assumed Blomberg's title of Commander in Chief, giving him total control over the army, navy and air force. Hitler now controlled everything that moved in Germany!

German Economy
During the 1930s the German economy staged a recovery, which could only be described as miraculous. The miracle was achieved by vast spending on infrastructure, the building of autobahns, railways and huge industrial output (much of it armaments). While Hitler took the credit for the autobahn programme, the first autobahn was, in fact, built by Konrad Adenauer, the Mayor of Cologne and future postwar Chancellor. The autobahn from Cologne to Bonn was built between 1929 and 1932, mainly using manual labour in an attempt to ease the unemployment crisis.

At this time unemployment dropped to virtually zero. Keynesian economics were being applied simultaneously by Hitler in Germany and Roosevelt in America. The two countries did not envisage that in less than ten years they would be major players on opposite sides in a new world war!

Needless to say, Hitler's popularity soared. He could do no wrong. With the help of a young architect called Albert Speer, he staged a series of rallies at Nuremberg, which attracted crowds of hundreds of thousands and were truly spectacular. Flags, torches, banners and weapons of war were part and parcel of the occasions. The rest of the world looked on nervously!

Joseph Goebbels was Hitler's Propaganda Minister. Both Hitler and Goebbels received Catholic schooling and became very familiar with the structure of the Catholic Church. Even though Hitler became extremely anti-Catholic, he much admired the discipline and the organisational structure of the church. Between himself and Goebbels, they developed an organisation as powerful as — and in some respects similar to — the Catholic Church. The parades at Nuremberg in 1933 were reminiscent of the church's Eucharistic Congress in Dublin in 1932 attended by 700,000 people. However, it is more likely that the church learned from the German National Socialists (Nazi Party), rather than the other way around.

Berlin hosted the Olympic Games in 1936. Richard Strauss provided the music for a choir of 3,000, and many of the 100,000 attendees (including some teams) saluted when Hitler entered the stadium. World leaders kept a sharp eye on the event, intrigued by the economic miracle performed in Germany while apprehensively monitoring the German build-up to war. The Olympics didn't go exactly as Hitler wanted. He refused to shake the hand of Jesse Owens, an African American who won four gold medals in athletics: a big blow to the Führer's Aryan race theory!

From 1936 onwards Hitler was preparing seriously for World War II.

The Jews, the Aryan Race and the Holocaust
The Aryan race was a concept influential in western culture in the period of the late 19th and early 20th centuries. The idea of the northern origins of the Aryans was particularly influential in Germany who saw the Aryans as a blue-eyed, blond-haired 'master race'. In the Nazi concept of an Aryan Race, there was no room for what were considered 'imperfect people'. This meant that Jews, gypsies, cripples and homosexuals had to be removed from Germany.

Anti-semitism, which was rife in the early part of the century, increased as a result of the Aryan race theory. By the time Hitler had completed *Mein Kampf,* he fully endorsed the theory that the Jews were responsible for everything that was wrong in Germany. In 1933 all Jewish civil servants and academics were dismissed. In 1935 the Nuremberg race laws were passed whereby Jews lost their German citizenship and were banned from marrying non-Jewish Germans. The Jews who left Germany of their own accord were those who could afford to do so: business people, doctors, dentists, scientists, etc. It did not seem to occur to Hitler that such skilled people were assets that Germany could ill-afford to lose (Albert Einstein went to America).

However, most Jews had neither the money nor the opportunity to escape. Neither had they a destination since many countries were now closing their doors to Jews.

Kristallnacht (the Night of Broken Glass) occurred on 9 November 1938. Thousands of shops and houses owned by Jews were destroyed by Nazis and hundreds of synagogues set on fire. Many Jews were arrested and taken to concentration camps, where millions of them died. 7,500 out of 9,000 Jewish shops were destroyed and almost 2,000 Jews were killed.

One of the most horrifying aspects of the Holocaust was the use of Jewish children in medical experiments under the supervision of the notorious Dr. Josef Mengele. The experiments usually meant a long and painful death for these children. On 1 September 1941 Reinhard Heydrich signed a decree making it compulsory for all Jews over the age of 6 to wear a yellow Star of David in public with the word 'Jude' (German for Jew) sewn onto it.

When Germany occupied Norway, the Netherlands, Luxembourg, Belgium and France in 1940, and the Balkan countries in 1941, anti-semitic measures were also introduced in these countries, although the severity varied from country to country.

Armed Forces: Germany 1919–39
During the interwar years Germany went through two distinct political phases: the Weimar Republic and the Nazi Party. During both phases the objective was the same: to overturn the Treaty of Versailles and restore Germany to the world power it once was. Hitler had only six years (1933–39) to achieve a military miracle, but he was helped in no small way by Germany's (and Prussia's) military experience spanning many centuries, including her tradition of compulsory military service.

The election of Paul von Hindenburg as President of the republic in 1925 ensured a continuation of Germany's military traditions. When Blomberg was appointed Supreme Commander in the Weimar Republic, Germany had a troika (including Hitler) with a common purpose: the rebuilding of Germany as an armed force. However, things changed in the mid-1930s. Hindenburg died in 1934 and Hitler became head of state. When Blomberg was forced to resign in 1938, Hitler became Supreme Commander. He was now both head of state and commander of the armed forces!

Hitler's rearmament programme began in earnest in 1935, when the inhabitants of the Saar chose by plebiscite to rejoin Germany. The army began a major programme of conscription in contravention of the Treaty of Versailles. At the same time the Luftwaffe was reformed and over the next four years became a major air force to rival Britain's

RAF. In parallel with this, Hitler instigated a major expansion programme in the Kriegsmarine (German navy).

When his senior generals suggested that Germany would not be ready for war until 1942 at the earliest, Hitler gave them the deaf ear. In fact, he did not take advice from anyone nor did he discuss his war plans with anybody. All of his major decisions, including the Anschluss (political union) with Austria, the remilitarisation of the Rhineland and his policy towards Czechoslovakia were made without consultation with his senior commanders.

Hitler's massive rearmament programme bore little relation to German resources. In 1938 he was warned by his generals that Germany had exhausted her financial reserves and that she would have to intensify her trade and return to the world economy. This would mean a slowdown in Hitler's plans for war. Hitler ignored the generals. He believed that the economy was somebody else's problem and he pushed ahead with his massive expansion plans for army, navy and air force. It transpired that the finance required came from Swiss banks *[see Bergier Commission under Switzerland in Chapter 10, page 165]* and from major German industries.

In 1936 Hitler began to test the opposition. He was not sure how far he could go before France and Britain would react. He decided to take it one day at a time or, to be more precise, one country at a time: Austria, Czechoslovakia and Poland in that order. His first move, however, was within Germany itself. The Rhineland had been demilitarised by the Treaty of Versailles. On 7 March 1936 German troops entered the Rhineland and waited for a reaction from France and Britain. There was none. After all, France and Britain were not very concerned about what happened within Germany's boundaries. The Treaty of Locarno was ignored.

Between 1936 and 1939 Hitler sent troops and planes to assist another dictator, General Franco, in the Spanish Civil War. The planes he sent were German Condor aircraft, which carried out a horrific attack on Guernica. Later, Hitler regretted getting involved when Franco refused to support him in World War II.

Hitler's next move came in 1938. Austria was an ally of Germany in World War I, and even after Versailles there was a strong pro-German pro-Nazi feeling within Austria. Many Austrians were in favour of Anschluss with Germany and when German troops entered Austria on 12 March 1938 there was no opposition: in fact, they were welcomed by many.

Czechoslovakia, formed after World War I, was a mixture of nationalities. Twenty per cent were German and these were located in an area around the perimeter of Czechoslovakia called the Sudetenland. They pressed for self-government in 1938, encouraged by Germany. Hitler saw this as another opportunity and on 29 September Germany invaded the Sudetenland. The Czech government sought help from Britain and France. France was willing to help but would not go it alone. Neville Chamberlain, the British Prime Minister, wished to avert war at all costs: memories of World War I were still very vivid. He adopted a policy of appeasement (i.e. letting Hitler have the Sudetenland in return for an assurance that he would go no further). But Hitler did not abide by the Munich Agreement and in March 1939 Germany occupied the remainder of Czechoslovakia.

Hitler had now succeeded in recovering the Rhineland in addition to taking over Austria and Czechoslovakia without a bullet being fired. His next move, however, was Poland and this would be an altogether different proposition.

One of Hitler's big complaints about the Treaty of Versailles was the awarding of the Polish Corridor (West Prussia) and the port of Danzig to Poland, giving her access to the Baltic. This meant isolating East Prussia from the rest of Germany. It also meant that a percentage of Germans ended up living in Poland against their will. Hitler was determined to reverse this position at the earliest opportunity.

Poland's only hope was that Russia would come to her aid, but when Hitler and Stalin signed a non-aggression pact in August 1939 (to everyone's surprise), Poland — sandwiched between Germany and Russia — was in trouble!

The explanation behind the pact, which became known as the Molotov-Ribbentrop Pact, was simple. Hitler wanted to keep Stalin onside while he attacked the West. In the pact, Hitler and Stalin agreed to divide Poland between them and they also agreed that Stalin could take the Baltic states of Latvia, Estonia and Lithuania.

Poland's only allies now were France and Britain, both of whom threatened war on Germany if she invaded Poland. Ribbentrop, the German Foreign Minister, believed they were bluffing and urged Hitler to call their bluff!

Germany invaded Poland on 1 September 1939. France and Britain declared war on Germany on 3 September. The bluff had been called and World War II had begun! There were many in Germany who were deeply unhappy: memories of World War I were stark. Hermann Göring, Commander in Chief of the Luftwaffe (German air force), laid the blame squarely at Ribbentrop's feet.

ITALY 1919–39

Italy emerged from World War I a very unhappy victor. She had not entered the war initially but was persuaded to do so by the Allies in 1915 with promises of territory. When the war was over, those promises were quickly forgotten. Italy suffered 1.5 million casualties in the war and her economy suffered greatly. The 1919–20 period was characterised by mass strikes, high unemployment and political instability. The climate was ideal for the emergence of Benito Mussolini and his Fascist Party.

Mussolini was born in Forli in 1883. He was a small aggressive youth known for his violent nature (he stabbed his girlfriend when he was eighteen). To avoid compulsory military service, he moved to Switzerland where his political ambitions started. He became an avid writer and a supporter of left wing socialism. He returned to Italy in 1904, served out his military time and continued his political writing in a weekly publication. By the time World War I started in 1914, Mussolini had become the editor of an Italian daily newspaper.

Although Italy was in an alliance with Germany and Austria-Hungary, she initially remained neutral in the war. Mussolini later surprised everybody by publishing an article advocating that Italy join the war on the side of the Allies, which she did in 1915.

In 1919 Mussolini saw the instability after World War I as an opportunity and organised a group of war veterans to come together and form the Fascist Party (the word 'fasces' means a bundle of rods and became a symbol of power in Italian history). And so, the Fascist Party was born, ten years before Hitler's Nazi Party! Fascism is defined as an authoritarian and nationalistic right-wing system of government. It includes a belief in the supremacy of one national or ethnic group, contempt for democracy, an insistence on obedience to a powerful leader and a strong demagogic approach. At this time Italy was a monarchy under King Victor Emmanuel III.

In October 1922 Mussolini took advantage of a general strike to announce his demands to the Italian government to give the Fascist Party political power or face a coup. With no immediate response, a group of 30,000 fascists began a long trek across Italy to Rome (which became known as the March on Rome) demanding power for the fascists. They also demanded the resignation of the Prime Minister and his replacement by Mussolini. King Emmanuel was faced with a critical decision. Although the Italian army was considerably stronger than the fascists, the King, who feared Mussolini, chose the fascists over the Italian Socialist Party to form a government. Mussolini was appointed Prime Minister and, from then on, became known as '*Il Duce*'(the leader).

Over the next five years the Italian Fascist Party went from strength to strength but not always democratically. The members used violence and intimidation to gain control of the parliament. In 1926, Mussolini succeeded in getting a law passed declaring that he was accountable to the King alone, making him the sole person able to determine the parliament's agenda. In 1928 all political parties (except the Fascist Party) were banned and thereafter all political candidates had to be nominated by the Grand Council of Fascism. The best that can be said about Mussolini on the domestic scene is that he did improve transport and other public services in Italy.

Foreign Politics

Mussolini promised to make Italy the world power it once was, building a 'new Roman Empire' (Mare Nostrum) around the Mediterranean Sea. In this he was singularly unsuccessful. In 1923 Italy took over the Greek Island of Corfu. In 1925 she forced Albania to become a de facto protectorate. She also had plans to take over Italian-populated areas of France (Nice and Corsica), but with the rise of Nazism Mussolini became more concerned with the potential threat to Italy from Germany.

During the Spanish Civil War, Italy sent arms and 60,000 troops to assist Franco's nationalist faction. This was to secure Italy's naval access to Spanish ports and increase Italian influence in the Mediterranean.

Mussolini and Hitler first met in 1934. They were both aware of the other's ambitions for power and Mussolini was not enamoured with the idea of playing second fiddle to Hitler. He opposed Germany's plans to annex Austria and promised the Austrians military support if Germany took action.

On 3 October 1935, Mussolini invaded Abyssinia (Ethiopia) and forced Emperor Haile Selassie into exile. It was a hollow victory over a significantly inferior nation. The only nation to back Italy was Nazi Germany. The invasion made little sense since Abyssinia is located at the Horn of Africa a long way from Italy. She was also a member of the League of Nations, which condemned the action. While Britain and France condemned the invasion, they took no action: a fact that Hitler noted with interest!

Italy and Germany signed the Rome-Berlin peace pact on 25 October 1936. A year later, Italy opted out of the League of Nations. At this point, Mussolini had no option but to back Hitler and he abandoned his support for Austria. He gave Hitler verbal support in Nazi Germany's actions in Austria, the Sudetenland and Czechoslovakia while he sought to prove his own strength by invading Albania in April 1939. This invasion pleased Mussolini: he had added Albania to his empire. Mussolini's plan was to use Albania as a base to take over the Balkans.

As war approached in 1939, the Fascist regime stepped up an aggressive press campaign against France claiming that Italian people in Nice and Corsica were being ill-treated. In May 1939 Mussolini signed a formal alliance with Germany, known as the Pact of Steel (name chosen by Mussolini). Mussolini felt obliged to sign despite his belief that Italy would not be ready for war for several years and because of his personal desire to prevent Hitler becoming the dominant leader in Europe.

Mussolini was taken aback, however, when Germany and Russia formed a pact agreeing the partitioning of Poland in August 1939 without consulting him.

Armed Forces: Italy 1919–39
Italy was badly prepared for World War II when it started and the blame for this can be laid squarely at the feet of Mussolini. Instead of building up Italy's armed forces, he wasted her limited resources on the Ethiopian and Albanian campaigns and on assisting Franco in the Spanish Civil War.

Mussolini persuaded the Italian army not to interfere while he grew his Fascist Party. He promised them increased power, a promise he never fulfilled. There was major conflict between the army, navy and air force over the allocation of resources. If Mussolini's dream of a new fascist Mediterranean Empire was to become a reality, resources would have to be provided to the navy and air force at the expense of the army. The outcome was that all three of Italy's armed forces were under-resourced and Italy was very badly prepared for World War II when it started.

Mussolini's invasion of Abyssinia and his support for the nationalists in the Spanish Civil War were little more than ego trips for Mussolini himself. Most of Italy's military funding was spent on these campaigns and resulted in Mussolini informing Hitler that Italy would not be ready for war until early 1943. Hitler simply ignored him.

In support of Hitler during the Holocaust, Mussolini's regime systematically confiscated Jewish property and dismissed Jews from jobs in the civil service, schools, universities and banking. 8,000 Jews were deported from Italy to their deaths in concentration camps in Germany and in Poland.

JAPAN 1919–39

In World War I Japan joined the Allied forces but played only a minor role in fighting German colonial forces in East Asia. At Versailles in 1919, Japan's proposal to include a 'racial equality clause' in the covenant of the League of Nations was rejected by the United States, Britain and Australia.

Ever since Japan opened up to trade with the western world at the beginning of the 1800s, arrogance and racial discrimination towards the Japanese plagued Western-Japanese relations and were again major factors in the deterioration of relationships in the decades preceding World War II. A typical example was the passing of the Immigration Act by the US Congress in 1924 prohibiting further immigration from Asia.

After the end of World War I, Japan's economic situation deteriorated. The Great Kantō earthquake, which struck eastern Japan on 1 September 1923, resulted in the deaths of more than 100,000 people and massive structural damage.

A European nation looking at the landmass of Japan at the beginning of the twentieth century could be forgiven for thinking, *"Japan could be a suitable colony for us."* How wrong they would be! The Japanese might have a small landmass but they were proud, independent, ambitious and extremely capable. Japan had one major weakness: a lack of natural resources (oil and minerals) of her own. She had a further weakness in that senior army officers, responsible only to the Emperor, ran the country. There were no politicians who might have foreseen the results of various military offensives.

If there was one word to describe Japan, it would have to be 'belligerent', and Japan was completely unfazed by the size of the opposition, whether it was China, Russia or the US. The first Sino-Japanese War took place from 1894 to 1895 during the Meiji (enlightenment) period in Japan (1868–1912). After six months of continuous successes by the Japanese army and navy, China surrendered in 1895. For the first time in 2,000 years, regional dominance in East Asia shifted from China to Japan. There was a public outcry in China, resulting in a series of domestic revolutions. Meanwhile, Japan moved on. In 1903 Japan requested that Russia recognise her interest in Korea and Manchuria. Russia's refusal resulted in a naval war between the two, culminating in the Battle of Tsushima in 1905 when the entire Russian fleet was wiped out. European powers were not the only ones to sit up and take notice!

On 25 December 1926 Hirohito became Emperor of Japan on the death of his father and would continue to reign until his death in 1989. He proved to be a capable foil for the belligerent officers of both the army and navy, who operated independently and who were happy to go to war with minimal cause. Hirohito was looked up to more as a God than a political leader!

On 18 September 1931 Japan occupied Manchuria, and the occupying forces became known as the Kwantung Army. Manchuria became Manchukuo and the following year it was declared an independent state, controlled by the Kwantung Army through a puppet government.

In 1933 Japan withdrew from the League of Nations after the League heavily criticised her actions in China.

Japan saw herself as the 'Germany of the East': in fact, she was given the nickname 'The Prussia of Asia'. She was surrounded by the colonies of other countries, many of whom had substantial natural resources, which Japan needed so badly. The British controlled India, Burma, Malaya and Sarawak. Hong Kong had been a British colony for years, while to the south lay the Dominions of Australia and New Zealand. The French controlled Indochina and the Dutch East Indies, while the United States controlled the Philippines and other Pacific island bases, including Hawaii. A Japanese officer made the point that 450 million natives of the Far East were living under the domination of less than a million whites! Japan's ambition knew no bounds: she saw no reason why she could not control East Asia and the entire Pacific while Germany controlled West Asia and Europe! The army ran the country and could see nothing but victories ahead!

On 7 July 1937 the second Sino-Japanese War broke out. This marked the start of World War II in the Pacific. Many historians maintain that this was the actual start of World War II. The war was the result of a decades-long Japanese imperialist policy aimed at dominating China politically and militarily, and securing her vast material reserves and other economic resources, particularly food. The Japanese forces succeeded in occupying almost the entire Chinese coastal area and in doing so committed some appalling atrocities against the Chinese population. During the fall of the capital Nanking in December 1937, the Japanese massacred more than 200,000 prisoners and civilians, and raped more than 20,000 women and girls. The brutality of the Japanese was unbelievable: many of their captives were bayoneted to death. Some were even buried alive. This became known as the Nanking Massacre. However, the Chinese government never formally surrendered and the war continued on a reduced scale until 1945.

When China was not occupied fighting Japan, she was engaged with her own civil war: nationalist China under Chiang Kai-shek versus communist China under Mao Tse-tung. For the duration of the Pacific War, it suited the Allies to side with Chiang Kai-shek's nationalists, who then kept a minimum of ten Japanese divisions engaged for the duration of the war.

On 29 July 1938 the Japanese invaded the USSR and suffered their first defeat at the hands of the Red Army in the Battle of Khalkhin Gol River. The commander of the Soviet Army was Georgy Zhukov, who went on to become the Commander in Chief of the Soviet Army in World War II.

Japan concluded that she would be better employed concentrating on the Pacific. As things turned out, this proved to be a fortuitous decision. Had Japan continued to attack the Russians on this front, Russia would have found herself under attack on two fronts in World War II: Germany on the Eastern Front and Japan on a southern front. If that had happened, the outcome of the war might have been very different!

Armed Forces: Japan 1919–39
ARMY
To be in the army in Japan was considered an honour and manpower requirements were easily met during the interwar years. There was, however, a considerable degree of indoctrination, and military training became a regular part of the secondary school curriculum. Military recruits were taught that there was no more honourable way to die than fighting for your country!

While the regular army numbers remained static at seventeen divisions between 1924 and 1931, its patriotic fervour reached new heights during this period. Major expansion programmes were undertaken from 1931 onwards and by 1940 Japan had an army of fifty divisions (one million soldiers).

NAVY
In the Five-Power Naval Limitation Treaty of 1921/22 signed in the aftermath of World War I, Japan agreed to accept the third position in the 5:5:3 capital ship ratio after Great Britain and the United States (France and Italy were allocated ratios of 1.75). This meant that Japan had to restrict the size of her navy to three-fifths that of Great Britain and the US. Japan geared her shipbuilding programme accordingly. However, she was resolute that naval professional efficiency was not to be sacrificed. She scrapped ten ships and proceeded with the building of a more modern fleet. She developed her own Eight-Eight Fleet programme, the objective of which was to build a capital fleet of eight battleships and eight battlecruisers, all of modern design. She also modernised major docklands at Yokosuka, Kure and Sasebo. To overcome the restrictions of the Naval Limitation Treaty, Japan

continued building smaller naval vessels and merchantmen (trading ships), as well as modernising existing capital ships.

In 1922 Japan built her first aircraft carrier. It was the first ship in the world to be built as a purpose-built aircraft carrier. Japan had the foresight to see that aircraft carriers would be the key to controlling the vast Pacific. In 1924 Japan (after a detailed study of the German U-boat) began the construction of new diesel-powered submarines.

With the abrogation of the Naval Limitation Treaty in 1934, Japan began a naval construction programme aimed at achieving parity with the United States and Great Britain. She commenced a programme of building the most modern battleships in the world. The navy, mindful of the superior battleship strength of its chief potential adversary, the United States, persuaded its government to finance the unorthodox development. During the interwar years, the total tonnage of capital ships, aircraft carriers, cruisers, destroyers and submarines in the Japanese navy increased substantially.

AIR FORCE

Japan was unusual in that it had not one but two air forces: the Imperial Japanese Army Air Force and the Imperial Japanese Navy Air Force. The reason for the two air forces was quite simple: communication and cooperation between the army and navy was very poor and both felt the need to have their own aerial backup. The Army Air Force was to provide tactical air support for ground troops. The Navy Air Force was responsible for long-range strikes in the Pacific and it was not until the later stages of the Pacific War that both forces combined.

The first aircraft factory in Japan — the Nakajima Aircraft Company — was built in 1916, but it was not until World War I was over that Japan developed serious interest in aircraft for military use. By the end of the 1920s Japan was producing her own designs to meet the needs of the army and by 1935 she had a large inventory of technically-advanced aircraft. By 1941 the Japanese Army Air Force had about 1,500 combat aircraft designed for takeoff and landing on aircraft carriers. These were mainly Zero fighters, which were the dominant aircraft in the early years of the war in the Pacific. They enjoyed air superiority due to the combat experience of their crews and the lack of preparedness of the Allied forces. The Allies were playing catch-up until 1943.

However, as the war continued the industrial limitation of the country in comparison with the Allies, as well as the bombing of the Japanese home islands, resulted in Japan being unable to maintain a competitive volume of aircraft. Many experienced crews were lost in combat. New ones could not be trained due to lack of fuel and time available, and towards the end of its existence the Army Air Force resorted to 'kamikaze' (suicide) attacks against overwhelmingly superior Allied forces. Crashing a plane into a battleship proved to be very effective, but each assault resulted in the loss of a plane and a pilot, and replacements were not readily available.

CHAPTER 10

The Doomed Quest To Avoid Another War

Spain

Belgium

Poland

Yugoslavia

Turkey

Switzerland

Spain — Spanish Civil War

The Spanish Civil War was fought between July 1936 and April 1939. The belligerents were the revolutionary Nationalists led by the newly-emerged General Francisco Franco and the democratic government's Republican Party. The war, which was widespread throughout Spain, seriously divided the country. Major atrocities were perpetrated by both sides resulting in the deaths of 500,000 people.

Germany (using her Condor aircraft) and Italy supported Franco's Nationalists, while the Republicans received support from the Soviet Union. Britain and France did not become involved. 50,000 volunteers from various European countries travelled to Spain to support the government in what they perceived to be a battle against the emerging fascism and Nazism.

In April 1937 Germany's Condor Legion — in support of Franco — bombed Guernica, an undefended Republican area in the north of Spain, killing more than 2,000 people. This action provoked worldwide condemnation.

Franco emerged victorious from the war in 1939 and ruled Spain as a dictator up to his death in 1975. His Falange Party took control of a country that was destroyed by the civil war and in need of extensive rebuilding.

The question is often asked: why did Franco not support Hitler in World War II? Hitler did try to enlist Franco's support, but Hitler described a meeting with Franco as *"more painful than a visit to the dentist"*. In return for his support, Franco demanded control of Gibraltar and all of North Africa. Hitler refused.

In truth, Spain was a broken country physically and economically. She was in no position to get involved in World War II after her own civil war and declared herself neutral.

Picasso's famous painting 'Guernica' reminds us of the horrors of the Spanish Civil War.

Belgium

The number of war campaigns that took place in Belgium during several wars resulted in her being nicknamed 'The Cockpit of Europe'.

Belgium was neutral in World War I but this did not deter Germany. Germany ignored the neutrality of both Belgium and Luxembourg and invaded both countries as part of her plan for a surprise attack on France, which she hoped would result in Germany quickly taking Paris.

Belgium, however, put up stubborn resistance and much of the fighting on the Western Front took place on Belgian soil. The result was that Belgium emerged from the war in ruins. The towns of Ypres and Liège were completely destroyed while damage in Flanders as a result of the Battles of Ypres and the Battle of Passchendaele was horrific. Belgium spent much of the interwar years rebuilding her country.

In the Treaty of Versailles in 1919, the area of Eupen-Malmedy was returned to Belgium. The Vennbahn railway (which ran partly through German territory) was transferred to Belgium while two former German colonies in Africa — Rwanda and Burundi — were mandated to Belgium by the League of Nations.

Taking into account the damage to the country in World War I, it shows something of the resilience of the Belgian people that the first postwar Olympic Games were held in Antwerp in 1920.

In 1925 the Treaty of Locarno was signed in Switzerland, who remained neutral through the two world wars. The treaty recognised Germany's borders with France and Belgium and was signed by Germany, France, Belgium, Britain and Italy.

Belgium maintained her neutrality throughout the 1930s, but World War II began in 1939, and in 1940 Germany invaded all three Low Countries: Belgium, the Netherlands and Luxembourg.

Poland

Poland did not exist as an independent state during World War I, but her geographical position between Germany and Russia meant that much fighting — along with huge human and material losses — occurred on Polish territory. After the war and the collapse of the

Russian, German and Austro-Hungarian Empires, Poland became an independent republic. The Treaty of Versailles gave Poland back the lands of West Prussia, Posen and Upper Silesia. It also gave her the Polish Corridor, giving her access to the port of Danzig (Gdansk) and the Baltic Sea. This was a bitter one for Germany to accept since it involved separating East Prussia from Germany. Independent Poland, which had been absent from the map of Europe for 123 years, was reborn.

Revolutionary Józef Piłsudski was chief of state from 1918 to 1922, at which stage he handed power over to others and resigned. However, he became very unhappy with the management of the new republic over the next four years and in 1926 he resumed active participation in government. He was immediately appointed Minister for Defence, a position he was to hold until his death in 1935.

Establishing Poland's borders with her neighbours — Germany, Russia, Austria, Ukraine and the Baltic states — proved a formidable task and in several cases resulted in a territorial war. The most important of these was the Polish-Soviet War (1919–21), which ended with a compromise peace treaty at Riga in early 1921.

As the Great Depression gained momentum in the 1930s, anti-Semitism began to rise in Poland in parallel with Germany. Poland was home to more than three million Jews (ten per cent of Poland's population), the largest Jewish population in Europe at the time. Impoverished Jews were sustained in part by the charity of working Jews.

Polish agriculture suffered from the usual handicaps of Eastern European nations at that time: technological backwardness, low productivity, lack of capital and access to markets. Despite this, Poland could claim some noteworthy achievements during the interwar years: economic growth; the revival of Polish education and culture after decades of official curbs; and, above all, reaffirmation of the Polish nationhood that had for so long been disputed. Much of this could be attributed to Piłsudski.

Foreign policy was more straightforward than domestic since the major political parties all agreed that Germany was a potential threat and that France was the natural ally of Poland. Relations with the Soviet Union remained hostile, but Piłsudski was willing to negotiate and in 1932 the two countries finally established diplomatic relations. Soon afterwards Hitler came to power. Piłsudski could see what was coming and he proposed that Poland join forces with France and launch a pre-emptive strike against Germany. France, with memories of World War I still vivid, declined. Had France responded positively to Piłsudski's proposal, perhaps World War II could have been averted!

In 1934 Poland and Germany signed a non-aggression pact, but Hitler was only going through the motions. His focus was on regaining control of the Polish Corridor which would reconnect Germany with East Prussia.

Piłsudski died in 1935 and was a huge loss to Poland.

The Poles were in an invidious position sandwiched between two of the most powerful nations in the world: Russia and Germany. They feared both: *"With the Germans, we fear losing our liberty,"* said one of their leaders, *"with the Russians, we could lose our soul."* They believed their best option was to play one off against the other.

However, Hitler began to apply pressure towards the end of 1938. After the invasions of Austria and Czechoslovakia, Poland feared that she would be next. At this stage, Poland had declared allies in both Britain and France. Both, however, were ill-prepared for war and Poland's only real hope was Russia. At this stage, Hitler showed an unexpected degree of cunning: he persuaded Stalin to enter into a non-aggression treaty with him on 19 August 1939. There was method in Hitler's madness: he agreed that Germany and Russia would not only share Poland but also that Russia could take the Baltic states of Latvia, Estonia and Lithuania. Hitler was now free to attack westwards, knowing he need not fear an attack from the east as happened in World War I.

On 1 September 1939 German troops crossed the Polish border. A day later both France and Britain declared war on Germany. World War II had begun!

Yugoslavia

Yugoslavia was a confusing entity during the early part of the twentieth century. It consisting initially (from 1918) of Croatia, Serbia, Slovenia and Macedonia; and was known as the Kingdom of Serbs, Croats and Slovenes. This was basically the area known as the Balkans during World War I.

Josip Broz Tito, whose nom de guerre was 'Tito', first came to notice when he was conscripted into the Austro-Hungarian army in 1913. He was a very capable soldier and quickly moved up through the ranks, becoming the youngest Sergeant Major in the Austro-Hungarian army in 1915. Later the same year, Tito was captured by the Russians and sent to a work camp in the Ural Mountains. He broke out and in 1918 he joined the Communist Party of Yugoslavia (CPY).

The CPY's influence on Yugoslavia grew rapidly. After government elections in 1920, it became the third strongest party in government. In

Polish revolutionary Józef Piłsudski, Chief of State 1918–22, Minister for Defence 1926–35.

Map 14: Interwar Europe

1921 the party was declared illegal. Throughout the 1920s Tito continued to work underground despite pressure on the communists by the government.

King Alexander I banned national political parties in 1929, assumed executive power and renamed the country the 'Kingdom of Yugoslavia', which then became a dictatorship. However, the King's policies encountered opposition from other European powers stemming from developments in Italy and Germany, where fascists and Nazis rose to power, and the Soviet Union, where Stalin became absolute ruler. None of these three regimes favoured the policies pursued by King Alexander I, who attempted to create a centralised Yugoslavia. The effect of Alexander's dictatorship was to further alienate the non-Serbs from the idea of unity. During his reign, the flags of Yugoslav nations were banned.

King Alexander I was assassinated in Marseille during an official visit to France in 1934. He was succeeded by his 11-year-old son Peter II and a regency council headed by his cousin Prince Paul.

In the 1930s things were changing politically with the emergence of Germany and Russia as major world powers. Supported and pressured by fascist Italy and Nazi Germany, Croatian leader Vladko Maček and his party created the Banovina of Croatia in 1939. This was a province which would still be governed by Yugoslavia in matters of defence, security, foreign affairs, trade and transport but would have autonomy over internal affairs. The entire kingdom was to be federalised, but World War II put paid to this plan.

Meanwhile, Tito had progressed to the position of Secretary-General of the outlawed CPY party. He went on to lead the Yugoslav guerrilla movement, the Partisans, during World War II.

Turkey
Turkey — or the Ottoman Empire as it was then — participated in World War I on the side of Germany and the Axis forces. Her choice was determined by her fear of Russia. Her sole major victory in the war was at Gallipoli where she routed the Allied forces. The leader of the Ottoman forces at Gallipoli was the renowned Mustafa Kemal Pasha (Pasha is a higher political or military rank, similar to a British peerage or knighthood). However, in the Middle East in 1917/18, they were comprehensively defeated by the British.

In 1920 the Ottoman government signed the Treaty of Sèvres with the Allies, drastically reducing Ottoman territory to where it covered only part of modern Turkey but also giving most of the control of the Ottoman nation over to the Allies. As a condition, the Sultan and his government were allowed to stay in power but subservient to the

Allies. This provoked the Turkish revolutionaries to begin their armed campaign against the Allies and the Ottoman forces still loyal to the Sultan. Meanwhile, the Greeks landed in western Anatolia in Turkey to assert territorial claims that they had been promised by the Allies.

However, the Turkish revolutionaries never accepted the Treaty of Sèvres. Under the leadership of Kemal they continued their fight, which became known as the Turkish War of Independence or the Greco-Turkish War of 1919–22.

In 1922 they drove the Greeks out of Turkey. On 24 July 1923 the Treaty of Sèvres was replaced by the Treaty of Lausanne, which gave the Turks a fairer deal. The Allies acknowledged the end of the Ottoman Empire and the birth of the modern Turkish republic.

One of the effects of the emergence of the Turkish nation at this time was called the Great Catastrophe. The Turks exiled one million Orthodox Greeks in exchange for 400,000 Turkish Muslims. The exchange resulted in considerable violence and a huge number of deaths on both sides.

Mustafa Kemal became the first President of the Republic of Turkey in 1923, a position he would hold until his death in 1938. Kemal embarked on a programme of political, economic and cultural reforms, seeking to transform the former Ottoman Empire into a modern, westernised and secular nation-state. Under his leadership, thousands of new schools were built (ninety per cent of the population was illiterate in 1923). Turkey officially became a secular state in 1928 and in 1934 women were granted the right to vote.

One of Kemal's reforms was the introduction of western-style names and on 1 April 1934 the parliament granted him the name Atatürk, which means 'Father of the Turks'. He died in 1938; he was a great loss to his country. While the Turks were a major ally of Germany in World War I, they retained their neutrality during World War II.

Switzerland
Switzerland remained neutral during World War I and her neutrality — which was respected by both Allied and Axis forces — facilitated the growth of the Swiss banking industry.

Vladimir Lenin, in his stance against World War I, took up residence in neutral Switzerland in 1914 and remained there until 1917, when he returned to lead his Bolsheviks in the October Revolution in Russia.

In 1920 Switzerland joined the League of Nations. During the interwar years Switzerland's banking system went from strength to strength. In 1934 the Swiss Banking Act was passed. This allowed for anonymous numbered bank accounts, in part to allow individual Germans (including Jews) to hide or protect their assets from seizure by the newly-established Third Reich.

Switzerland again declared herself neutral during World War II, but her neutrality has been extensively questioned ever since.

Bergier Commission

In 1996 a special commission called the Bergier Commission was set up by the Swiss parliament to establish conclusively the relationship between the Nazi regime and the Swiss banks. The commission was completely independent, consisting of members from Poland, America and Israel along with members from Switzerland itself. It presented its findings in 2002.

The commission reached the following conclusions:

1. Nazi Germany's war effort was facilitated mainly by Swiss banks from 1938 onwards (some financing was also provided by large German industrial concerns). Huge amounts of gold looted from the central banks of Germany's defeated neighbours (mainly Belgium, the Netherlands and Luxembourg) and from wealthy individuals, including Jews, were sold to the Swiss banks for Swiss francs, which were then used to make strategic purchases for the German war effort. Between 1940 and 1945, the German state bank sold gold valued at over 100 million francs through Swiss commercial banks and the Swiss National Bank!

2. Switzerland conformed to Nazi policy regarding the Jews from 1933 onwards. In 1938 the Swiss government requested the Nazi authorities to stamp all passports of German Jews with a 'J'. Thousands of refugees were then sent back to Germany, where they ended up in concentration camps.

CHAPTER 11

The Struggle To Break Away From British Rule

During the interwar years, Britain ceded independence to several countries, including Ireland, India and Egypt.

Ireland

Ever since the Act of Union between Britain and Ireland in 1800, Ireland had been seeking independence from Britain and in 1912 Irish representatives at Westminster, led by John Redmond, were offered a form of Home Rule. However, not everyone in Ireland wanted independence. The six Unionist/Protestant counties in the north of Ireland wished to remain part of the United Kingdom while the remaining twenty-six Republican/Catholic counties wanted independence. There was open conflict between John Redmond's Irish Volunteers and Edward Carson's Ulster Unionists. Carson was born in Dublin to a Protestant family, and the minority Protestants in Ireland feared that Home Rule in Ireland would mean 'Rome Rule' i.e. that Ireland would be ruled by the Catholic Church. The Unionists opposed Home Rule and they had the support of the House of Lords. Diehard Republicans, however, wanted a united island of Ireland: nothing less was acceptable! The onset of World War I in 1914 resulted in the problem being shelved until after the war (nobody expected it to last for four years).

More than 200,000 Irish soldiers fought on the side of the Allies in the war, 40,000 of whom (including the grandfather of the author of this book) died in the war. Many of those who fought were followers of Redmond and they fought in the belief that Britain would more readily grant Home Rule to Ireland out of gratitude when the war was over.

However, in 1916 a small group of Republicans from the Irish Republican Brotherhood saw Britain's involvement in the war as Ireland's opportunity to rebel against British rule. They had little support from the populace at large, many of whom had fathers and brothers fighting on Britain's side in the war. Neither did they have the support of Eoin MacNeill, the leader of the Irish Volunteers, who also wanted Home Rule but by peaceful means! MacNeill tried to call off the planned armed uprising by placing a notice in the Easter Sunday newspapers to that effect, but the rebel leaders decided to press on regardless.

The uprising had support from Germany, who was quite happy to discommode Britain, her enemy in the war, by supplying arms to the rebels. A shipment of arms organised by Roger Casement, a member of the Gaelic League, was intercepted off the Kerry coast by British naval forces. Casement was arrested and jailed in London.

In what became known as the Easter Rising, the revolutionaries — led by Pádraig Pearse and James Connolly — seized control of several important buildings, including the General Post Office (GPO) in the centre of Dublin. The British response under General John Maxwell, a colonial officer whose only understanding of conflict was brute force, was swift and ferocious. He moved in with heavy artillery and the rebels were forced to surrender in a very short time. The heavy artillery destroyed O'Connell Street (then called Sackville Street), the main street in Dublin.

Initially there was little public support for the insurgents, but Britain's treatment of the captured leaders turned this opinion. Fourteen of the leaders were taken to Kilmainham Gaol, where they were executed by firing squad between 3 and 12 May. A fifteenth, Thomas Kent, was executed at Cork Detention Barracks. One of the leaders, James Connolly — who had been badly injured in the Easter Rising — was carried out on a stretcher then strapped to a chair to be executed!

The only leaders spared were Éamon de Valera — who had American citizenship and whose execution would not go down well in the US — and Countess Markievicz because she was a woman. There was one further execution. Three months after the Kilmainham Gaol executions, Roger Casement was hanged as a traitor in London. The executions proved to be the spark that fuelled Irish nationalistic feelings towards Britain. Who knows what the future relationship between the two countries might have been had those leaders been imprisoned rather than executed?

Towards the end of the war the Sinn Féin ("we ourselves") party under de Valera came to prominence seeking independence by peaceful means. However, not everyone was willing to wait. In 1919 the Irish Republican Army (IRA) under Michael Collins began a campaign of terror designed to drive the British out of Ireland.

What followed became known as the Irish War of Independence. In 1919 the British sent over auxiliary troops, known as the 'Black and Tans' (so-called because of the colour of their uniforms), to assist the Royal Irish Constabulary (RIC) police force. Throughout 1920 the IRA and the Tans matched brutality with brutality. On 21 November 1920 Michael Collins ordered the execution of eleven men who were accused of spying for the British. The IRA carried out his order and in the process killed three British soldiers. The British exacted their revenge that Sunday afternoon. In what became known as the original 'Bloody Sunday', the British drove their armoured cars into Croke

Park stadium (headquarters of the Gaelic Athletic Association) where a football match was being played. They opened fire on the spectators and players, killing fourteen people and wounding many more. Later that day two IRA members were executed at Dublin Castle.

Britain desperately needed a solution to the Irish problem, which was causing them huge embarrassment in the eyes of the world. In December 1920 Lloyd George proposed the Government of Ireland Act, which revived the idea of Home Rule on the basis of Ireland being divided north and south. A truce was called in the hostilities. The Irish were invited to London to negotiate a treaty. De Valera — instead of going himself — sent a deputation led by Arthur Griffith and Michael Collins to negotiate a treaty with a British team led by Lloyd George and Winston Churchill. On 6 December 1921 Griffith and Collins signed the Anglo-Irish Treaty, which established the Irish Free State (26 counties) as a dominion of the British Empire. Collins commented afterwards, *"I have just signed my own death warrant."* Despite the objections of de Valera and the strong Republication element, the Irish government ratified the treaty. A new Irish Free State was born, and the United Kingdom of Great Britain and Ireland ceased to exist.

However, this was to be a milestone in Ireland's turbulent history. Sinn Féin and the IRA refused to accept the treaty and this marked the start of the Irish Civil War. Ireland was divided right down the middle between pro-treaty and anti-treaty factions. In some instances families were divided and brother fought brother. The Free State Army, led by Michael Collins, fought against their former colleagues in the IRA. The IRA was forced to retreat into the mountains, from where its soldiers carried out a guerrilla campaign. On 22 August 1922 Michael Collins was shot dead by the IRA in a roadside ambush in County Cork. A short time later the IRA laid down its arms. The Irish Civil War was over and, in its short lifetime, it had cost the lives of 1,000 people.

William Cosgrave and his Cumann na nGaedheal party (the party of the Irish) became the government party from 1922 to 1932. De Valera broke away from Sinn Féin and formed the Fianna Fáil (Warriors of Ireland) party, which won the 1932 election and formed a new government with de Valera as its leader. The Fianna Fáil party would go on to become the major force in Irish politics for the rest of the twentieth century. Throughout his tenure de Valera pursued a policy of parochial politics, which was disastrous for the country.

In 1937 de Valera and his government prepared a new constitution for Ireland. The 'special position' of the Catholic Church in Ireland was acknowledged in the new constitution, thereby confirming the fears of Carson's Unionists. The constitution brought an end to more than 500 years of British intervention in Ireland.

When the Anglo-Irish Treaty was signed in 1921, it was agreed that Britain would retain control over the ports of Lough Swilly, Berehaven (Castletownbere) and Queenstown (Cobh). These became known as the 'Treaty Ports'. As World War II approached in 1938, Britain (under Neville Chamberlain) wanted Ireland to become involved on the Allies side. Ireland (under de Valera) wanted the partition of Ireland removed. Britain was faced with a dilemma: the Ulster Unionists refused point blank to the removal of partition. Chamberlain, in an attempt to solve the problem, agreed to return control of the Treaty Ports to Ireland. This was a huge 'sop' (it reduced considerably the risk of Ireland being bombed by Germany). Despite this, de Valera insisted that Ireland would remain neutral in the war. For the duration of the war, de Valera resisted pressure from Winston Churchill (who became British Prime Minister in May 1940) and from US President Roosevelt to become involved on the side of the Allies. However, 50,000 Irishmen volunteered to fight for the Allies while an additional 200,000 emigrated to England seeking employment.

While Ireland remained neutral, it was very much a case of 'allied neutrality'. British and American pilots who landed in Ireland for any reason were allowed to travel to Northern Ireland, from where they were repatriated to their own country. German pilots, on the other hand, were interned in the Curragh camp in County Kildare for the duration of the war.

India
India became a British colony in 1858, but it was not until the end of the nineteenth century that strong nationalistic feelings began to emerge.

The Indian National Congress was founded in 1885. This was a Hindu organisation, which grew rapidly and went on to become India's largest political party. Hindus comprised eighty per cent of the population of India. Muslims, the next strongest religion, formed the Muslim League to ensure their voice would be heard. There would be much conflict between the two!

In 1915 Mahatma Gandhi arrived back to India from South Africa where he had been one of the leaders of a civil rights movement for all oppressed peoples against the white South African government. His ideas and strategies for non-violent civil disobedience against the British quickly built up a large following. Britain was frustrated by the non-violent policies and her solution was to jail Gandhi. He spent several periods in jail, but his policy of non-violence never changed.

India supported Britain in World War I, hoping — like Ireland had hoped — that she would be rewarded with independence. Britain conceded that India should be granted independence but on a gradual basis, and in 1919 the Government of India Act introduced a dual mode of administration, in which both elected Indian legislators and British officials shared power. Decisions on international affairs, however, were made by the British Viceroy.

The early 1920s saw the emergence of new generations of Indians from within the Congress Party, including Jawaharlal Nehru and Chandra Bose, who would later become the prominent voices of the Indian independence movement. Under the presidency of Nehru at its historic Lahore session on 31 December 1929, the Indian National Congress adopted a resolution calling for complete independence from Britain.

In 1930 Gandhi led his famous Salt March to the coast in protest against having to buy heavily-taxed salt. The march covered 240 miles (400 kilometres) and ended with the marchers making their own salt from seawater.

In the early 1930s a series of round table conferences were held in London with Gandhi present in an attempt to progress independence. However, the conferences ended in failure and Gandhi returned to India to continue his 'policies of disobedience'.

In 1935 the Government of India Act was passed. However, it would take another two years for provincial autonomy to become a reality: elections were held in 1937, resulting in the Congress emerging as the dominant party.

At Lahore in 1940, in what became known as the Lahore Resolution, the Muslim League demanded the division of India into two separate states, one Muslim, the other Hindu; generally referred to as the 'two-nation theory'.

The volatile political climate between Hindu and Muslim was now making the possibility of a separate state of Pakistan more of a reality.

When World War II started in 1939, the British Viceroy declared India's entry into the war without consulting provincial governments. India was furious and the entire Congress resigned from local councils in protest. However, a huge number of Indians (2.5 million) supported Britain during the war. This arbitrary entry into the war was strongly opposed by Chandra Bose, who had been elected President of the Congress twice: in 1938 and 1939. So vehement was Bose in his opposition that he led the Azad Hind (Free India) movement into the war to fight on the side of Germany and Japan against Britain. This resulted in the bizarre situation of India fighting on both sides in the war!

In 1945, when the war was over, Britain finally agreed to India's independence.

On 3 June 1947 Viscount Louis Mountbatten, the last British Governor-General of India, announced the partitioning of British India into India and Pakistan. On 14 August 1947 the Indian Act of Independence was passed and Jawaharlal Nehru was elected the first Prime Minister of India. Twenty-four hours later Pakistan (located in the north-west and the north-east) was declared a separate nation. Many Indians found themselves in the 'wrong country' due to their religion and were forced to relocate, a process that led to considerable violence and many deaths. The north-eastern section of Pakistan would later become Bangladesh.

Chandra Bose was killed in a plane crash in 1945.

Egypt

Egypt is a transcontinental country linking North Africa with south-west Asia. It is bordered by the Mediterranean Sea to the north, the Gaza Strip and Israel to the north-east, the Red Sea to the east, Sudan to the south and Libya to the west. It is a very populous country with a great majority of her eighty million people living near the Nile River. The large areas of the Sahara desert are sparsely populated.

The Suez Canal, also known by its nickname 'the Highway to India', is an artificial sea-level waterway connecting the Mediterranean Sea and the Red Sea. There are no locks on the canal since the water level at both ends is the same. It was financed jointly by France in partnership with Egypt and was built mainly by forced Egyptian labour.

It was opened in 1869 after ten years of construction work. It allows passage for ships between Europe and Asia without going around the Horn of Africa, resulting in huge savings in time and distance (distance from London to Mumbai [Bombay] reduced from 12,300 miles to 7,200 miles). It had a huge effect on world trade and played an important role in the increased European colonisation of Africa.

The canal is owned and maintained by the Suez Canal Authority of Egypt. Under international treaty, it may be used *"in time of war as in time of peace, by every vessel of commerce or of war, without distinction."*

In 1930 the headquarters of the British Royal Navy's Mediterranean fleet was moved from Malta to Alexandria in Egypt (Malta was considered too exposed and too vulnerable).

In 1936 King Farouk I ascended to the throne of Egypt and his contentious reign would continue until 1952.

During World War II one of Germany's objectives was to take control of the Suez Canal. However, her defeat in North Africa and the continuous presence of British troops at the canal ensured that this never happened.

Part Three — World War II

(1939–1945)

CHAPTER 12

1939
World War II Breaks Out

World War II commences with Germany's invasion of western Poland followed by Russia's invasion of eastern Poland, the commencement of the Winter War between Russia and Finland, and several sinkings at sea. The Phoney War commences.

There were two main theatres of war in World War II: Europe and the Pacific Ocean, but the war involved many nations throughout the world. The war was also fought in two distinct phases: (i) the conquests by the Axis forces (Germany, Italy and Japan) in Europe and the Pacific between 1939 and 1942 and (ii) the fight-back of the Allied forces between 1942 and 1945.

The one big difference between World War I and World War II was mobility. There had been huge developments in tanks and aircraft during the interwar years and World War II saw little of the trench stagnation that had bogged down World War I.

More than fifty million people died in the war, many of whom were civilians.

WORLD WAR II BELLIGERENTS

Allied Forces	Axis Powers
Soviet Union	Germany
United States (1941–45)	Japan (1937–45)
Britain	Austria
France	Italy (1940–43)
Poland	Hungary (1941–45)
China (1937–45)	Romania (1941–44)
Yugoslavia (1941–45)	Bulgaria (1941–44)
Norway (1940–45)	Finland (1941–44)
Netherlands (1940–45)	Croatia (1941–45)

Belgium (1940–45)   Czechoslovakia

Greece (1940–45)

Italy (1943–45)

British Empire:

> ▸ Canada
> ▸ India
> ▸ Australia
> ▸ New Zealand
> ▸ South Africa

When World War I began, it was greeted all over Europe by jubilant cheering crowds. Most people were in favour of the war. The beginning of World War II was totally different. When Germany invaded Poland, there was a stunned silence: nobody wanted war. People remembered only too well the awfulness of World War I!

Poland

When German tanks rolled into Poland on 1 September, the world witnessed a new form of warfare: *blitzkrieg* (lightning war). It was aptly-named. The speed of the invasion was determined not by the speed of the infantry as in World War I but by the speed of the newly-developed tanks. When Britain and France declared war on Germany two days later, Germany was already on her way to a crushing victory in Poland. The Germans moved at lightening speed and the Poles, while not lacking in courage, were no match for them. The declarations of war by Britain and France were as far as it went at that time. Neither country was ready for war and no action was taken.

German forces were numerically and technologically superior to the Poles who, although not badly outnumbered, were totally outclassed. Poland had an army of 400,000 men, including eleven cavalry brigades. However, World War I had shown very clearly that horses were no match for tanks. In addition, while the Poles had several hundred tanks, many were obsolete. The Poles lacked anti-aircraft and anti-tank guns, but their real weakness was in the air. The small number of aircraft they had was no match for Germany's Luftwaffe, the new German air force. German Stuka dive-bombers paved the way by bombing the Polish air force while it was still on the ground.

Many of the German pilots had gained valuable experience in Germany's Condor Legion in the Spanish Civil War. When Germany attacked, both the terrain and the weather were in her favour. The ground was level and dry, facilitating swift progress. The word 'panzer' became synonymous with fast-moving, well-equipped army units. German forces, under Heinz Guderian and supported by East Prussia, swept down through Poland from the north heading for Warsaw. They reached Warsaw on 8 September but, faced with sterling resistance from the Poles, were unable to take the city. Their southern forces, under Gerd von Rundstedt and supported by Slovakia, moved rapidly eastwards heading for the major cities of Krakow and Lublin.

The killer punch to Poland came on 17 September when Russia invaded Poland from the east. Polish forces were now surrounded by their two considerably more powerful enemies! Warsaw was targeted with a heavy bombardment from both ground and air and was quickly reduced to ruins. Warsaw capitulated on 27 September and fighting ceased some days later. There was, however, no formal surrender, and Polish resistance units remained active throughout the war.

The Polish government retreated into Romania (neutral at the time), while many Polish pilots who survived fled to Britain and joined the Royal Air Force.

As the German army entered the war, Hitler instructed his forces to show no mercy, and they took his instructions literally.

Hitler and Stalin, meanwhile, set about obliterating the Polish people. Apart altogether from the Jews, Hitler deemed the Poles an inferior race which should be exterminated. Huge numbers were incarcerated in concentration camps and many of them died there. Stalin, meanwhile, prompted by his NKVD chief Lavrenti Beria, decided to exterminate all of the Polish leaders. In April 1940, 22,000 of Poland's top military officers, political officials, priests, doctors, lawyers, engineers and writers were taken to the **Katyn Forest** near Smolensk and brutally murdered. They were shot dead and their bodies buried layer upon layer in pits in the forest floor. Russia later tried to pin the blame on Germany for the deed that could only be described as the ultimate in depravity! Russia eventually accepted responsibility in 1990.

70,000 Polish soldiers died in the attack on Poland along with countless numbers of civilians. 700,000 Polish troops were captured and sent to concentration camps, where many of them died.

WESTERN FRONT 1939

Hitler was pleasantly surprised when France and Britain did not answer Poland's distress call when she was invaded by Germany in September 1939. Neither country was ready for war even though they had ample warning. To be ready for this day, both Britain and France would have had to commence preparations years previously. This they had not done.

Britain was never going to move until France moved first. France, however, was content to sit behind her Maginot Line *[see Chapter 9, page 127]* and wait for the German attack. Such was Hitler's satisfaction at his enemies' reluctance to fight that on 9 October he ordered his officers to draw up plans to invade both the Low Countries and France. By the end of October plans were finalised and the invasion of Belgium was set for 10 November. However, on 7 November severe winter weather set in and the invasion was postponed. It was a measure of Hitler's lack of confidence at this stage that the winter weather in northern Europe deterred him from fighting, while two years later he was not deterred by the Russian winter!

PHONEY WAR

The Phoney War refers to the period from October 1939 to April 1940. Each side feared a bombing campaign by the other, but in fact entering the winter neither side was sufficiently advanced with their war preparations. The result was that they continued their preparations while keeping a watchful eye on each other. There was no action. In anticipation of a bombing campaign by Germany, Britain evacuated large numbers of children from the major cities: more than one million children were evacuated from London alone at the beginning of September. The children were moved to the homes of relatives and friends in safer countryside areas. By April 1940 the anticipated bombing had not happened and the children, many of whom had come from the dockside areas in London, were permitted to return to their homes.

The one positive action that Britain took was to move 150,000 British Expeditionary Forces (BEF) to Belgium to support Belgium and France in September 1939. There was no further action from Britain or France during the Phoney War.

Even though Germany was blockaded, she had little difficulty getting foodstuffs during this period. Supplies of food and raw materials were readily available from Sweden, Russia and Italy.

In Britain's case the majority of her food came from overseas and was frequently seized by the German navy. Rationing was introduced.

THE WINTER WAR — FINLAND AND RUSSIA

While both sides sat it out in the Phoney War on the Western Front, a 'real' war broke out in Finland on 30 November 1939, when Finland was invaded by Russia.

Stalin and Hitler never trusted one another even though the two signed the Molotov-Ribbentrop Pact in 1939. Stalin feared an attack by Germany through Finland (Leningrad was just inside the Russian border) and he decided to take over Finland. After all, Finland was a small country compared to Russia so he figured it should not take long to defeat her. On 30 November Russia attacked Finland and bombed Helsinki. 3,000 Russian tanks invaded Finland, who had none.

The Soviets had huge superiority in men, tanks and planes. However, the Finns were experts at fighting in winter weather. Their ski troops moved silently, dressed in white as camouflage in the snow and, under the command of Marshal Carl Gustaf Mannerheim, they led the Russians a merry dance. The Russians were leaderless. This was the first occasion on which Stalin had to pay the price for purging his officers in 1937!

The Russians lost 1,500 tanks and ten times as many soldiers as the Finns in the early months of the war. However, sheer weight of numbers forced the Finns to surrender eventually on 16 March 1940. They were forced to cede the Isthmus of Karelia (located between Finland and Russia) but theirs was a moral victory. Russia lost 150,000 men against Finnish losses of 50,000. The Winter War, as it was called, was a huge loss of prestige to the Soviets, who were expelled from the League of Nations because of the illegal attack.

In the meantime — as in the invasion of Poland — Britain and France 'fiddled while Rome burned'. Daladier, the French Prime Minister, had wished to confront Germany when she attacked Czechoslovakia in 1938. He had taken no action then and he took no action now. He was dismissed from office.

At this stage in World War II, Hitler was possibly the only person who was aware of his own future plans to attack Russia. In this regard his confidence got a boost when he saw the very poor performance by Russia against the Finns. He knew that Finland would be fighting on Germany's side against the Soviet Union. One thing he did not learn, however, was the importance of winter clothing for winter warfare!

Hitler and Churchill (back in his old job as First Lord of the Admiralty) were both aware of the importance of Norway as overseer of both the North Sea and the North Atlantic, and through which Sweden's iron ore was channelled to all of the belligerent countries. But Hitler moved first!

WAR AT SEA 1939

Both sides had learned the importance of naval warfare in World War I. The Allies became aware that the only way to overcome the U-boat threat was to use a convoy system crossing the Atlantic.

In World War II the war at sea got off to a flying start. On 3 September the liner *Athenia* was hit by a German torpedo and sunk off the Irish coast en route to Canada. 112 passengers were lost. The message from Germany was clear. They considered all Allied shipping fair game.

On 14 October the Germans scored a psychological victory when one of her submarines penetrated the Royal Navy's main base at Scapa Flow in the Orkneys (where it was also located in World War I). The sub torpedoed and sank the battleship *Royal Oak,* causing 880 deaths. Apart from the loss of life, the pride of the British navy was severely dented!

Attacks on British ships in the North Sea continued. In mid-October the British navy moved its base from Scapa Flow to the Clyde on the west coast of Scotland, which was a more sheltered and better-protected base.

Britain had one major victory at sea in 1939. The German cruiser *Admiral Graf Spee*, named after the German captain of World War I, was stationed in the south Atlantic preying on merchant shipping: between September and December she sank nine ships. Early on the morning of 13 December, the *Graf Spee* inflicted heavy damage on British ships before eventually being damaged herself. She sought shelter in Montevideo harbour.

Convinced by false reports of superior British forces gathering outside the harbour, the German captain Hans Langsdorff scuttled his ship on 17 December and then shot himself. This was a much-needed morale-boosting victory for the British navy!

1939 TIMELINE

30 Jan	Hitler threatens Jews during Reichstag speech.
15/16 Mar	Germany invades Czechoslovakia having previously invaded Austria (Mar '38) and the Sudetenland (Sept '38), both of which were pro-German.
28 Mar	Spanish Civil War ends.
22 May	Germany and Italy sign the Pact of Steel.
23 Aug	Germany and Soviets sign the Molotov-Ribbentrop Pact.
25 Aug	Poland and Britain sign a mutual assistance treaty.
31 Aug	British fleet mobilises, Civilian evacuation begins from London.
01 Sep	Germany invades Poland (from the west). World War II begins.
03 Sep	Britain, France, Australia and New Zealand declare war on Germany. Liner *Athenia* sunk by German torpedo.
04 Sep	British Royal Air Force attacks the German navy.
05 Sep	US proclaims her neutrality.
08 Sep	Germans advance as far as Warsaw.
10 Sep	Battle of the Atlantic begins. Canada declares war on Germany.
17 Sep	Russia invades Poland (from the east).
27 Sep	Warsaw surrenders to Nazis.
29 Sep	Nazis and Soviets divide up Poland.
09 Oct	Hitler orders his officers to prepare plans to invade France and the Low Countries.
14 Oct	Battleship *Royal Oak* sunk at Scapa Flow.
Oct	Nazis begin euthanasia on the Jews and on sick and disabled in Germany. Phoney War begins.
08 Nov	Assassination attempt on Hitler fails.
30 Nov	Soviets invade Finland.
13 Dec	German cruiser *Admiral Graf Spee* sunk in Montevideo harbour.
14 Dec	Soviet Union expelled from the League of Nations.

CHAPTER 13

1940
Germany's Attack Expands Westwards

War begins in earnest with Germany's invasion of Denmark, Norway, the Netherlands, Belgium, France and Luxembourg; the evacuation of Dunkirk; Italy's entry into the war; the Battle of Britain and the Blitz; the commencement of war in North Africa and the entry into the war of Romania, Hungary and Bulgaria.

Denmark and Norway

After Poland, Norway was Hitler's next target. Hitler's Kriegsmarine officers left him in no doubt about the advantages of controlling Norway. Her main ports overlooked the North Sea and the Atlantic Ocean, while the port of Narvik was the main port for exporting iron ore from Sweden (which remained neutral) to Germany. Hitler at this time was planning the invasion of western Europe and did not wish to have any threat hanging over him from the north.

Hitler was spurred into action on 16 February by the *Altmark* Incident. The *Altmark* was a German tanker carrying 300 British prisoners of war, who had been captured in an earlier naval engagement involving the German cruiser *Admiral Graf Spee* in South America. She was on her way back to Germany, when she was boarded by the Royal Navy in neutral Norwegian waters and the prisoners were all released. Six German sailors were killed in the incident, which proved to Hitler that Britain was ready to invade Norway also. Hitler's reaction was to speed up his preparations so that he could take over Norway before Britain did.

The Phoney War extended well into 1940 as a result of the capture by the Allies of detailed plans of the German operations from a crashed German plane in Belgium on 10 January. The Germans, aware that the Allies knew their plans, decided to prepare new plans, resulting in a substantial delay.

The Winter War between Russia and Finland ended on 12 March. The Phoney War came to an abrupt end on 9 April when Germany invaded both Denmark and Norway. At dawn the Luftwaffe, Panzer tanks and ground troops entered both countries. As in Poland, the speed of the action was decisive. The Danes were totally unprepared and surrendered immediately. The Norwegians fought back courageously but were outgunned in every respect. Norway was a monarchy and

King Haakon VII was aware of the value of Norwegian ports to both sides. When informed that they had been attacked, the King enquired, *"England or Germany?"*

Within a few days Norway's main ports, airports and cities were taken. The Norwegian navy fought courageously and did considerable damage to the German Kriegsmarine before they were overcome. The Norwegian ground troops retreated to the mountains, from where they kept up a war of attrition for the next two months.

The British promised aid, but from 10 May all Allied forces were fully occupied in the defence of Belgium, France and the Low Countries.

On 28 May a combined force of British, French and Polish troops captured Narvik, but at this stage the war in Europe had moved on. The Dunkirk evacuation was underway. Churchill ordered the evacuation of Norway, and Germany remained in control there for the remainder of the war. However, German control meant retaining 300,000 soldiers in Norway for the duration of the war. Norway finally surrendered on 10 June. King Haakon VII and his cabinet went into exile in Britain.

Vidkun Quisling was a Norwegian who admired the Nazis and did not oppose the German invasion of his country. He collaborated with the Germans and headed up a wartime government on their behalf. The word 'Quisling' became synonymous with 'traitor' thereafter.

There was outrage in Britain as a result of the abject failure in Norway. Even though the failure was Churchill's as First Lord of the Admiralty, Chamberlain took the blame and resigned as Prime Minister. When asked by King George VI who should succeed him, Chamberlain replied, *"Churchill"*.

Churchill became Prime Minister on 10 May and he immediately formed a National Government. The one big plus from the Norwegian campaign was the appointment of Churchill as leader. He was the only political leader who had the desire and the ability to guide Britain through World War II.

WESTERN FRONT 1940

Hitler was now ready to attack in western Europe. Britain and France assumed it would be a repeat of World War I and that the Germans would invade through the flatlands of Belgium. The Germans, however had an ace up their sleeve. The French Maginot Line extended from Switzerland to the Ardennes Forest in Belgium and Luxembourg, but there were no defences built from there to the English Channel.

Whereas the Allies considered the Ardennes Forest impenetrable to vehicular traffic, German General Erich von Manstein studied the densely-forested region in detail and noted a series of country lanes and tracks running through the trees. He suggested to Hitler that they could use these undefended tracks to invade France at Sedan and Belgium at Dinant. Both were located on the River Meuse. Hitler jumped at the idea. The only obstacle was the River Meuse, which would have to be crossed using temporary bridges and inflatables. For Germany to invade France along this route would be a huge blow to French pride, since France had been defeated by Prussia at Sedan in the 1871 Franco-Prussian War.

'Case Yellow' (Fall Gelb)
Germany prepared a detailed strategy to attack France, which involved dividing her army into three groups:
1. Army Group A to attack through Luxembourg and the Ardennes Forest.
2. Army Group B to attack through the Netherlands into Belgium and on into France.
3. Army Group C to keep the main French army pinned down along the Maginot Line.

The Nazis would invade the Netherlands, Belgium, Luxembourg and northern France in one operation!

Germany had an army of 135 divisions (2.7 million men) at their disposal with almost one million men allocated to Army Group A. The greatest asset the Germans had — apart from their vast army — was the Luftwaffe, which at this stage, was far superior to the air forces of Britain and France.

The invasions in all three areas started on 10 May 1940. Protestations of neutrality by all three Low Countries were ignored by Hitler.

The Netherlands was hit by Army Group B's Stuka dive-bombers, paratroopers, Panzer tanks and ground troops; and was overrun in five days. Rotterdam was bombed to the ground (a breakdown in communications meant that Rotterdam's willingness to surrender was not conveyed to the German bombers). Queen Wilhelmina and the Dutch government fled to London.

Army Group B swept down into Belgium taking Liège on the way. The Belgians retreated to a defensive line at the River Dyle where they were joined by troops who had recently arrived from France and Britain. However, they lacked leadership and were totally outnumbered by the Germans. Almost immediately, the British and French began to retreat, leaving the Belgians to soldier on alone against the Nazis. The Belgians surrendered on 28 May and King Leopold of Belgium became a German prisoner for the duration of the war.

Army Group A in the meantime had advanced rapidly through Luxembourg and the Ardennes Forest. They streamed through the undefended forest in never-ending columns stretching back fifty miles: it was described by one German general as *"the greatest traffic jam in history!"* Field Marshal Gerd von Rundstedt was the overall commander, supported by Heinz Guderian (Sedan) and Erwin Rommel (Dinant). There was little or no opposition since the French were not prepared for an attack in this area.

Meanwhile, Army Group C had kept the major sector of the French army pinned down along their much-vaunted Maginot Line without much difficulty!

Reflecting back on the static nature of World War I, it is difficult to grasp the speed of this entire operation. All three German army groups had commenced their various assaults on 10 May. By 15 May the Netherlands had succumbed to Army Group B, who then advanced into Belgium. Army Group A had slipped through Luxembourg and the Ardennes Forest and was now proceeding to surge across northern France. On 19 May its troops crossed the old battlefields of the Somme and on the following day they took Amiens. Their panzer trail split France north and south. The progress they achieved in ten days was remarkable!

Once the Germans broke through into France, the Allies expected them to head for Paris, but the Germans had another surprise in store for the Allies. Army Group A, instead of turning left for Paris, turned right to advance northwards towards the English Channel, and Guderian advanced until he reached the Channel on 22 May. Since the British and French troops were in retreat mode, the Germans took control of both Calais and Boulogne without much difficulty. This left Dunkirk as the only major port on the Channel remaining under the control of the Allies. Meanwhile, the French and British had been driven out of Belgium by Army Group B also in the direction of Dunkirk. The Germans now had the Allies surrounded and the only way out was through the port of Dunkirk.

THE EVACUATION OF DUNKIRK

Long before Lord Gort, head of the BEF, sent out the SOS, it was obvious to Churchill and the British government that their only option was a complete evacuation from Dunkirk. The alternative would be to fight to the bitter end or to surrender. Either way meant the end of the British army and, as Churchill well knew, every soldier would be vital if and when Hitler chose to invade Britain.

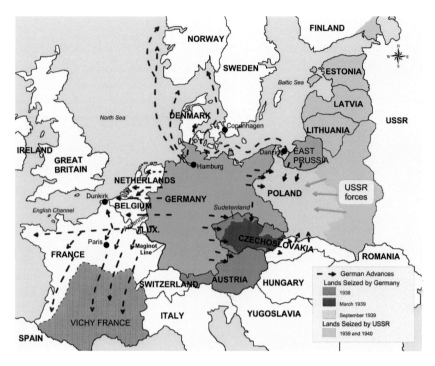

Map 15: German Advances in Europe 1938–40

Benito Mussolini and Adolf Hitler in Munich, Germany, 18 June 1940.

British troops line up on the beach at Dunkirk to await evacuation, 1940.

Londoners sleep on the platform and on the train tracks at Aldwych Underground station during heavy all night Nazi bombing raids during the Blitz, 8 October 1940.

On 19 May Vice-Admiral Bertram Ramsay was put in charge of the evacuation (code-named Operation Dynamo). Every boat/ship that was seaworthy enough to cross the Channel was called into action. French and British soldiers retreated into Dunkirk knowing that this was their only option.

Then came one of the great imponderables of World War II. Hitler called a ceasefire for a number of days thus allowing the retreating troops an opportunity to get away. His officers were furious, especially Göring, head of the Luftwaffe, who knew his air force could easily destroy the Allies despite the attentions of the RAF, which had finally engaged in battle having been notably absent during the invasions of Poland, Norway and the Netherlands.

We will never know for certain why Hitler took the action he did. Historians down through the years have come up with various suggestions. The most feasible would appear to be that Hitler wished to keep on the right side of Britain as he had in mind a future European/Asian continent ruled by Germany together with Britain and her empire.

One thing is certain: the evacuation of 340,000 men (British, French and Belgian) in a little over a week would not have succeeded were it not for Hitler's stay of execution. An added bonus was the 'flat calm' that existed in the Channel for a week, enabling boats of all sizes to participate in the evacuation. (The Allies would have been very grateful for a similar 'calm' for the D-Day landings in 1944.) Ramsay's concentration was on evacuating British troops. He only agreed to take French and Belgian troops when ordered to do so by Churchill.

Some historians have described Dunkirk as a victory for Britain. Churchill got it right when he said: "*Wars are not won by evacuations*". The entire operation was a humiliating defeat. They got the men out, but the entire weaponry of the British army had to be left behind on the beaches of Dunkirk.

THE FALL OF FRANCE

After Dunkirk, Hitler had a decision to make: would he take over the remainder of France or would he cross the English Channel to invade Britain? He chose the former, leaving Britain for another day.

In the wake of Dunkirk the French were totally demoralised and at a very low ebb. Five divisions (100,000 men) of their troops had been evacuated to Britain and the spirit had been completely knocked out of those who were left behind. Commander in Chief General Maxime

Weygand was left with fifty divisions to face up to the Nazi's 140 divisions (including ten Panzer tank divisions).

The Dunkirk evacuation was not the only evacuation from north-east France. Once the French people in the north-east realised the full extent of what was happening, they panicked. They remembered only too well how they had suffered during the German occupation in World War I.

Eight million people from the north-east and from Paris abandoned their homes and headed for the west and the south. While the Germans created a traffic jam into north-eastern France, the evacuees created a traffic jam out of the area. It was a pitiful sight! An interminable line of carts and wagons carrying men and women, babies and children, grandmothers and grandfathers, furniture and livestock wended westwards and southwards like a never-ending centipede. Lille, Rheims and Chartres were evacuated and became ghost towns: a fate that was about to befall Paris!

Germany's surge southwards through France, which began on 5 June, was little more than a mopping-up exercise. The Battle of France was as good as over. On 8 June with the Germans in sight of Paris, the French government — under Paul Reynaud — moved headquarters first to Tours and then to Bordeaux. To save the city from major bomb damage, Paris was vacated and declared an 'open city'. The Germans made their triumphal entry into a deserted Paris on 14 June, a day that will live forever in the memory of the people of France.

Part of the mopping up process was the takeover of the French west coast from Brest to Bordeaux, giving Germany key access to the Atlantic Ocean. The French regime collapsed completely. Reynaud resigned and was replaced by Philippe Pétain. However, this was not the general who performed so heroically in the Battle of Verdun in World War I. This was an 84-year-old man who craved peace in his retiring years. He remembered only too well the horrors of World War I. On 17 June he sought an armistice on behalf of the people of France.

Meanwhile, on 16 June, a belligerent young army officer, Charles de Gaulle, who had been Under-Secretary of State for National Defence in Reynaud's government, arrived in London from where he would direct the operations of the Free French Army for the next four years.

In a six-week period, Germany had overcome the Netherlands, Belgium, Luxembourg and France. This was probably the greatest feat ever in any war and would remain so until Germany invaded Russia in 1941. A humiliating armistice was signed on 22 June between Germany and France. At Hitler's insistence, it was signed at Compiègne in the same railway carriage used in 1918 at the end of World War I when Germany was in defeat.

France was divided in two, with Germany occupying the north and the west of the country, giving them control over the English Channel and the Atlantic Ocean. The remainder of France became a 'Free Zone' administered by Philippe Pétain under German direction. This Free Zone government had its headquarters in the town of Vichy and became known as the Vichy Government. They collaborated with the Germans, even to the extent of sending French Jews to Germany where they ended up in concentration camps.

This was a very unhappy period of French history. There was considerable bad feeling amongst the 'occupied French' against the Vichy Government: they felt there was far too much collaboration with Germany. The fall of Paris and Vichy France gave rise to a very strong French underground movement, which became known as the Maquis and would play a major role in the years ahead. It suited Germany to have the Vichy Government carrying out the financial administration not just of the Free Zone but of the Occupied Zone also.

Hitler paid a well-recorded visit to Paris at 5:00 a.m. on the morning of 23 June, accompanied by his architect Albert Speer and other officers. Why did he feel it necessary to make his visit at 5:00 a.m.? He constantly feared assassination!

On 6 July Hitler staged a triumphal march in Berlin to celebrate his victory in France. Many in the jubilant crowd thought they were celebrating the end of the war.

Meanwhile, the French people were devastated. They simply could not believe that the French army, which had performed so valiantly at Verdun in World War I, could have been swept aside so easily. The reason was quite simple: the Germans had moved on twenty years since World War I; the French had not moved on a single year. Their tanks still moved at the same speed as their infantry. Much of their weaponry, including their anti-aircraft guns, was obsolete while aircraft development was minimal. Apart from their Maginot Line, they simply had not prepared for the war and when it came, they were simply no match for the Germans.

THE END OF THE FRENCH NAVY

Britain was now fighting a lone battle in western Europe. She was the only non-neutral country not yet brought to her knees by Hitler.

One of the imponderables after the armistice was what to do with the French navy. A condition of the armistice was that the ships would be sailed to specific ports, where they could be disarmed and demobilised under German supervision. Hitler feared them falling into British hands, thus making the Royal Navy even more powerful! Churchill, on the other hand, did not trust the Germans. He was afraid that the ships would be added to the fleets of either Germany or Italy. Churchill had been beaten to it by Germany in Norway. He was not about to let it happen again. He was in a no-win situation, but he showed his mettle by deciding that the Royal Navy would take over the French navy. The French fleet was based in several ports and most ship captains yielded to the British without any resistance. However, a large number of ships, including two powerful battle cruisers, were based at Mers-el-Kébir in Algeria. The admiral in charge was given three options by the Royal Navy: sail the ships to neutral ports, scuttle them or hand them over to Britain's navy. The admiral refused to comply with any of the three options.

Churchill ordered the Royal Navy to open fire on her ally. The battleships were sunk and twelve hundred sailors were killed. France was stunned at what she considered to be an act of treachery.

Not surprisingly, relations between France and Britain during the remainder of World War II were difficult. The message to Hitler, however, was clear: Churchill was going to be a tough nut to crack!

THE BATTLE OF BRITAIN AND THE BLITZ

Churchill's Speeches

During the Battle of Britain, Churchill did a superb job keeping the British spirit up with his regular morale-boosting speeches on radio. The following are extracts from some of his speeches.

"I have nothing to offer but blood, toil, tears and sweat." — on his appointment as Prime Minister.

"Hitler knows he will have to break us in this island or lose the war. Let us therefore brace ourselves to our duties, and so bear ourselves that, if the British Empire and its Commonwealth last for a thousand years, men will still say, 'This was their finest hour.'" — at the commencement of the Battle of Britain.

"Never in the field of human conflict was so much owed by so many to so few." — referring to the Royal Air Force after the Battle of Britain.

Churchill was tremendously successful in building the spirit and morale of the British people and was without doubt the only man who could have led Britain through World War II.

Operation Sea Lion: Planned Invasion of Britain

On 16 July Hitler issued the instruction to proceed with Operation Sea Lion: the invasion of Britain. Needless to say, the morale of the Germans after their six-week blitz of western Europe was sky high. Britain was the only non-neutral country left unconquered in western Europe and Hitler could see no reason why it would not fall just as quickly.

However, the reason was staring him in the face: the 22-mile-wide English Channel! The Germans were a land army; they had little experience of the sea and they feared the unknown vicissitudes of the tides. The German navy was going to need the services of every ship and barge they could get their hands on (much the same as the British at Dunkirk) to cross the Channel and, moreover, they would need protection from the air.

Grand Admiral Erich Raeder, commander of the Kriegsmarine, made it clear to Hitler that the success of the invasion was dependent on the Luftwaffe achieving superiority over the Royal Air Force. While they had superiority in numbers, the Nazis were hampered by the distances they had to fly from the various airports they were using in France, Holland, Belgium and the Nordic Countries.

In advance of the planned invasion of Britain, Germany invaded the Channel Islands on 30 June 1940. Churchill made no attempt to stop them: he reasoned that the islands were of no strategic importance to Britain. Jersey and Guernsey remained occupied by the Germans until the end of the war.

Britain, meanwhile, had problems of her own. She was very short of armaments as a result of abandoning hers on the beaches at Dunkirk. America came to her aid and supplied armaments originally destined for France. They were supplied on a cash-and-carry basis: the goods had to be paid for in advance and transported in British ships.

From the time he took office, Churchill had endeavoured to bring America into the war, but American President Franklin D. Roosevelt remained adamant: America would remain neutral. Circumstances, however, would force Roosevelt to change his mind a year later!

Between the end of May and the middle of July, the British had not been idle. The production of Spitfire and Hurricane fighter aircraft, which were Britain's protection against Messerschmitt fighters and Luftwaffe bombers, was hugely increased. While many of Germany's pilots had experience in the Spanish Civil War, Britain was short of experienced pilots and appreciated the assistance of pilots from Poland and Czechoslovakia, countries which had been defeated earlier in the war.

From 1937 onwards Britain had been developing a network of radar stations located around the south-east coast of England and by summer 1940 the stations were functioning and proved vital.

Since British men were fully occupied in the army, British women manned the factories and the farms and proved themselves an essential cog in Britain's defence wheel. The children who had been dispatched to the countryside during the Phoney War were dispatched to safety once again. A volunteer defence force, the Home Guard, was formed on 14 May and proved invaluable — as air raid wardens, for example — once the bombing started. Air raid shelters and gas masks were supplied, even though the shelters were frequently abandoned in favour of the local Underground stations.

The air war began in earnest on 13 August. The Germans had 2,500 aircraft against Britain's 1,000. The Luftwaffe began its bombing campaign, sending more than 1,000 aircraft a day to target British airfields and radar stations (many of which, unfortunately, were located at the airfields). Losses were huge on both sides. The Germans quickly found that daytime bombing was too costly: the British radar system was very efficient in daylight. They switched to night-time bombing, which was safer but not as effective. Many of Britain's south-eastern airports were damaged by bomb craters, and the Spitfires and Hurricanes were being destroyed on the ground. Losses continued to be severe up to 24 August, at which stage Britain was close to defeat. Salvation, however, came from an unexpected source. On 24 August a German bomber accidentally bombed non-military targets in London (there was an unspoken understanding that no civilians would be targeted in the war). This was the excuse Churchill needed. He immediately ordered a retaliatory attack on Berlin. The following night eighty twin-engined bombers took off for Berlin. Only thirty planes reached Berlin: the rest got lost! Damage to Berlin was slight, but Berliners were aghast. Hitler had promised them that such an event would never happen. Hitler was furious and he now ordered the terror bombing of London. This was a mistake on his part. The switching of targets gave the British the opportunity to rebuild their airport runways and boost their air force.

The bombing campaign that followed became known as the Blitz! The Blitz began on the night of 7 September 1940 when more than 300 tons of bombs were dropped on London. Night after night the Luftwaffe bombers arrived, protected by Messerschmitt fighter aircraft. For fifty-four consecutive nights, the bombers hit London. By 31 December

London had been bombed 125 times. Every night, once darkness arrived, the aircraft warning sirens started up and Londoners headed for the nearest Underground station. The first wave of German bombers invariably carried incendiary bombs. These started fires, which gave the follow-on bombers targets to aim at.

By 31 October the Germans had lost 1,300 planes against British losses of 800 and Britain was shooting down German bombers faster than German factories could produce them. In the meantime, Hitler continued with the facade that he was going to invade Britain. He had not succeeded in defeating the RAF and without that victory Operation Sea Lion would not proceed.

He deferred the date of the invasion several times and on September 19 he ordered the dispersal of the invasion fleet. The planned invasion of Britain was off the agenda, permanently as it turned out. The history books make little mention of the Royal Navy during the planned invasion; basically they were on standby waiting for Hitler's forces to attempt a Channel crossing.

Certainly, the power of the RAF and the Royal Navy together would have ensured that the German army could never have crossed the Channel. Hitler's only hope was Britain's surrender and as long as Churchill was in control that would never happen.

42,000 people died in the Blitz and another 60,000 were seriously injured. Hitler continued to launch intermittent bombing raids on British cities throughout the winter and spring until May 1941. It would appear that he was trying to break the spirit of the British people — something he never achieved!

Between November 1940 and May 1941 Luftwaffe bombers targeted the cities of Coventry, Liverpool, Manchester, Glasgow and Belfast, along with several ports. During the same period, the RAF's Bomber Command dropped 50,000 tons of bombs on German cities. They did not do a great deal of damage, but they kept the Germans aware that the RAF was very much alive.

Coventry
On the night of 14 November, Luftwaffe bombers devastated Coventry, including the city's medieval cathedral, with the loss of over 500 lives. Hitler eventually signed off on the Blitz in Belfast in April and May 1941. The only logical reason for bombing Belfast was to target the Harland and Wolff shipyard and the Short Brothers aircraft factory. However, it was the civilian population that suffered most. There were two major raids on Belfast. On 15 April two hundred bombers attacked the city. Fifty per cent of the houses in Belfast were destroyed and 920

people lost their lives. A further attack on 4 May resulted in a further 150 deaths.

Dublin

On 31 May four German bombs were dropped on the North Strand area of Dublin killing twenty-eight people. This was either a navigational error or was a warning to neutral Ireland to stay out of the war.

Had Hitler been successful in his plan to invade Britain, he would have followed on by invading Ireland. His plan to do so, Operation Green, was already in place. Had that happened, he would have had control over the entire Eastern Atlantic seaboard from Norway to North Africa, and America's task of invading Europe from the Atlantic would have been infinitely more difficult, if not impossible. The Allies had Churchill and Britain to thank for preventing such a disaster.

ITALY ENTERS THE WAR

Not only was the Italian army unprepared for war, the country's economy was in a very poor state. In 1940 Italy's output in motorised vehicle production was only fifteen per cent that of France or Britain. In terms of industrial output, Italy produced two per cent of Britain's coal production and ten per cent of Germany's steel production. Mussolini further exacerbated Italy's problems by providing large numbers of weapons and supplies to Franco's forces during the Spanish Civil War (1936–39).

Towards the end of the 1930s, Italy did make a serious effort to catch up, particularly in armaments production, but it was very much a case of too little, too late.

The Italian navy was the strongest of Italy's armed forces but was locked into the Mediterranean by British-controlled Gibraltar at one end and the Suez Canal at the other.

If Mussolini's dream of a Roman Empire in the Mediterranean was to have any chance of succeeding, it was imperative that Italy would have to seize any additional land she could in the area. An obvious target was the island of Corsica. After a period of independence, Corsica returned to French rule in 1796, and during World War I the island's population fought on the side of the Allies. Mussolini realised that there was no hope of Hitler ceding him Corsica or any other territory unless he joined the war on the side of Nazi Germany.

Italy declared war on France and Britain on 10 June 1940. Following up his declaration of war, Mussolini launched an attack across the Franco-Italian Alpine border. Italy had thirty-two divisions and, although there were only five French divisions to oppose them, the Italian forces were driven back. Their equipment was obsolete; they were extremely short of motorised transport; and, more importantly, they lacked leadership. Italy suffered her first ignominious defeat in World War II.

Hitler and Mussolini met at the Brenner Pass on the Austrian-Italian border on 4 October to discuss strategy. Hitler told Mussolini nothing about his plans to invade Russia, and Mussolini told Hitler nothing about his plans to attack Greece. A strange partnership!

On 10 November the British Royal Navy launched an attack on the Italian fleet at Taranto, a major port located in the foot of Italy. Swordfish aircraft, launched from the aircraft carrier HMS *Illustrious,* attacked the Italian naval base, sinking three battleships. Hitler was not impressed by his ally's defence.

As it happened, Germany neither wanted nor needed any help from Mussolini. A German general, Field Marshal Werner von Blomberg, when asked his opinion about the war, is reputed to have said, *"Whoever has Italy on his side is bound to lose."*

AFRICA 1940

East Africa
Earlier in the century, Italy had taken control of Libya (1911), Abyssinia (Ethiopia) (1935) and Albania (1939). Libya gave Italy a gateway into North Africa and Albania a base in the Balkans. The takeover of Ethiopia on the Horn of Africa by Mussolini, although it linked Eritrea and Somaliland, made little sense. Ethiopia was a huge distance from the Mediterranean, which meant that getting supplies to it was very difficult, particularly as the Allies controlled the Suez Canal.

In June 1940 Italy launched an attack from her colony in Ethiopia on British Somaliland and, by sheer weight of numbers, achieved a rare success, forcing the British to retreat by sea to Aden. The success was short-lived. In January 1941 the British, with colonial help, fought back. Indian and African forces attacked the Italian forces in Ethiopia from Kenya and Sudan, while the British launched an amphibious assault from Aden to retake British Somaliland.

The Ethiopian capital of Addis Ababa fell in April 1941 and this was the end of the fighting in East Africa. The Ethiopian Emperor Haile Selassie returned to his homeland exactly five years after being driven out by Mussolini's forces.

North Africa

Immediately after declaring war in June 1940, Italy invaded Libya. This was Mussolini's opening move in the formation of his new Roman Empire — his 'Mare Nostrum' — to be located around the Mediterranean.

His intention was to invade Egypt and seize the Suez Canal, but his ambitions far outweighed the capabilities of his armed forces. Italian forces advanced from Libya into Egypt on 13 September: 200,000 Italian troops advanced as far as Sidi Barrani.

On 10 December a combined force of 30,000 British, Indian and Australian forces under General Sir Archibald Wavell attacked the Italians and drove them back as far as El Agheila in Libya, despite being vastly outnumbered.

GREECE 1940

Before he commenced his invasion of Russia, Hitler had planned to have the support of the Balkan countries. Mussolini threw a spanner in the works, however. Using Albania as a stepping stone, Italy invaded Greece on 28 October. This was another attempt by Mussolini to gain both prestige and territory. The first Hitler knew of the invasion was when Mussolini announced on the day of the invasion: *"Führer, we are on the march."* Once again, Hitler was not impressed by Mussolini.

The Greeks were more than a match for the Italians. They were more adept at fighting in mountainous terrain, and by mid-November had driven the Italians back into Albania. In the meantime, Churchill had diverted British forces from North Africa to assist Greece. Greece did not need them against the Italians; Churchill would have been better advised to keep his forces in North Africa to try to finish the war there. As it turned out, he created a lull in the fighting in North Africa, which gave Germany and Rommel the opportunity of becoming involved there.

Before 1940 drew to a close, Romania, Hungary and Bulgaria had joined Hitler's Axis Powers peacefully: they were well aware of the price Poland paid by resisting. Germany taking control of Romania was a big boost for Hitler. Control of Romania meant control of the Ploeşti oil wells.

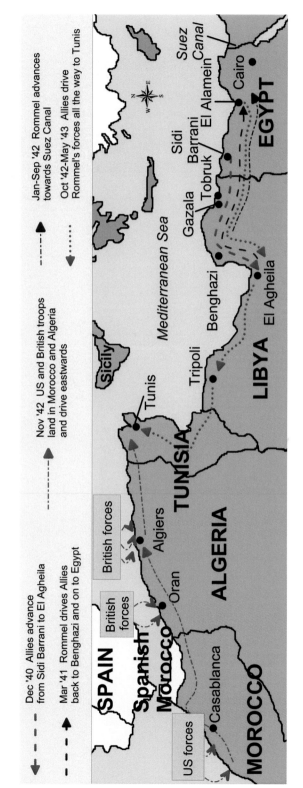

Map 16: Troop Movements in North Africa 1940–43

Near Algiers, Operation Torch troops hit the beaches behind a large American flag (left), 8 November 1942.

Yugoslavia and Greece refused to bow to the Nazi threat and in doing so knew that they would be Hitler's targets at the earliest opportunity.

WAR AT SEA 1940

Having failed to bomb Britain into defeat, Germany changed tactics: she would starve Britain into defeat by means of a blockade. She targeted British supplies by means of warships, U-boats and bombers. They operated mainly from the ports Germany had recently taken over along the west coast of France. The Kriegsmarine and the Luftwaffe re-located U-boats and Condor bombers to the area. They would target the Atlantic convoys, whose supplies of both foodstuffs and armaments were essential to Britain. Fortunately for Britain, the weather was very poor from November 1940 until the spring of 1941, and the blockade had little effect during that period.

1940 TIMELINE

Jan–Apr	Phoney War continues.
08 Jan	Rationing begins in Britain.
16 Feb	The *Altmark* Incident.
12 Mar	Finland and Soviets sign peace treaty.
16 Mar	Germans bomb Scapa Flow naval base.
09 Apr	Germany invades Denmark and Norway.
10 May	Germany invades Netherlands and Belgium.
	Germany invades France and Luxembourg.
	Churchill becomes Prime Minister after Chamberlain's resignation.
15 May	Netherlands surrenders.
19 May	Germans take Amiens.
22 May	Germans reach the English Channel.
26 May	Dunkirk evacuation begins.
28 May	Belgium surrenders.
03 Jun	Germany bombs Paris.
	Dunkirk evacuation ends.
10 Jun	Norway surrenders.
	Italy declares war on France and Britain.
14 Jun	Germans enter Paris.
16 Jun	Marshal Pétain becomes French Prime Minister.
18 Jun	Hitler and Mussolini meet in Munich.
	Soviets begin occupation of the Baltic States (Latvia, Lithuania and Estonia).
22 Jun	Armistice signed between France and Germany.
23 Jun	Hitler pays early morning visit to Paris.

28 Jun	Britain recognises Charles de Gaulle as the Free French leader.
01 Jul	German U-boats attack merchant ships in the Atlantic.
05 Jul	French Vichy Government breaks off relations with Britain.
03 Jul	Churchill sinks remainder of French fleet at Mers-el-Kébir in Algeria.
10 Jul	Battle of Britain begins.
16 Jul	Hitler decides to proceed with Operation Sea Lion (invasion of Britain)
23 Jul	Russia occupies Lithuania, Latvia and Estonia.
03 Aug	Italy invades British Somaliland in East Africa.
13 Aug	Germany commences bombing campaign over Britain.
17 Aug	Hitler declares a blockade of the British Isles.
24 Aug	Germany bombs central London.
26 Aug	Britain bombs Berlin.
03 Sep	Hitler plans Operation Sea Lion (invasion of Britain).
07 Sep	Blitz of London begins.
13 Sep	Italy invades Egypt through Libya.
15 Sep	Massive German bombing over Britain.
16 Sep	US military conscription bill passes.
19 Sep	Hitler orders dispersal of invasion fleet.
27 Sep	Tripartite Pact signed by Germany, Italy and Japan.
04 Oct	Hitler and Mussolini meet at Brenner Pass.
07 Oct	German troops enter Romania.
12 Oct	Hitler defers planned invasion of Britain until the spring.
28 Oct	Italy invades Greece.
05 Nov	Roosevelt re-elected President for third term.
10 Nov	British navy attacks Italian fleet at Taranto.
14 Nov	Germans bomb Coventry.
20 Nov	Hungary joins Axis Powers.
22 Nov	Greeks defeat Italian army.
23 Nov	Romania joins Axis Powers.
09 Dec	British begins offensive against Italy in North Africa.
29 Dec	Massive German air raid on London.
30 Dec	Bulgaria joins Axis Powers.

CHAPTER 14

1941
Germany Invades Russia;
Japan Attacks Pearl Harbor

WAR IN EUROPE 1941

Rommel arrives in North Africa. Germany invades Yugoslavia and Greece. Operation Barbarossa (Invasion of Russia) begins. Siege of Leningrad begins. Germans attack Moscow. Soviets counter-attack around Moscow. Japanese attack Pearl Harbor and several other colonies in the Pacific.

WAR AT SEA 1941

With the arrival of spring, the Germans intensified the Battle of the Atlantic. The U-boat campaign under the command of Admiral Karl Dönitz, a veteran of World War I, was stepped up and between 31 March and 31 May sank 140 ships, 98 of them British. (Dönitz lost two sailor sons in the war, one in a submarine). At the same time, the Luftwaffe sank a further 175 vessels, mostly merchant shipping. These were heavy losses and Churchill was seriously concerned that their sea link with America might be broken.

The British Royal Navy was forced to step up a gear in the Atlantic, sinking many U-boats. This intensity was maintained up to the end of the war.

At the end of May, the Kriegsmarine under Admiral Raeder got a boost with the delivery of the *Bismarck* (named after the Iron Chancellor), one of the world's biggest and most powerful battleships. She was immediately pressed into service in the North Atlantic, giving the Royal Navy even more cause for concern. Royal Navy ships confronted the *Bismarck* in the Denmark Strait on 24 May. The *Bismarck* opened fire on the HMS *Hood*, the pride of the Royal Navy, which blew up and sank with the loss of 1,400 men. This was a grievous blow to Britain.

Determined to avenge the loss of the *Hood*, the Royal Navy gathered its forces to confront the *Bismarck*. It also enlisted the assistance of the RAF to find and destroy the *Bismarck* before it reached the safety of a

German-controlled French port. The *Bismarck* was located 400 miles from the port of Brest. She was attacked from the air by torpedo-bombers launched from an aircraft carrier, and her steering gear disabled. The next morning, 27 May, two British battleships arrived to finish her off. Having been pounded with shellfire for two hours and then torpedoed, the mighty *Bismarck* eventually sank with the loss of 2,200 men. The *Hood* had been avenged!

Hitler now had a decision to make. He had failed to defeat Britain in the Blitz and so far in the Battle of the Atlantic, and he had no wish to experience another *Bismarck*. Furthermore, he was about to attack Russia on the Eastern Front and this was the priority for his Luftwaffe. He decided to leave the Atlantic to his U-boats. As a result, the pressure on Britain in the Atlantic during the remainder of the war was significantly reduced.

THE BALKANS 1941

Germany's invasion of both Yugoslavia and Greece commenced on 6 April 1941. The invasion had been planned the previous autumn when Hungary, Romania and Bulgaria had agreed to join the Axis forces, but Yugoslavia and Greece refused. Hitler wanted a united Balkans behind him when he attacked Russia.

The Balkans was important to Hitler for several reasons. The eastern boundary of the Balkans was Russia, which was Hitler's next target. Furthermore, Germany had two main sources of oil: Russia's Crimea and the Ploeşti oil fields of Romania. Hitler was about to sever his access to the former; it was vital that he retained continuous access to the latter.

Yugoslavia
Yugoslavia was a huge country comprising Croatia, Slovenia, Bosnia-Herzegovina, Montenegro and Serbia. The German attack on Yugoslavia in 1941 commenced with an all-out bombing attack on Belgrade. Ignoring the fact that April 6 was Palm Sunday on the religious calendar and that Belgrade was thronged with pilgrims, the Germans attacked. The attack by Stuka dive-bombers was merciless. 17,000 people of various nationalities were killed. Ground forces from the Axis countries swept through Yugoslavia in support of the bombers and on 17 April Yugoslavia surrendered. King Peter II fled the country, and military resistance temporarily ended.

Josip Broz Tito now came to the fore in Yugoslavia. On 1 May Tito issued a pamphlet calling on the people of Yugoslavia to unite in the battle against occupation. On 27 June the central committee of the

Communist Party appointed Tito Commander in Chief of all national liberation forces in Yugoslavia.

Much of the fighting that took place in Yugoslavia during the war years was a civil war between Tito's Partisans supported by the Allies and the rival monarchic Chetnik movement, led by Draža Mihailović, supported by Germany's Axis forces. The Yugoslavs knew only one way to fight — with maximum brutality — and more than a million people died in Yugoslavia during World War II.

GREECE 1941

Mussolini's invasion of Greece had failed miserably in 1940. An added reason for Hitler to invade Greece in 1941 was to salvage some pride for Mussolini!

Despite the fact that Britain had come to Greece's aid, the Nazi's *blitzkrieg* tactics, backed up by the other Axis troops, devastated Greece in a very short space of time and on 23 April 1941 the Nazi flag was raised over the Acropolis in Athens. Prime Minister Alexandros Koryzis committed suicide.

On 28 April the Royal Navy evacuated British forces to the island of Crete, abandoning all of her armaments in Greece.

Battle of Crete

Hitler was well aware of the strategic position of the island of Crete in the Eastern Mediterranean. He decided to take it under his control before heading for Russia. However, it did not turn out to be the formality he anticipated.

Crete was defended by 30,000 troops from Britain, Australia and New Zealand, the majority of whom had just been evacuated from Greece. They were supported by some 10,000 Greek troops. The Allies, with the backing of the Royal Navy, were well equipped to defend Crete against a sea invasion by the Germans. However, not for the first time, the Germans outwitted them. German General Kurt Student was the expert in modern parachute warfare, having led the German airborne troops to victory in Norway and Belgium earlier in the war. His plan was to fly over the Royal Navy and to parachute onto the island. On 20 May German paratroopers landed on the island in substantial numbers but suffered many casualties (paratroopers were easy targets). There were, however, sufficient survivors to take control of the airfield at Maleme. Within a week the Germans had flown in substantial troops to take over the island and by 31 May Britain and her Allies were organising another evacuation, this time to Egypt.

Both sides learned valuable lessons in Crete. Air cover was now vital for successful invasions, whether on land or sea. The German Luftwaffe inflicted substantial damages to the Royal Navy during the battle, sinking three cruisers and six destroyers, much to Churchill's chagrin. Hitler was not happy either having lost several thousand paratroopers in the battle. He forbade any further large-scale parachute operations, which was good news for Malta and Cyprus. Crete was the final nail in Europe's coffin before Hitler headed for Russia.

However, the question is often asked: did the time Hitler spent in the Balkans fatally delay his invasion of Russia?

NORTH AFRICA 1941

Following the drive by the Allies under Wavell from Sidi Barrani in Egypt to El Agheila in Libya in December 1940, the Australians took control of Tobruk on 22 January 1941.

Two major decisions at the beginning of 1941 changed the face of the war in North Africa. Early in 1941 Churchill diverted several divisions of British troops from Libya to assist Greece and on 6 February Hitler sent Erwin Rommel to Libya to take control of the German/Italian forces, who became known as the Afrika Korps.

Rommel was one of Hitler's finest generals, having originally come to prominence in 1917 in World War I. He also played a major role in the invasion of France in 1940.

Rommel possessed tremendous energy and drive. He believed in leading from the front. He wouldn't ask his troops to do anything he wouldn't do himself. He was the master of the unexpected. Opposing forces were never sure what his next move would be — hence his nickname 'Desert Fox'. He didn't lack courage either physically or morally: he was one of the few German generals who, when he considered it necessary, refused to obey Hitler's orders. It didn't take him long to make his mark in the deserts of North Africa, even though his troops were vastly outnumbered!

Desert Warfare
It didn't take both sides long to discover that desert warfare was totally different to any warfare they previously experienced. The protagonists had to deal with the scourge of heat, thirst, flies, sand and sandstorms. The sand was pervasive. It got into the food they were eating. It got into every orifice of the body and it got into the engines of the tanks, jeeps and trucks.

The battlefields of North Africa extended across the entire width of the continent: a distance of some 3,000 miles. The logistical problems of moving men, food, armaments and fuel over such a huge distance were formidable.

In March 1941 Rommel attacked and forced the British back into Egypt. However, he was unable to dislodge the 30,000 Australian troops from the fortress of Tobruk in Eastern Libya near the Egyptian border. By keeping control of Tobruk, the Australians (the self-styled 'Rats of Tobruk') deprived the Germans of a vital supply port. Tobruk was a strategically-important deepwater port on the Mediterranean coast close to the Egyptian border. It was a major fortress, and whoever controlled Tobruk controlled all incoming services by sea in the area.

Both Wavell and Rommel spent the spring of 1941 training and reorganising their respective troops. Wavell got a big boost when a huge supply convoy reached Alexandria in Egypt through the Mediterranean on 12 May. The convoy contained 240 tanks and forty Hurricane planes. Churchill believed that this would be enough to drive the Axis forces out of North Africa completely. However, it is not possible to hide a convoy of this size, and Rommel was ready and waiting. The tanks were new Crusader tanks, which were untested and many suffered mechanical failure in the desert sand. Those that remained operational ran foul of Rommel's anti-tank guns. After three days of fighting, the Allies had lost ninety tanks while Rommel had lost only twenty-five. The Desert Fox was showing his mettle! Churchill reacted with a change of leadership. On 21 June he swapped Wavell with the head of the British forces in India, General Claude Auchinleck. On the same date on the Eastern Front, Germany invaded Russia.

Auchinleck was precise but cautious and spent the next few months preparing his Operation Crusader to defeat the Germans. The objective was to take control of the Cyrenaica area of Libya and to relieve Tobruk, which was under continuing siege by the Germans. The offensive began on 18 November, and fighting was intense. Rommel was forced to retreat his forces westward, and on 7 December Tobruk was relieved. While both sides lost approximately 300 tanks, Axis casualty figures were 38,000 compared to 18,000 for the Allies, who achieved a much-needed victory. The Siege of Tobruk had lasted from 10 April to 7 December.

MALTA 1941

Malta is a small British-controlled island seventeen miles long by nine miles wide, located sixty miles south of Sicily. It lies directly between

Italy and North Africa. It has a fine deep-water harbour at Valetta and would have been a very valuable base for Hitler's Axis forces had they succeeded in taking it.

Having lost so many in the Battle of Crete, Hitler had decided that the use of paratroopers was not the way to take over an island. He decided to bomb Malta into submission. However, he had not bargained for the resolute nature of the Maltese, similar to the British during the Blitz. Rommel believed that the Axis forces would not succeed in North Africa without taking over Malta.

The bombing of Malta began on 11 June 1940 when Italy attacked the island. When the Germans moved into Sicily in December, the bombing of Malta intensified and continued almost on a daily basis until the war in North Africa ended in May 1943. When Hitler began the attack on Russia in June 1941, the pressure on Malta was reduced. This gave the Allies the opportunity to attack the Axis supplies to Rommel in North Africa. On the other hand, Axis submarines were very active in attacking British convoys bringing much-needed supplies to beleaguered Malta.

Malta suffered her most intense period of bombing between December 1941 and May 1942 when 10,000 tons of bombs were dropped on the island. Despite the fact that on a nightly basis the Maltese people took to underground tunnels, cellars and catacombs, almost 1,500 Maltese civilians were killed. 35,000 houses and numerous public buildings were damaged or destroyed, but the planned invasion of Malta never took place.

By the summer of 1942, however, the island was close to starvation and fuel supplies were at a very low level. On 10 August a convoy of fourteen merchant vessels under heavy escort entered the Mediterranean at Gibraltar bound for Malta. They were attacked by air and by sea. Casualties were substantial. Only five ships (some severely damaged) made it to Malta. Malta was saved by the heroism of the Santa Maria Convoy. The attacks on Malta ceased when the war in North Africa ended in May 1943.

The bravery and courage of the people of Malta was honoured when King George VI awarded the island of Malta the George Cross on 15 April 1942.

RUDOLF HESS

Rudolf Hess was the German officer who typed out Hitler's *Mein Kampf* when they were in Landsberg Prison together after the failed

Beer Hall Putsch in 1923. Hitler, who was fond of Hess (calling him *"Mein Hesserl"),* appointed him deputy Führer of the Nazi Party in 1933.

Hess was very interested in astrology and, as World War II progressed, Hess and his astrology friends began to see a future littered with millions of corpses. Aside from his astrological beliefs, Hess had courage. He believed if he could broker a peace with Britain, he could save millions of lives!

He was an accomplished pilot and on 10 May he 'borrowed' a Messerschmitt plane and flew to Scotland with the intention of making contact with the Duke of Hamilton, a Scottish peer known to Churchill, with the aim of initiating peace talks. Hess had never made a parachute jump, but he took his plane up to a suitable height and jumped. The plane crash-landed in the countryside and it was no surprise that Hess broke an ankle on landing. He was arrested and interviewed by Britain's Minister for Aircraft Production, Lord Beaverbrook, who made it clear to Hess that peace at this stage in the war was not possible. Hess was imprisoned in the Tower of London until the end of the war, after which he was transferred to Spandau Prison in Russia. He remained there until he committed suicide in 1987 at the age of 93. When Hitler was made aware of the flight to Scotland, he was apoplectic with rage!

OPERATION BARBAROSSA: THE INVASION OF RUSSIA

Hitler had initially planned to invade Russia in May, but his decision to come to the assistance of his ally Mussolini in the Balkans and in North Africa delayed the start of Operation Barbarossa (named after Frederick the Great) by a month. This delay would prove costly in the months ahead. The invasion of Russia commenced on 22 June when an incredible force of four million men (three million Germans and one million of her allies from Italy, Romania, Hungary and Bulgaria) crossed the Russian border. Stalin had plenty of forewarnings but took no defensive action. It would appear that the arrogant Russian leader did not believe that Hitler would break the Molotov-Ribbentrop Pact of 1939! Either way, he was caught off guard and the purge of his army officers, which he carried out in 1937, came back to haunt him.

Hitler's plan was to hit the Soviets on three fronts:
1. Army Group North to head for Leningrad (St. Petersburg)
2. Army Group Centre to attack Moscow
3. Army Group South to target Kiev in Ukraine

The logistics of Operation Barbarossa were enormous. The battlefront was 920 miles long. It took 500,000 motor vehicles and 300,000 horses to move the troops. Food, motor fuel and fodder for the horses were needed in enormous quantities. The territory they had to cross, while flat, was poorly served by both road and rail. The longest railway in the world, the Trans-Siberian Railway (5,700 miles long) connecting Moscow with Vladivostok on the Sea of Japan, proved very useful during the early years of the war when Hitler could depend on Stalin's goodwill. The railway was used on a daily basis to transport goods (particularly rubber originating in French Indochina) from Japan to Germany. However, the day Hitler invaded Russia marked the end of this arrangement.

On 22 June the three army groups crossed the Russian border. The *blitzkrieg* tactics were used once more, with the Luftwaffe carrying on a relentless bombing campaign. The bombing was initially directed at Russian airfields where aircraft were conveniently parked up in rows. In the first 24 hours, it's estimated that more than a thousand Russian planes were destroyed!

Army Group North, under the command of Field Marshal Wilhelm von Leeb, attacked out of East Prussia, invading the Baltic states of Lithuania, Latvia and Estonia. They were assisted by the Finnish army, whose sole motive was to avenge their defeat by Russia in the Winter War. The Russians achieved almost total success. On 1 July the group reached the Latvian capital of Riga. The Germans were initially welcomed in the Baltic states, where their presence was thought to be better than the oppression of Stalin! (This was also the sentiment in Ukraine.) On 19 August Army Group North reached Leningrad (now St. Petersburg), which was surrounded and placed under siege. The siege lasted 920 days. By the time it was eventually lifted in January 1944, some 200,000 civilians had been killed by German bombardment, and more than 600,000 had perished from starvation and disease. Anticipating a major battle, Stalin sent General Georgy Zhukov, his most able general, to Leningrad in September to organise its defence, but once it became clear that there would be no battle (Hitler had decided to starve Leningrad into submission) Zhukov was recalled to Moscow.

Army Group Centre, whose target was Moscow, made rapid progress under the command of Field Marshal Fedor von Bock, taking the Belarusian capital of Minsk on 30 June followed by Smolensk a week later. From there, it was to be the big prize: the Russian capital Moscow. If Hitler could successfully take Moscow, it would be the beginning of the end for Stalin! At this stage, however, Hitler stalled the advance on Moscow in order to prioritise the taking of Kiev in the south before tackling the capital. Army Group Centre was diverted to the Kiev area. This was one of Hitler's big mistakes.

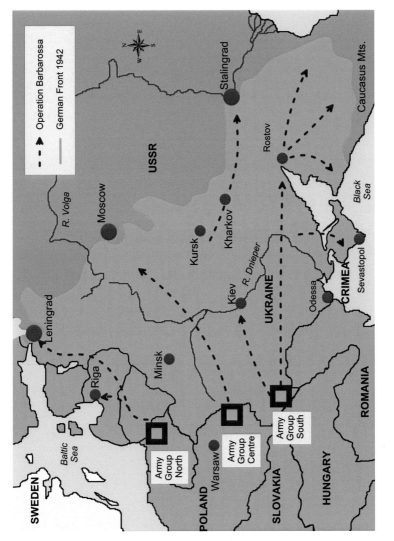

Map 17: Operation Barbarossa — Invasion of Russia 1941–42

SS Chief Heinrich Himmler visiting a Prisoner of War camp during World War II.

Army Group South, under the command of Field Marshal Gerd von Rundstedt, assisted by Romania and Hungary, reached the Ukrainian capital of Kiev in mid-July, and on 5 August they laid siege to Odessa on the Black Sea. Hitler was not just interested in the city of Kiev but in the natural assets of the area — namely oil, coal and agriculture. Rundstedt had a major victory taking Kiev in September before seizing the summer wheat crop in Ukraine. The industrial region of Kharkov was taken in October followed by Rostov in November. The initial welcome for the Germans in Ukraine evaporated very quickly with the seizing of their wheat crop and the murder of 33,770 Ukrainian Jews at Babi Yar. Babi Yar was one of the worst horror stories of World War II.

Babi Yar

Babi Yar was a ravine outside Kiev. The Nazis seized the opportunity to use it as a mass grave. When the Nazis encountered some underground resistance in Kiev, they blamed the Jews and proceeded to round up all the Jews in the area. More than 30,000 Jews — men, women and children — were marched to the ravine, forced at gunpoint to strip, climb down into the ravine, and lie face downwards. They were then shot in the back of the head. Over two days — 29 and 30 September — 33,770 Russian Jews were murdered; layer upon layer of bodies!

Two years later, when the war was moving in the opposite direction and the Russians retook Kiev, a few locals who had survived the massacre informed the Russians of the massacre and led them to the ravine, where they unearthed the bodies.

By the end of 1941 it is estimated that 500,000 Soviet Jews were murdered by the German army.

Nazi Advance

The initial progress of Operation Barbarossa was astonishing; the Germans had every reason to be euphoric. Russian casualties were huge. In a matter of weeks, 10,000 Russian aircraft and ninety per cent of their tanks were destroyed. More than five million Russians were killed, wounded or taken prisoner. Before the invasion started, Hitler's instruction to his German army was to show no mercy. As a result many civilians were raped and murdered. Those taken prisoner were incarcerated in concentration camps (many of the camps were no more than wire cages), where most of them died from cold and hunger.

Stalin had been caught unawares (despite many warnings) when Operation Barbarossa commenced. He was initially stunned as he witnessed the magnitude of the casualty figures. However, as he digested the full reality of Russia's situation, he moved quickly.

Industrial Relocation

As the Germans advanced, Stalin ordered that all industrial factories in west Russia be moved to the east. More than one thousand factories, complete with industrial plant, were disassembled and moved (mainly by rail) eastwards behind the Ural Mountains where they restarted production a safe distance away from the Nazis. This was an unbelievable feat of logistics, and in a short space of time the Soviets were operational and churning out armaments like never before! This extraordinary movement of factories to the east was key to the Russian fightback.

As the Russians retreated, Stalin instigated a 'scorched earth' policy. All food and shelter which could be of benefit to the Nazis was destroyed. This was a mistake and would backfire on the Russians later in the war.

This initial German success was not achieved without cost. The Russians, although poorly-led and poorly-equipped, defended fiercely. By the end of September the Nazis had suffered more than 500,000 casualties, which increased to one million by the end of 1941.

The drive on Moscow was not resumed until 2 October, when Operation Typhoon was launched. During the delay, two major events occurred. The Russians took full advantage of the delay to regroup while the weather took a turn for the worse. The rain in early October churned the ground into a sea of mud, making progress difficult. Tanks had to be abandoned in favour of horses. The Nazis were approaching the gates of Moscow when winter weather arrived in November. Frost and snow hampered their efforts. Hitler had not foreseen the possibility of fighting in such conditions (he believed the war would be over) and German troops had not been issued with winter clothing. They suffered severely as a result of the freezing conditions. By the end of the year, 100,000 serious cases of frostbite were reported. Of these, 14,000 men had to have a limb amputated. It was also extremely difficult to keep tanks and motorised vehicles moving in such conditions. It would appear that Hitler had learned nothing from Napoleon's invasion of Russia in 1812.

On 5 December without any warning, the Russians launched a counter-attack. They were under the command of General Georgy Zhukov, who first came to prominence leading the Russian army to victory over the Japanese in the Battle of Khalkhin Gol River in 1938. After the battle, the Japanese decided to stick to the Pacific.

Zhukov would prove in the years ahead to be a very able commander indeed. During the previous weeks, Zhukov — unknown to the Germans — had assembled a force of one hundred divisions, many new to battle, who were well-equipped and warmly-clad. This new force attacked a tired and cold enemy over a two-hundred-mile front. Success was immediate. The Germans were driven back more than one hundred miles and the threat to Moscow was lifted.

Stalin remained in Moscow throughout the battle and played a crucial role in organising its defences. In this respect, he differed from Hitler who never appeared at a war front.

Hitler had failed to take both Leningrad and more particularly Moscow: he would pay for this in the years ahead! Several German generals blamed Hitler's concentration on the industrial and agricultural lands around Kiev for the defeat at Moscow. Certainly, the two months Germany lost — one in Kiev and one in the Balkans — were major factors in his defeat at Moscow.

Two days later came an event which truly turned the war into a world war. On 7 December Japan attacked the American fleet at Pearl Harbor in the Pacific Ocean *[see War in the Pacific 1941, page 223]*.

UNITED STATES OF AMERICA 1941

From the day World War II started in Europe in 1939, President Franklin D. Roosevelt had viewed the proceedings with apprehension. He kept insisting that America was neutral and would not get involved in the war. He resisted Churchill's pleas to join the war, but he gave Britain as much help as possible without actually getting directly involved.

In 1940 Roosevelt agreed to give Britain fifty-year-old destroyers in return for some colonial bases. From the start of the war, he supplied Britain with arms and other goods on a cash-and-carry basis. He followed this in 1941 with the Lend-Lease Act, which allowed Britain to purchase arms on credit. Without his assistance, Britain would have been bankrupt long before the war ended.

As the war in Europe progressed to the stage where the Nazis took over France, Roosevelt had good reason to be apprehensive. Hitler now controlled the Atlantic seaboard from Norway to France (with the exception of Britain and neutral Ireland) and all that separated the Nazis from the east coast of America was the Atlantic Ocean.

In August 1941 Roosevelt and Churchill met on board a warship off the coast of Newfoundland in Canada. They signed an agreement of war aims, called the Atlantic Charter. At this point, the Americans were clearly committed to the war against Germany in every way, short of actual involvement in the fighting.

However, it was not the war in Europe that would drag the US into World War II but the Japanese attack on the American fleet in Pearl Harbor.

Long before Pearl Harbor, Roosevelt had convinced Congress of the need to increase numbers in the armed forces and the production of armaments. The factories, which the Americans had built for the mass production of automobiles, switched to the manufacture of tanks and aircraft.

Aircraft production increased from 6,000 in 1939 to 13,000 in 1940, rising to 26,000 in 1941. Only the US (or Russia) could rival such a spectacular increase in industrial output!

1941 TIMELINE — EUROPE

22 Jan	Tobruk in North Africa falls to British/Australian troops.
11 Feb	Britain advances into Italian Somaliland in East Africa.
12 Feb	German forces under Rommel arrive in Tripoli.
07 Mar	British forces arrive in Greece.
11 Mar	Roosevelt signs the Lend-Lease Act.
27 Mar	A coup in Yugoslavia overthrows the pro-Axis government.
06 Apr	Nazis invade Greece and Yugoslavia.
14 Apr	Rommel attacks Tobruk.
17 Apr	Yugoslavia surrenders to the Nazis.
27 Apr	Greece surrenders to the Nazis.
28 Apr	British forces evacuated from Greece to Crete.
01 May	German attack on Tobruk is repulsed. Tito takes over leadership of the Yugoslav guerrilla movement.
10 May	Rudolf Hess flies to Scotland. Heavy German bombing of London.
11 May	Britain bombs Hamburg.
12 May	Huge convoy relieves Alexandria.
15 May	British counter-attack begins in Egypt.
20 May	German paratroopers land in Crete.
24 May	British war ship HMS *Hood* sunk by *Bismarck*.
27 May	*Bismarck* sunk by British navy.
28 May	Germans invade the Island of Crete.
31 May	Allies evacuate Crete.
14 Jun	US freezes assets of Germany and Italy in America.
22 Jun	Operation Barbarossa, Nazi attack on Russia, begins.
28 Jun	Nazis capture Minsk.
Jul	Japan invades Indochina.
03 Jul	Stalin orders 'scorched earth' policy.
10 Jul	Germans cross the River Dnieper in Ukraine.

12 Jul	Mutual assistance agreement between British and Soviets.
14 Jul	British occupy Syria.
26 Jul	US freezes Japanese assets in America.
01 Aug	US announces oil embargo against Axis Powers.
14 Aug	Roosevelt and Churchill announce the Atlantic Charter.
20 Aug	Siege of Leningrad begins.
01 Sep	Nazis order Jews to wear yellow stars.
03 Sep	First use of gas chambers at Auschwitz.
19 Sep	Nazis take Kiev.
29 Sep	Nazis begin murder of 33,770 Jews at Babi Yar in Kiev.
02 Oct	Germans begin attack on Moscow.
16 Oct	Germans take Odessa.
24 Oct	Germans take Kharkov.
30 Oct	Germans reach Sevastopol in Crimea.
13 Nov	British aircraft carrier *Ark Royal* is sunk off Gibralter by German U-boat.
20 Nov	Germans take Rostov.
27 Nov	Russians retake Rostov.
05 Dec	Hitler defers German attack on Moscow.
06 Dec	Soviets launch major counteroffensive around Moscow.
07 Dec	Tobruk finally relieved of German siege.
11 Dec	Hitler declares war on the US.
16 Dec	Rommel begins a retreat to El Agheila in North Africa.
19 Dec	Hitler takes complete control of the German army.

WAR IN THE PACIFIC 1941

US places embargo on oil and steel to Japan. Japan bombs Pearl Harbor. US and China declare war on Japan. Japan invades Thailand, Malaya, Singapore, Burma, the Philippines, British Borneo, Guinea, Guam, Wake Island and Midway Island. Britain surrenders Hong Kong to the Japanese.

CHINA

The war in the Pacific which began in 1937, two years before the war in Europe, was the result of a decades-long Japanese imperialist policy aimed at dominating China politically and militarily. It aimed to secure China's vast raw material reserves and other economic resources, particularly oil, food and labour.

The war was fought in East Asia, the Pacific Ocean and on the islands in the Pacific. In East Asia, the Japanese scored a major victory in Shanghai in 1937 and by the end of the year they had captured the

Chinese capital of Nanking, carrying out an appalling massacre in the process. By 1939 the war had reached stalemate after Chinese victories in Changsha and Guangxi but continued intermittently right up until 1945. The Chinese cause was not helped by the civil war between the Chinese nationalists under Chiang Kai-shek and the Chinese communists under Mao Tse-tung.

PACIFIC OCEAN

All that separated America and Japan was the Pacific Ocean, but it was an enormous ocean: covering about one-third of the Earth's surface area. Its boundaries are America to the east, Asia to the west, Australia to the south and the Arctic to the north. Distances in the Pacific are difficult to grasp, as indeed they were in North Africa. Hawaii is 2,000 miles from San Francisco and 3,300 miles from Yokohama. Hong Kong is 1,400 miles from Singapore, while the Dutch East Indies lies 2,500 miles south of Japan.

Prior to 1940 most of the islands in the Pacific and East Asia had been colonised by the European countries of Britain, France and the Netherlands; by America; or by Japan itself. Britain's Commonwealth included India and Burma; Malaya and Singapore; Sarawak and North Borneo; New Guinea and the Solomon Islands; Australia and Hong Kong. France controlled Indochina. The Netherlands had control over the oil-rich Dutch East Indies and South Borneo. America controlled the Philippines, Hawaii and Guam. Japan's empire included Korea, Manchukuo, Taiwan and eastern China. The Caroline Islands, the Marshall Islands and the Mariana Islands were also mandated to Japan.

Japan was a small nation with huge ambition. If you revert back to the interwar years in this book, you will see that Japan had ambitions to control East Asia and the entire Pacific with Germany controlling West Asia and Europe. She spent much of the 1930s building up her navy, particularly her fleet of aircraft carriers, and by 1941 she had one of the most powerful navies in the world.

However, Japan had two major concerns. Firstly, she sought more territory. In this respect, she was not achieving great success against either China or Russia. However, she could see that commitments in Europe against the Axis countries in World War II would ensure that Britain, France and the Netherlands would be unable to come to the aid of their colonies in the Pacific if they were attacked.

Testing the waters, Japan demanded that Britain close the Burma Road, a supply route through Burma to China and, against US wishes, the British complied. (The Burma Road was a 700-mile long road running

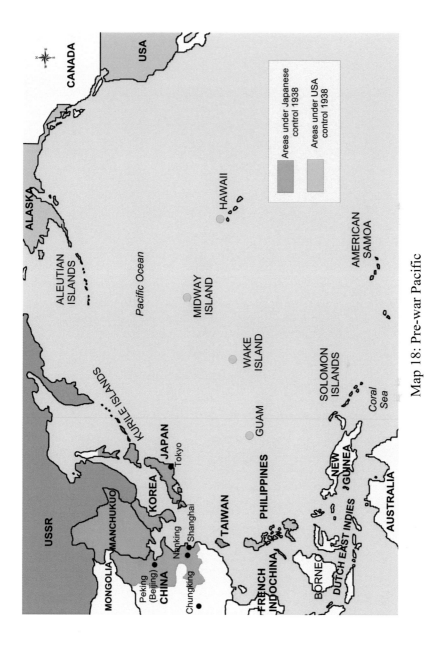

Map 18: Pre-war Pacific

Japanese attack on Pearl Harbor, Hawaii, 7 December 1941.

through mountain territory from Lashio in Central Burma to Kunming in south-west China. Goods, armaments, etc. were transported from the port of Rangoon by rail to Lashio.) *[see Map 21, page 245]*

After the invasion of French Indochina by Japan in July 1941, the US responded by placed an embargo on oil and steel supplies to Japan. This severely hurt Japan, but instead of backing down she responded by signing a tripartite pact with Germany and Italy in September 1940. Roosevelt was not enamoured by the Tripartite Pact, which he saw as a threat to the United States.

The second problem Japan had was oil or to be more precise the lack of oil. She knew where the oil was: in several of the Pacific Islands, particularly the Dutch East Indies. However, it was not readily available to Japan — she would have to take it! She also set her sights on the rubber plantations in Malaya.

Early in 1941, the European Powers with territory in the Pacific met with the Americans to discuss their joint concern regarding Japan's ever-increasing aggression. Britain agreed to reopen the Burma Road, while the US sent a volunteer air squadron to assist China's air defence.

In April Japan signed a neutrality agreement with Russia, which eased the tension at the Manchukuo/Russian border!

In June 1941 Hitler's army invaded Russia. With the Russian army now fully occupied in Europe, Japan was free to concentrate her attentions on East Asia and the Pacific. Her first act of aggression was to occupy French Indochina, which she did at the end of July 1941. She knew she would meet little resistance since French Indochina was, through Vichy France, basically under German control.

The American government responded quickly to this aggression. On 17 August a communication was dispatched to the Japanese government with the following demands: that Japan end the war with China, remove her forces from Indochina, withdraw from the Tripartite Pact and agree to solve problems by peaceful means. The Japanese did not take kindly to this diktat — they responded by attacking the Americans at Pearl Harbor.

PEARL HARBOR

In Japan at that time, the military controlled everything. In October 1941 former army Chief of Staff General Hideki Tojo was appointed Prime Minister. Tojo's ambitions included conquering the US and

European colonies in the Pacific. In August 1939 Admiral Isoroku Yamamoto was appointed commander of the Japanese fleet. He was a commander of considerable imagination and daring. Having lived in the US, he was aware of the strength the Americans could muster when required, and he was not in favour of going to war against them. However, if war was inevitable, his plan was to move quickly and to destroy the American fleet while it was still at anchor in its Pacific base at Pearl Harbor in Hawaii.

It was an audacious plan and it took some time for Yamamoto to convert the naval general staff to his way of thinking. However, they were finally persuaded and all agreed that the success of the plan would depend on silence and secrecy!

Towards the end of 1941, Japanese naval forces were far superior to those of the Allies in the Pacific. Japan had ten aircraft carriers (which were the key to the Pacific) while the US had three. In terms of battleships the sides were of equal strength, but the Allies' ships were deployed in the Atlantic and the Middle East as well as the Pacific.

Japan, moreover, had clear superiority in the air. She had 1,400 Zero fighter aircraft designed specifically to operate from aircraft carriers. The Americans, British and Dutch between them could muster no more than 700 aircraft in the Pacific, none of which were of modern design like the Japanese Zero fighters.

The Japanese were planning the attack on Pearl Harbor for a full year beforehand. Pilots were trained as dive-bombers and taught the skills of launching shallow-water torpedoes. Aerial photographs gave them every detail of Pearl Harbor and its surrounds.

On 6 December Japan ordered six aircraft carriers carrying 400 aircraft to converge 300 miles north of Pearl Harbor under cover of a weather front. For some months, the Americans were aware that the Japanese were planning something (they suspected an attack in the Philippines), but little did they realise that their base at Pearl Harbor was the target.

The Japanese launched their attack on Sunday, 7 December. Sunday was a rest day for the Americans and many were having a lie-in!

At 8:00 a.m. the first wave of Japanese bombers, launched from the aircraft carriers, attacked. They bombed the harbour and American aircraft parked up on nearby airstrips. A huge number of ships were sunk, but the biggest loss was six major battleships, which were torpedoed in the harbour. An hour later, a second wave of bombers arrived to finish off the job.

By 10:00 a.m. Pearl Harbor was a devastated battle zone. The sinking of the six battleships resulted in the loss of 2,400 men. 160 aircraft were destroyed on the ground. The Japanese were exultant: their success at Pearl Harbor was unprecedented!

The only saving grace for the Americans was that none of their three aircraft carriers were in the harbour that morning. The battleships that were hit sank in shallow water while vital naval infrastructure, including their repair dockyard and their oil supplies, escaped unscathed.

The political repercussions were swift! The following day, 8 December, President Roosevelt addressed America's Congress. He spoke of *"a date which will live in infamy,"* and he now had no difficulty getting Congress' agreement to declare war on Japan. America was finally at war, much to Churchill's relief, and World War II was now truly a world war.

Events moved swiftly after Pearl Harbor. On 8 December the US, Britain, Australia and the Netherlands declared war on Japan. Four days later, Germany and Italy declared war on the Americans in support of their ally Japan. This was widely considered to be a strategic blunder, since it negated the benefit Germany gained by Japan's distraction of the US.

America now had the same problem that she'd had in World War I. She had to build an army. She immediately embarked upon a programme of conscription and training. Conscription proved to be an easy task. Many Americans had been unemployed since the Great Depression in the 1930s and were only too glad to be conscripted. However, it would take a year to build and train the new American army. During that year and for several years to come, American factories vastly increased their production of armaments, including planes and ships — in particular, aircraft carriers.

Late in December 1941 Winston Churchill met with President Roosevelt in Washington in what became known as the Arcadia Conference to discuss plans for the war. They realised with the forces available to them, it would be impossible to fight the Germans in Europe and the Japanese in the Pacific at the same time. They took the decision to concentrate on Europe first and deal with the Pacific later.

In conjunction with Pearl Harbor, the Japanese immediately embarked on a programme of major expansion southwards, taking new territories and sourcing raw materials, particularly oil and rubber. They invaded Thailand and the US bases on Guam and Wake Islands. Britain, Australian and Dutch forces, drained as they were by the war in Europe, could only offer token resistance.

The Japanese planned the setting up of a new Japanese-controlled Greater East Asia Co-Prosperity Sphere, which was a little ironic considering how they treated some of their neighbours in the past.

Japan had two major victories in the Pacific before the end of 1941. On 10 December the British dispatched two battleships, the HMS *Prince of Wales* and the HMS *Repulse,* to Singapore as a show of strength. Japanese bombers flying from Indochina attacked and sank both ships. If Churchill had been unaware up to that moment of the strength of the Japanese air force, he was now left in no doubt.

The first target of the Japanese expansion plan was Hong Kong. A British possession for more than a century, the Japanese considered Hong Kong to be a token of European intrusion into Asia and on 8 December they attacked the port.

Hong Kong was poorly defended by a small force of Royal Hong Kong volunteers, aided by some Canadian troops. They defended bravely but by Christmas Day they had no option but to surrender. Hong Kong is sometimes referred to as the 'British Pearl Harbor', but there was no comparison. Before the end of 1941, the Japanese invaded Malaya, Singapore, Burma, British Borneo and the Philippines.

1941 TIMELINE — PACIFIC

Jul	Japan occupies French Indochina.
Aug	US places embargo on oil and steel supplies to Japan.
Sep	Tripartite Pact agreed between Japan, Germany and Italy.
07 Dec	Japan bombs US base at Pearl Harbor in Hawaii.
	Japan attacks Thailand, Malaya, Singapore, Wake Island and Midway Island.
08 Dec	The US, Britain, Australia and the Netherlands declare war on Japan.
09 Dec	China declares war on Japan.
10 Dec	Japan invades the Philippines and Guam.
	En route to Singapore, two British battleships, *Prince of Wales* and *Repulse,* are sunk by Japanese bombers.
11 Dec	Japan invades Burma.
16 Dec	Japan invades British Borneo.
18 Dec	Japan invades Hong Kong.
22 Dec	Japan invades Luzon, the main island in the Philippines.
25 Dec	Britain surrenders Hong Kong to the Japanese.
26 Dec	Manila declared an open city.
27 Dec	Regardless of open city status, Japan bombs Manila.

CHAPTER 15

1942
Hitler Launches 'Final Solution' Against Jews;
Japan Moves Swiftly Through the Pacific

WAR IN EUROPE 1942

War in North Africa continues with Montgomery taking control of the Allies in August. American troops and General Eisenhower arrive in Britain. Senior SS officer Reinhard Heydrich is assassinated. Germany takes Crimea and drives towards Stalingrad. Soviets counter-attack at Stalingrad. American troops arrive in North Africa. Pacific War begins in earnest.

NORTH AFRICA 1942

After Rommel's reverses towards the end of 1941, it did not take him long to bounce back. He went on the offensive on 21 January 1942, recapturing Benghazi and most of the territory he had lost only a month previously. However, the two sides spent much of the spring of 1942 regrouping their forces. Churchill did his best to prod Auchinleck into action, but it was Rommel, heavily outnumbered, who went on the offensive. Four weeks of intensive fighting took place, starting in mid-May and culminating in Rommel retaking Tobruk on 21 June, after breaking through the Gazala Line on 26 May (the Gazala Line was a line of defence from Gazala on the coast west of Tobruk running south to Bir Hacheim in the desert). Hitler rewarded Rommel by promoting him to the rank of Field Marshal: the youngest in the German army.

Rommel's forces now advanced into Egypt and on 30 June reached **El Alamein**, only sixty miles from Alexandria. Rommel was now poised to deliver a crippling blow to Churchill by taking Alexandria, gaining control of the Suez Canal and driving the British out of Egypt. He could then turn northeastwards to conquer the valuable oil fields of the Middle East and link up with the German forces besieging the equally-valuable Caucasian oil fields. However, such a move would require substantial troop reinforcements and Hitler simply did not have Rommel's vision and understanding of global warfare. Despite the efforts of Rommel and naval commander Erich Raeder to convince Hitler of the strategic value of Egypt, no troops were forthcoming.

Hitler's problem at this stage was that Germany was fully committed in Russia.

From Churchill's point of view, the Axis forces were too close to the Suez Canal for comfort. On 4 August he flew to Egypt to check the position for himself. Once again, he decided that a change of leadership was necessary. He replaced Auchinleck with General Harold Alexander in the Middle East and with General Bernard Montgomery in North Africa. 'Monty' quickly became very popular with his men. He was brave and decisive, treated his troops fairly and was just the boost the British Army needed at this time. He proved an able foil to Rommel.

On 1 July 1942 the **First Battle of El Alamein** commenced with a heavy artillery bombardment by the Allies. The depleted and hungry Axis forces were heavily outnumbered and were forced to retreat. Though Rommel managed to inflict higher casualties on the Allies than he himself suffered, the British were able to replace casualties quickly. There were no replacements for the Axis forces! Rommel's forces — and indeed Rommel himself — were exhausted. However, there was still some fight left in his Axis troops. On 30 August the Germans launched an attack at **Alam el Halfa**, but on this occasion the Desert Fox was outfoxed! Monty lured the Axis forces into a mine-strewn area with patches of quicksand and on 2 September Rommel was forced to withdraw his troops. He had suffered substantial losses and realised that the war in North Africa was unwinnable without air support. This was not forthcoming as the Luftwaffe was totally committed on the Russian front.

The continuing pressure on Rommel was affecting his health and he took sick leave in Italy and Germany from late September. He was called back from sick leave when the **Second Battle of El Alamein** began on 23 October. Before Rommel arrived back, General Georg Stumme, who was in control of the Axis forces in his absence, died of a heart attack. On his return, Rommel discovered that their fuel situation was disastrous, which meant that the only war he could fight was a static war. He was also heavily outnumbered. Monty's troops dominated. Heavy aerial and artillery bombardment on 24 and 25 October destroyed Rommel's army and he had no option but to retreat.

Hitler's instruction to Rommel was clear: *"Show your troops no other way than that which leads to victory or death."* Rommel, however, did not believe in needlessly sacrificing his men. He kept his troops together as they retreated westward along the coast road. They reached Benghazi on 20 November and Tripoli a week later. El Alamein was the turning point in the war in North Africa.

Operation Torch began on 8 November 1942 when a fleet of Allied ships began to deliver thousands of troops onto the beaches and ports of France's two North West African colonies, Morocco and Algeria.

Churchill and Roosevelt were under pressure from Stalin to open a second front in western Europe, but — rather than launch a full-scale invasion at this stage — Churchill compromised by agreeing to clear the Germans completely out of North Africa and then attack Italy. The Allied forces that invaded Morocco and Algeria were mainly American, since the British were understandably personae non gratae in the two French colonies. Memories of the sinking of French ships at Mers-el-Kébir in Algeria by the British after the invasion of France, and the consequent loss of French lives had not been forgotten.

General George C. Marshall

General George C. Marshall had been appointed Chief of Staff by President Roosevelt when America entered the war and he became Roosevelt's right-hand man throughout, attending the various conferences with him and keeping him informed on all war matters.

Marshall had experience in World War I in 1918 in northern France, where he shared the responsibility of bringing the war to an end with General Pershing. He held senior positions throughout the interwar years and was promoted to Chief of Staff in the US Army when World War II started in 1939. Marshall appointed General Dwight D. Eisenhower as Commander in Chief of the Allied forces in Europe in 1943.

General Marshall reluctantly agreed to deal with North Africa as a precursor to an invasion of Europe. On 8 November 60,000 American troops under General Eisenhower landed in the two French colonies. Half of the invading forces had sailed directly from the US, the remainder from British ports. They were supplemented by thousands of French residents who supported de Gaulle's Free French movement. Hitler, believing that Vichy France had collaborated with the Allies, ordered his troops back into the French unoccupied zone on 11 November. France in her entirety was once more under Nazi control!

HITLER'S TROUBLES IN GERMANY

Germany — The Final Solution to the Jewish Question
Hitler was fighting two wars in Europe at the beginning of 1942: the war against Russia and the war (as he saw it) against the Jews. There were times when he became so besotted with 'the Jewish question' that

he neglected the war in Europe. Initially, it was a case of 'exporting' the Jews but as time passed, fewer countries accepted them. Hitler's policy then changed to a policy of extermination, which became known as the Holocaust. Initially Jews were shot. Then they were gassed in motor vehicles. Hitler, however, was not happy with the slow pace of these operations. In July 1941 Nazi leader Hermann Göring issued a directive in which he ordered SS officer Reinhard Heydrich to submit a plan for the 'Final Solution' to the Jewish question.

The Wannsee Conference in Berlin was held in January 1942 during a lull in the fighting in Russia. Fifteen senior Nazi officers commanded by Heydrich and Adolf Eichmann attended the conference held on the shores of Lake Wannsee. Their brief from Hitler, who did not attend, was to plan the extermination of eleven million people — more than the total death toll in World War I!

Heydrich arrived at the meeting with details of the Jewish population in every country in Europe and an extermination plan. The fifteen officers who attended were intelligent, educated men, yet nobody objected! The Wannsee Conference proved, if ever proof was needed, that people who are at war will carry out operations which would be inconceivable to them in peacetime!

Their Final Solution was to increase the number of concentration camps and to install gassing and incineration facilities in all camps. The most notorious camps were at Auschwitz and Treblinka. The Holocaust and World War II proceeded in parallel. Between 1939 and 1945, the Final Solution resulted in the deaths of six million Jews! The job of implementing this operation was given to Heinrich Himmler, head of the Nazi Party.

As a result of the Holocaust, there were repercussions for Nazi Germany both during and after the war. During the war, the energy and resources diverted to this vast scheme of mass murder weakened Nazi efforts in the war against the Allies and also drained the German economy.

Death of Reinhard Heydrich
In September 1941 Hitler moved Heydrich to Prague to keep control over the Czech protectorate. His base was Prague Castle.

The Czech underground movement, controlled by former President Eduard Beneš in London was very active. Early in 1942, they parachuted two resistance fighters, Jan Kubiš (Czech) and Jozef Gabčík (Slovakian) into Prague under cover of darkness. Their mission was to assassinate Heydrich (they couldn't get near Hitler). Heydrich arrogantly drove through Prague on a daily basis with a driver but no

General Bernard L. Montgomery watches his tanks move up, North Africa, November 1942.

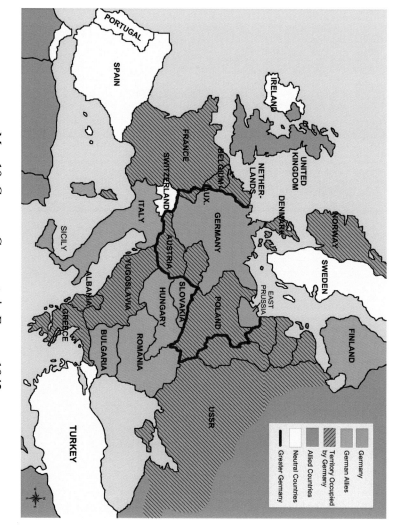

Map 19: German Conquests in Europe 1942

bodyguard. On 27 May Kubiš and Gabčík carried out their attempted assassination. They had chosen a sharp bend in the road below the castle, where the car would have to slow down. As Heydrich's car reached the bend, Gabčík stepped forward and raised his weapon to fire, but the gun jammed! As Heydrich reached for his own gun, Kubiš produced a grenade from his briefcase and rolled it under the car. It exploded, severely injuring Heydrich who died in hospital from his wounds on 4 June.

Lidice
When informed of the assassination, Hitler went berserk (Heydrich was one of his best generals) and ordered the execution of 30,000 Czechs in reprisal. When his anger abated, he reconsidered and instead ordered that the village of Lidice ten miles from Prague be wiped off the map. Lidice had a population of 500 people and Hitler believed that some of the villagers were complicit in the assassination of Heydrich. On the night of 9 June German troops entered the village, roused all the residents out of bed and forced them to assemble in the town square. The 300 women and children were taken away to Ravensbruck concentration camp. The 200 boys and men were lined up against the town wall in groups of ten and shot dead. The village was then bulldozed to the ground — quite literally wiped off the map as Hitler had ordered!

Kubiš and Gabčík — together with five local resistance fighters — took refuge in a local church. It took the German SS until 18 June to find them. They were trapped in the church cellar, and since they were armed, they made it very difficult for the Nazis to take them. The Nazis eventually drowned them using fire hoses to fill the cellar with water.

Hitler did not anticipate the reaction worldwide. Newspapers and radio ensured that the rest of the world was made aware of the atrocity that was Lidice. Several towns and villages around the world were renamed Lidice, while for the duration of the war the word 'Lidice' was daubed on Allied bombs dropped on German cities and on Russian tanks during the invasion of Germany. Hitler was not allowed to forget Lidice.

White Rose Group
While many in Germany did not support Hitler, few had the courage to express their feelings openly. To do so was to sign one's own death warrant! The White Rose resistance group consisted of students from the University of Munich together with their philosophy professor Kurt Huber. Between June 1942 and February 1943, the students distributed leaflets anonymously calling for active opposition to Hitler. The six most recognised members of the group, along with Professor Huber, were arrested by the Gestapo, tried for treason and executed in 1943. The two best-known members of the group were brother and sister

Hans and Sophie Scholl. Today, the members of the White Rose Group are honoured in Germany amongst its greatest heroes because they opposed the Third Reich in the face of almost certain death.

WESTERN FRONT 1942

Dieppe

During the spring of 1942, things were quiet on the Western Front. Stalin was pushing hard for an extra front to be opened up by the Allies to take some pressure off the Russians. Churchill also believed there should be some action on the Western Front before the summer. In conjunction with the Canadians, a decision was taken to carry out a cross-channel invasion of the French coastal town of Dieppe. The primary purpose was to see what lessons could be learned in advance of the main cross-channel invasion, which was to take place a year or two later. It proved to be an expensive lesson. At 5:00 a.m. on 19 August, 6,000 troops (mainly Canadian) began the assault. At 11:00 a.m., Admiral Louis Mountbatten, who was in charge of the operation, had to order a retreat. The Allies suffered 3,600 casualties. They lost thirty-three landing craft and ninety-six aircraft.

While the Allies can claim that the experience gained would serve them well in the years ahead, it was also true that the attempted invasion gave the Germans an indication of what to expect when the real invasion came!

Operation Frankton

A special detachment of the British Royal Marines was formed in July 1942 and based at Portsmouth under the command of Major Herbert 'Blondie' Hasler. The marines were aware that the port of Bordeaux was used extensively by the Germans to deliver necessary goods and arms to their troops in France.

Hasler devised a plan to attack German shipping in Bordeaux using submarines and canoes. The plan was to transport six canoes by submarine from Portsmouth to the mouth of the Gironde Estuary, where the canoes would be launched to paddle the sixty miles up the estuary to Bordeaux. Each canoe would be manned by two volunteer marines and carry eight Limpet mines (magnetic) to attach to ship hulls. Permission for the raid was granted on 13 October by Admiral Louis Mountbatten, Chief of Combined Operations.

The mission, which became known as Operation Frankton, was beset by problems from the start. When the canoes were being launched from the submarine, one was badly damaged and was then unable to take part in the operation. The sixty-mile canoe journey had to cope with a wall of water sweeping down the estuary at intervals. Three canoes were lost, with only two (including Hasler's) reaching their destination. Those two immediately set about fixing the Limpet mines to six ships, all of which were sunk, albeit in shallow water.

Of the ten men who started the operation, two drowned while six were captured and executed by the Germans. Only Hasler and his mate Bill Sparks survived. With the assistance of the French underground movement, they crossed the border into Spain, from where they eventually returned home to Britain.

The operation was considered a success in that it gave the Kriegsmarine something to worry about.

EASTERN FRONT 1942

Invasion of Russia

In December 1941 Hitler sacked his army Commander in Chief Walther von Brauchitsch and assumed the role of Supreme Commander of the German armed forces himself. From this point on he would heed nobody's advice. (In 1942 General Franz Halder, the German army Chief of Staff, was removed from office for arguing strategy with Hitler and spent the rest of the war in Dachau concentration camp.)

Hitler neglected to see, or did not wish to see, that his failure to take both Moscow and Leningrad — and the subsequent casualties — had seriously dented the power and spirit of the German forces. By the spring of 1942, they had suffered a million casualties (including 30,000 officers) and the loss of 3,000 tanks. Hitler planned to continue on regardless, convinced that the German army still had the power to conquer Russia.

He regrouped and planned a three-pronged attack as before.

Army Group North, supported by the Finns, would continue the siege of Leningrad, where hundreds were dying weekly from starvation. Throughout the siege, the Luftwaffe continued to bomb the city while the Soviets failed to break the siege. Late in 1941 the Russians succeeded in opening a road across the ice of Lake Ladoga to the east of the city. However, the amount of foodstuffs that got through was totally insufficient to feed the city's three-and-a-half million inhabitants. Every creature in the city, including the city's pigeons, was killed for food. Things got so desperate that a small number of people resorted to cannibalism in an attempt to stay alive. The stalemate continued right up to 1944, when the Russian army drove Hitler's forces back towards Germany.

Army Group Centre still aspired to taking Moscow, but Zhukov and the Russian army were now in total control of the capital. Hitler had missed his opportunity! Army Group Centre was diverted to help Army Group South.

Hitler decided to divide Army Group South into northern and southern battle groups. The target of the northern battle group was Stalingrad while the southern battle group would target the oil wells at Baku and Maikop in the Caucasus and in Crimea. The oil supplies in the Caucasus were vital to both the German and the Russian armies. On 9 August the Germans succeeded in taking Maikop, but the oil wells had been torched by the Russians as they departed. Baku, on the other hand, proved to be a bridge too far, being 500 miles away over rugged, mountainous territory. The overall plan by Hitler to take control of Russian oil was not successful.

The Germans fought a long hard battle for control of Crimea in May and June and on 3 July Sevastopol finally surrendered. General Manstein, who had made his name in the Ardennes at the beginning of the war, was rewarded by Hitler with promotion to Field Marshal.

Earlier in the spring, the Soviets came alive under Marshal Timoshenko and tried to retake Kharkov, which they had lost to the Germans six months earlier. Their initial success was quickly reversed when the German 6th Army under General Friedrich Paulus arrived from the north. The Soviets were driven back eastwards with substantial losses.

Stalingrad
Hitler was now ready to attack Stalingrad, Stalin's namesake city (the plan was code-named Operation Blue). In July the 250,000-strong German 6th Army under Paulus drove towards Stalingrad. On 23 August in support of her infantry, the Luftwaffe carried out a massive bombing raid, reducing the city to rubble. The Germans quickly discovered that their *blitzkrieg* — so effective in the open — was useless within the confines of the city of Stalingrad.

Throughout September and October, the two armies carried out intense guerrilla warfare, street by street and then house by house. Losses on both sides were huge. The Soviets were driven back eastwards over the River Volga.

Stalin now made a key decision. He moved his top general, Georgy Zhukov, from Moscow and placed him in control of the defence of

Stalingrad. Zhukov immediately set about rebuilding the Russian army, calling on their limitless supply of ground troops. The relocated Russian factories were now producing unbelievable numbers of tanks and aircraft.

Zhukov pulled a masterstroke on 9 November. The western perimeter of Germany's Axis forces comprised Italian and Romanian troops, who did not have the same commitment as the Germans themselves. Zhukov targeted these forces, who quickly surrendered. The Russians now attacked the Germans from both northwest and southwest. Paulus' 6th Army, with its back to the Volga River, was completely surrounded.

Manstein's attempt to come to Paulus' rescue was repulsed. The only service the Luftwaffe was able to provide was to fly in supplies, but the supplies that got through were totally inadequate to feed the German 6th Army. To make matters worse, winter arrived and Paulus' troops were ill-prepared for it. If the German soldiers were not killed in action, they either starved to death (as happened in Leningrad) or were destined to die from cold and hunger in a concentration camp.

Paulus requested permission from Hitler to surrender, but Hitler refused point blank! He ordered the German 6th Army to fight until "*victory or death*". However, Paulus could take no more. He declined to obey Hitler and on 1 February 1943 he surrendered.

The Germans had started the Stalingrad offensive with 250,000 men. 92,000 surrendered into captivity, which few of them survived. The remaining 160,000 were either killed in action or starved to death.

The Battle of Stalingrad was over and Germany's defeat at Stalingrad was the turning point of World War II in Europe.

1942 TIMELINE — EUROPE

01 Jan	United Nations Declaration signed by 26 Allied nations.
13 Jan	Germans begin a U-boat offensive along east coast of America.
14 Jan	US and Britain conclude Arcadia Conference.
20 Jan	SS leader Heydrich holds the Wannsee Conference to coordinate the Final Solution to the Jewish question.
21 Jan	Rommel's counteroffensive begins with capture of Benghazi.
26 Jan	First American troops arrive in Britain.
23 Apr	German air raids begin against cathedral cities in Britain.
08 May	German summer offensive begins in Crimea.
26 May	Rommel pierces and goes around the Gazala Line.
27 May	Heydrich fatally wounded in assassination plot in Prague.
28 May	German ground forces invade Crete.

30 May	British bomber raid against Cologne.
Jun	Mass murder of Jews by gassing begins at Auschwitz.
05 Jun	Germans besiege Sevastopol in Crimea.
10 Jun	Nazis liquidate Lidice in reprisal for Heydrich's assassination.
21 Jun	Rommel captures Tobruk.
25 Jun	General Dwight D. Eisenhower arrives in London.
30 Jun	Rommel reaches El Alamein near Cairo, Egypt.
01–30 Jul	First Battle of El Alamein.
03 Jul	Germans take Sevastopol.
05 Jul	Soviet resistance in Crimea ends.
09 Jul	Germans begin a drive towards Stalingrad.
22 Jul	Jews deported from Warsaw Ghetto to Treblinka.
04 Aug	Churchill flies to Egypt to assess the situation.
07 Aug	British General Bernard Montgomery takes command of Eighth Army in North Africa.
12 Aug	Stalin and Churchill meet in Moscow.
19 Aug	Allies attack German-held Dieppe across English Channel.
23 Aug	Massive German air raid on Stalingrad.
02 Sep	Rommel driven back by Montgomery in Battle of Alam el Halfa.
13 Sep	Battle of Stalingrad begins.
23 Oct	Second Battle of El Alamein begins.
01 Nov	Allies break Axis lines at El Alamein.
08 Nov	Operation Torch (US invasion of North Africa) begins.
09 Nov	Soviet counteroffensive at Stalingrad begins.
11 Nov	Germans and Italians invade unoccupied Vichy France.
13 Dec	Rommel withdraws from El Agheila.
31 Dec	Battle of the Barents Sea between German and British ships.

WAR IN THE PACIFIC 1942

Japan invades the Philippines, Dutch East Indies, Solomon Islands and Singapore; and advances into Burma. Japan attacks Darwin in Australia. General MacArthur and Admiral Nimitz are appointed to head American troops in the Pacific. United States defeats Japan in Battle of the Coral Sea, Battle of Midway and Battle of the Solomon Islands. US also victorious at Guadalcanal Island.

Pearl Harbor was only the beginning of Japan's aggression in the Pacific. She was fully intent on taking advantage of the commitments of the Allied countries — Britain, France, the Netherlands, Australia and the US — in the war in Europe. Most of the Japanese troops were soldiers experienced from their continuing war with the Chinese and

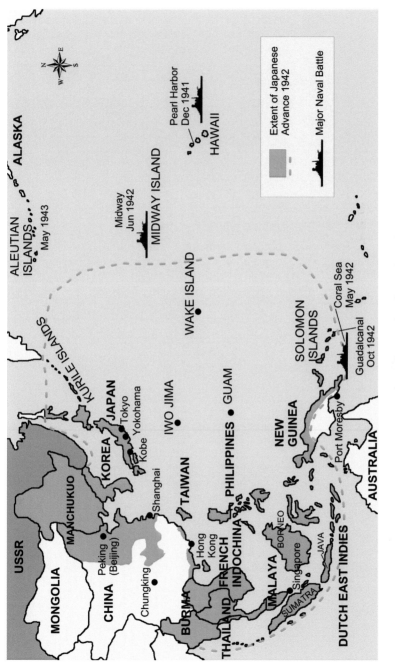

Map 20: The Aftermath of Pearl Harbor

Torpedoed Japanese destroyer *Yamakaze* sinking, photographed through the periscope of a US Navy submarine, 25 June 1942.

they put this experience to good use. In parallel with Pearl Harbor, they attacked several locations in the Pacific, including Hong Kong.

Thailand (1942)

At the beginning of the war in the Pacific, the Japanese put pressure on the Thais to allow the passage of Japanese troops on their way to invade both Malaya and Burma. This was not popular with many Thais, but their government thought it preferable to outright Japanese conquest. After Thailand agreed to let Japanese troops pass through the country, the Japanese then occupied Thailand, who later declared war on the Allies.

Malaya and Singapore (8 December 1941–15 February 1942)

On 8 December 1941, the Japanese attacked overland from French Indochina (which they had seized in July 1941) through Thailand and Burma. Two days later the Allied battleships HMS *Repulse* and HMS *Prince of Wales,* which had arrived to help, were attacked and sunk. The Japanese had 100,000 troops, 200 tanks and 550 aircraft; they were also reinforced by troops put ashore on the east coast of Malaya. They were faced with 92,000 troops from Britain, India, Australia and Malaya itself under the command of General Arthur Percival. However, these troops were poorly-equipped, having no tanks and few aircraft. The Allied forces had little experience of fighting in the climate of the Pacific equator. Poor reconnaissance meant they were burdened with unsuitable winter clothing and equipment while the Japanese were lightly dressed and equipped to enable them to move quickly (on bicycles where necessary).

By the end of January, the Japanese had seized many towns and villages in Malaya along with rich rubber plantations. Percival withdrew his forces to the city of Singapore. On 8 February 1942, the Japanese began an assault on the city, and on 15th Percival was forced to surrender. His 130,000 men experienced the first example of Japanese prisoner-of-war camps, where violence, cruelty, neglect and starvation were standard practice.

Borneo

Borneo, the largest island in the Pacific (it is eight times bigger than Ireland), had been under British and Dutch control since the mid–1800s. The British controlled the north (North Borneo, Sarawak and Brunei) while the Dutch controlled the south (part of the Dutch East Indies).

The Japanese invaded North Borneo and the Dutch East Indies on 11 January 1942. The big interest in North Borneo was the rich oil fields in Sarawak and Brunei. Despite these riches, there was virtually no defence and the Japanese took North Borneo after just eight days.

The Allies (mainly the Dutch) provided a much more vigorous defence in South Borneo, where the fighting continued throughout the month of December. However, the Japanese drove the Dutch and British back, taking the airfield at Kuching in the process. During the early months of 1942 the Allies took refuge in the tree-covered mountains before eventually surrendering on 1 April 1942.

The Philippines (mid-December 1941–6 May 1942)
The Philippine Islands were America's main base in the Pacific, having been colonised in 1898. In the 1930s the Filipinos developed their own army and, as war approached in December 1941, there were 110,000 Filipino and 30,000 US troops on the islands under the command of General Douglas MacArthur. They were supported by 300 outdated aircraft. On 9 December 1941 Japanese bombers attacked the airbase without warning and destroyed more than 100 aircraft on the ground.

The Allied troops now had little backup. The Japanese proceeded to effect landings on the main island of Luzon throughout December almost unopposed and around Christmas large-scale landings took place near the capital Manila. MacArthur's troops were no match for the Japanese air force and were driven back mercilessly. They were forced back onto the mountainous Bataan Peninsula. Fighting continued throughout March and April 1942, at which stage the Japanese had taken control of the entire island of Luzon. MacArthur was transferred to Australia in March to co-ordinate the Allies campaign in the Pacific and was replaced by General Jonathan M. Wainwright. Before he left, General MacArthur uttered the immortal words, *"I shall return,"* — a promise he was to keep!

Bataan Death March
The Japanese sent in additional troops and on 9 April the Americans surrendered the Philippines. The Japanese now had a problem of what to do with 60,000 American and Filipino POWs (prisoners of war). They decided to force-march them to Camp O'Donnell, one of their POW camps located eighty miles away. Without food or water, the march was characterised by physical abuse and murder inflicted by the Japanese soldiers. Several thousand prisoners died on the march, which was later judged by an Allied military commission to be a war crime by the Japanese. Fighting continued for a further month on the fortress island of Corregidor off Bataan, but on 6 May the remaining troops surrendered. The Japanese were now in total control of the Philippines.

Dutch East Indies (mid December 1941–9 March 1942)
The Dutch East Indies, known today as Indonesia, was always a primary target for the Japanese. The big attraction was oil, which the Japanese needed very badly. Also, the taking of the islands strategically brought the Japanese within 500 miles of Darwin on the Australian

mainland and at this stage no target was too big for 'the Prussians of the Pacific'!

The invasion of the islands of the Dutch East Indies — Sumatra, Java, Timor and Bali — took place between December 1941 and March 1942. The Dutch were assisted by their American, British and Australian Allies. The Japanese were well-prepared, and the invasion followed the now customary pattern: heavy air raids followed by well-protected seaborne landings.

The Japanese attacked from two locations. A western force attacked southwards from French Indochina, while the Eastern and Central forces sailed from the recently-occupied southern Philippines. Both forces were well-protected by both the Japanese navy and the Japanese air force. The invaders quickly seized airfields and oil wells.

In the Battle of the Java Sea, the Japanese navy sealed victory at the end of February. After this defeat, the position of the Allies became untenable and on 9 March they surrendered. The Japanese would remain in control of the Dutch East Indies until she surrendered at the end of the war in September 1945.

Now, with their fuel problem resolved, the Japanese navy could continue its Pacific campaign while its army was in a strong position to resume its continuing conflict with China.

Burma (February–May 1942)
Surrounded as it was by India, China and Thailand, Burma was a key country in East Asia in World War II. Overland supplies to China had to come through Burma. The only way Japan could attack India was through Burma.

Lack of roads in this inhospitable, mountainous, monsoon-ravaged country was a major problem. The **Burma Road** (717 miles long) between Lashio in Burma and Kunming in China was built in 1937/38 during the Second Sino-Japanese War. Goods en route to China had firstly to be transported by rail from Rangoon to Lashio.

The **Ledo Road** was built by the Americans between 1942 and 1944 connecting Ledo in India with the Burma Road. The name was later changed to Stilwell Road in honour of the American General Joseph Stilwell, who was responsible for building the road. There were mixed views on whether the road should have been built or not. It was over one thousand miles long and it tied up a huge amount of resources. Churchill described the project as *"an immense, laborious task, unlikely to be finished until the need for it had passed."* The alternative method of delivering goods from India to China was by air over the eastern end of the Himalayan Mountains known as 'The Hump'.

The **Burma Railway** — also known as the Death Railway — was built by Japan in 1943 to facilitate movement of her troops in World War II. It ran from Bangkok in Thailand to Rangoon in Burma. It was built by forced labour. 180,000 Asian labourers and 60,000 Allied POWs were used in its construction. The labourers were treated appallingly by the Japanese: 92,000 Asian labourers and 12,000 POWs died during the project, hence the name Death Railway.

Japan saw Burma (now known as Myanmar) as a back door entrance not only to China but also to India. While India had been seeking independence for some time (she was not successful until 1947), to lose India (the 'jewel in the British crown') in 1942 would have been a major disaster for Britain and her allies.

By the same token, Burma was essential to Japanese strategy. Control of the Burma Road would give them control over the sole overland route to China. It would also give them protection against any possible invasion by the Allied forces through India. Furthermore, Burma was rich in minerals, including rubber and oil.

After the fall of Malaya and Singapore, the Japanese campaign in Burma began in earnest. The Japanese were experienced fighters, with first-class air force backup. The Allies were a ragged assortment of troops from Britain, India, China and a token force of Americans. There were some Burmese troops, but whether they hated the Japanese more than they hated their colonial bosses — the British — was debatable. British General Bill Slim, who was one of the most highly-regarded generals in World War II, commanded the Allies. However, he was limited by the quality of the troops at his disposal.

The Japanese were much better geared than the Allies for the harsh environment: heat, humidity, flies, leeches, and the diseases of malaria and dysentery were the order of the day. There were few roads and only a single railway. The troops travelled mostly via the great rivers the Irrawaddy and the Sittang, while much of the fighting took place in dense jungle in monsoon conditions (monsoon rainfall was ten times heavier than rainfall in Europe).

From the start of the war in the Pacific in early 1942, the Allies were in retreat northwards from Rangoon. When the Japanese entered Rangoon on 8 March, the Allies had already evacuated. On 29 April the Japanese cut the Burma Road link: a big blow to China! In May, during the monsoon season, retreating British and Indian forces were driven as far as Imphal near the Indian border while the Chinese were forced northwards to their own border. While advancing northwards, the Japanese seized Mandalay, Burma's second city. That ended the war in Burma for the time being, resulting in the expulsion of British, Indian and Chinese forces from Burma.

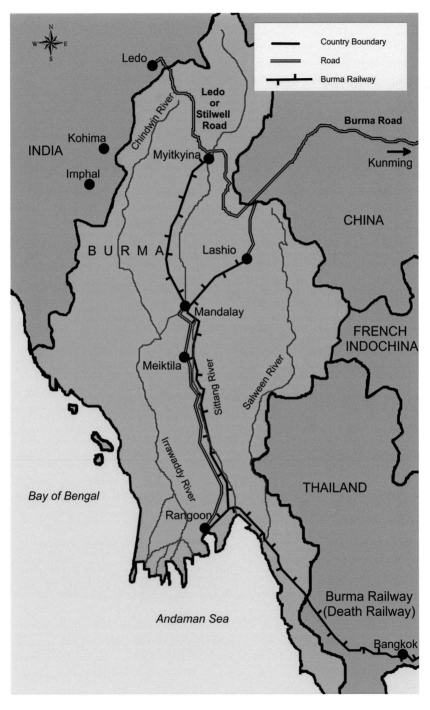

Map 21: Burma 1942–45

Japanese aircraft carrier *Hiryu* manoeuvring during a high-level
bombing attack by USAAF B-17 bombers during the
Battle of Midway, 4 June 1942.

India fought on both sides in the Burma campaign. The anti-British Indian National Army, led by Chandra Bose, fought on the side of the Japanese, but the majority of Indians fought on the side of the British in the belief that they would be granted independence after the war.

Australia (19 February 1942)
As a member of the Commonwealth, Australia more than played her part in both World War I (Gallipoli) and in World War II. As with many nations throughout the world, the Great Depression in the 1930s severely impacted on Australia. During the Depression years, Australia made little or no investment in her armed forces. As a result, she was not in any position to resist the Japanese when they attacked her northern coastal city Darwin in February 1942.

Concurrent to their invasion of the Dutch East Indies, the Japanese unleashed a Pearl Harbor-style attack on Darwin on 19 February 1942. 240 Japanese aircraft attacked ships and planes in Darwin's harbour and airfields in an attempt to prevent Allied forces using them as bases. Four of the Japanese aircraft carriers used at Pearl Harbor were used again at Darwin. The attack was a complete surprise. The Japanese inflicted heavy losses on the Allied forces at little cost to themselves. Many Allied ships and aircraft were destroyed and 250 men were lost.

Australia was now well and truly drawn into the war, and Prime Minister John Curtin immediately ordered Australian troops fighting in the Middle East to come home and defend their own country. He agreed, however, that Australian troops fighting in the Pacific would do so under the command of US Supreme Commander in the area, General MacArthur.

After the bombing, Darwin was abandoned as a base in favour of Port Moresby in Papua. The Australian New Guinea Administrative Unit was set up to run the territory for the duration of the war under the command of Major General Basil Morris. Port Moresby was gradually transformed into a large Allied base, with five operational airstrips; hospital and administrative buildings; fuel and logistical supplies.

Bombing of Tokyo (18 April 1942)
Japan's success in Asia and the Pacific between December 1941 and April 1942 was unprecedented. By April, having previously taken control of Manchukuo, Korea, Taiwan and French Indochina, they now added Hong Kong, Thailand, Malaya, Singapore, the Philippines, Borneo, Dutch East Indies and Burma. This unbelievable achievement in terms of speed and area covered was comparable only to the conquests of Nazi Germany in Europe in 1940. The remarkable success was achieved at a minimal cost. In four months Japan lost only 15,000 of her armed forces. Japan at this stage needed advice and

guidance, but politicians — as we understand them in the West — were non-existent in Japan.

Victory can also be addictive. Japan at this stage could have called a halt to her advances and concentrated on consolidation. But the adrenaline was flowing, and the more militant amongst the bellicose Japanese commanders set two more targets: firstly to drive Australia out of the war and secondly to score a deciding victory over the Americans in the Pacific. These targets would have to be achieved quickly before the US caught up with the Japanese in terms of numbers of aircraft carriers and of troops. At the same time, the perceived threat of invasion led to a major expansion of the Australian military.

Above all else at this stage, the Allies needed a morale boost. Under the command of General MacArthur and Admiral Chester Nimitz, the Americans decided to attack the Japanese where it hurt most: on their home ground. This audacious plan was the brainwave of Major General James Doolittle and became known as the **Doolittle Raid**. It took place on 18 April 1942. As the American bombers did not have the range to fly from an aircraft carrier located 400 miles from Japan and fly back again, their plan was to bomb Tokyo and then fly on to land in China, which was their ally. Fifteen of the sixteen bombers actually reached Japanese-occupied China, but the bomb damage was minimal. However the raid was a significant propaganda victory for the US, who delivered the clear message to the Japanese: we can reach you!

Battle of the Coral Sea (7–8 May 1942)
The first stage in Japan's plan to defeat Australia was to take the island of New Guinea. On 7 May she planned to attack Port Moresby, the island's capital. However, the American intelligence operation had cracked the Japanese naval code (just as the Allies cracked the German Enigma code in Europe) and knew the Japanese plan in advance. Admiral Nimitz sent two aircraft carriers with their compliment of 140 bombers to the battle site in the Coral Sea and surprised the Japanese. One American aircraft carrier was lost. However, the Japanese lost one aircraft carrier and a second was badly damaged. They also lost a considerable number of aircraft. The Japanese called off the planned attack on Port Moresby. The Australians were safe for the moment. The battle was unique in that it took place between two carrier-based air forces. It was also significant in that it was the first victory for the Allies in the Pacific. The fightback in the Pacific had begun!

The Marines
The American Marine Corps was initially formed at Guantanamo Bay in Cuba in 1911. It was reactivated in July 1914 to take part in World War I in France and reactivated again in 1940 to participate in the war in the Pacific in World War II.

The marines had a dual responsibility: to carry out amphibious assaults and to conduct subsequent land operations. During World War II, these responsibilities were ideally suited to the numerous islands of the Pacific Ocean. The marines were renowned for their courage and fighting ability.

Battle of Midway (4 June 1942)

Early in 1942, Japan planned to establish herself as the principal naval power in the Pacific. All she had to do was to drive the Americans completely from the area — easier said than done!

Midway Island, as the name suggests, is located midway between America and Asia in the central Pacific. The Japanese decided to seize the island and establish a base there, to give warning of any future attack on Japan by the US (they had learned a lesson from the Doolittle Raid).

The Japanese at this stage had developed the finest navy in the world.

General Yamamoto (the architect of the attack on Pearl Harbor) did not consider it necessary to use all of his resources at Midway Island. Four of his ten aircraft carriers were assigned to the battle, together with 600 aircraft and an array of battleships, cruisers and destroyers.

Admiral Nimitz's American forces consisted of three carriers, 230 planes and seventy-five assorted warships. Although heavily outnumbered, the Americans held one trump card: their decoders could tell them every move the Japanese planned!

Yamamoto tried to deflect America's attention by diverting some of his forces to the Aleutian Islands some distance away in the northern Pacific, but Nimitz remained focused on the job in hand. He decided not to get involved in a head-on confrontation; he attacked Japanese forces en route to Midway. However, he could not avoid the main battle on 4 June, when Japanese carrier-based aircraft attacked the island base, causing major damage. Many American ground-based bombers and fighters were destroyed both on the ground and in the air. Nimitz, however, was a shrewd tactician and he produced a masterstroke to decide the outcome of the battle. While the attention of the Japanese was focused on America's low-level torpedo bombers, Nimitz had assembled thirty-five Dauntless dive-bombers high up in the air, totally undetected by the Japanese!

When the order was given to attack, the dive-bombers wreaked havoc on the Japanese carrier fleet. Three of their four carriers — *Kaga, Akagi* and *Soryu* — were destroyed. Their fourth carrier *Hiryu* went on the attack with her Zero aircraft sinking one of the American carriers

USS *Yorktown*. The Americans got their revenge later in the day when they destroyed the *Hiryu*.

The outcome of the battle was a clear victory for the US. While the Americans lost one aircraft carrier and 150 aircraft, the Japanese lost four carriers and 330 aircraft. The victories at the Coral Sea and Midway proved to be the turning point of World War II in the Pacific.

As things turned out, the Battle of Midway proved to be the last great naval battle for two years.

The Battle of Guadalcanal

The Pacific Front was vast and in July 1942 Allied responsibilities for the area were divided between General MacArthur and Admiral Nimitz. MacArthur, with his headquarters in Australia, was given command of the south-west Pacific area. This included Australia itself, the Philippines, Dutch East Indies, New Guinea and the Solomon Islands.

Nimitz and his US Navy, who were strengthened by a new marine corps, were given a brief to control the southern Pacific area, that is, the southern sector of the biggest ocean in the world. On 2 July the Joint Chiefs of Staff set them both primary targets.

Nimitz's target was to take the island of Guadalcanal in the Solomon Islands, while MacArthur's target was first New Guinea, then New Britain en route to attacking the Japanese base at Rabaul.

The Japanese attacked first. Targeting the now major base of Port Moresby, they landed on the northern coast of New Guinea and got within thirty miles of the port before Australian and American forces drove them back. Fighting was intense, but the Allies continued to push the Japanese back until they eventually succumbed in January 1943. This marked a first victory on land for the Allies in the Pacific.

Meanwhile, the marines had landed on the island of Guadalcanal, one of the Solomon Islands, where they attacked an airstrip the Japanese were building. The airstrip became known as Henderson Field (Henderson was the name of an American soldier, who had died earlier in the war).

The fighting in Guadalcanal was ferocious, and the US troops and marines learned for the first time how difficult it was going to be to defeat the Japanese, who believed that "*to die fighting for your country is the honourable way to die*". Surrender was shameful and unacceptable!

The Japanese forces on Guadalcanal eventually succumbed in December 1942 after major losses. The tide had now turned in the Pacific!

The Sullivan Brothers

One of the great tragedies of the war was the deaths of the five Sullivan brothers from Waterloo, Iowa, in the US. George, Frank, Joe, Matt and Albert joined up in January 1942 with the stipulation that they serve together. However, as the Pals Battalions discovered in World War I, if you fight together, you may well die together. The five brothers died when their ship, the light cruiser USS *Juneau*, was sunk in the Battle of Guadalcanal in November 1942.

1942 TIMELINE — PACIFIC

02 Jan	Japan captures Manila.
07 Jan	Japan attacks Bataan in the Philippines.
11 Jan	Japan invades Dutch East Indies and Borneo.
16 Jan	Japan advances into Burma.
18 Jan	Japanese-German-Italian agreement signed in Berlin.
19 Jan	Japan takes North Borneo.
23 Jan	Japan takes Rabaul on New Britain.
30 Jan	The British withdraw into Singapore. The siege of Singapore then begins.
01 Feb	First US aircraft carrier offensive of the war as USS *Yorktown* and USS *Enterprise* establish bases in the Gilbert and Marshall Islands.
02 Feb	Japan invades Java.
08 Feb	Japan invades Singapore.
14 Feb	Japan invades Sumatra.
15 Feb	Britain surrenders Singapore.
19 Feb	Japanese air raid on Darwin, Australia.
22 Feb	President Franklin D. Roosevelt orders General MacArthur out of the Philippines to take command of the South West Pacific Theatre from Australia.
26 Feb	US aircraft carrier USS *Langley* sunk by Japanese bombers.
27 Feb	Japanese victorious in Battle of the Java Sea.
07 Mar	British evacuate Rangoon in Burma.
08 Mar	Dutch surrender on the island of Java. Japanese enter Rangoon.
09 Mar	Allies surrender in Battle of the Java Sea.
18 Mar	President Roosevelt appoints General MacArthur and Admiral Nimitz to take control of US forces in the Pacific.

03 Apr	Japan attacks US and Filipino troops at Bataan in the Philippines.
06 Apr	US troops arrive in Australia.
09 Apr	US forces on Bataan surrender to Japanese.
10 Apr	Bataan Death March begins.
18 Apr	Surprise Doolittle Air Raid on Tokyo by US.
29 Apr	Japanese cut the Burma Road link and take central Burma.
01 May	Japan takes Mandalay in Burma.
05 May	Japanese prepare to invade Midway and Aleutian Islands.
06 May	Japan takes island of Corregidor in the Philippines.
07/08 May	Japanese defeated in Battle of the Coral Sea.
12 May	The last US troops holding out in the Philippines surrender on Mindanao.
20 May	Japan completes defeat of Burma.
04/05 Jun	Key US victory in Battle of Midway.
07 Jun	Japan invades Aleutian Islands in northern Pacific.
21 Jul	Japanese land troops near Gona on New Guinea.
07 Aug	US marines invade Guadalcanal Island.
08 Aug	US marines take the unfinished airfield at Guadalcanal and name it Henderson Field.
08/09 Aug	Major defeat for US off Savo Island, north of Guadalcanal.
17 Aug	US marines attack Makin Atoll in Gilbert Islands.
21 Aug	US marines repulse first major Japanese ground attack on Guadalcanal.
24 Aug	US defeat Japan in the Battle of the Solomon Islands.
30 Aug	US troops invade Adak Island in the Aleutian Islands.
12–14 Sep	Battle of Bloody Ridge in Guadalcanal.
15 Sep	Japanese submarine attack on US warships near Solomon Islands.
27 Sep	British and Indian offensive in Burma.
11/12 Oct	Battle of Cape Esperance off Guadalcanal. US defeats Japan.
13 Oct	The first US Army troops land on Guadalcanal.
14–17 Oct	Japan bombards Henderson Field in Guadalcanal from warships.
26 Oct	Battle of Santa Cruz off Guadalcanal.
14/15 Nov	Further clashes off Guadalcanal between US and Japan, resulting in the deaths of the five Sullivan brothers.
23/24 Nov	Japanese air raid on Darwin, Australia.
02 Dec	Enrico Fermi conducts the world's first nuclear chain reaction test for the US.
20–24 Dec	Japanese air raids on Calcutta, India.
31 Dec	Emperor Hirohito of Japan gives his forces permission to withdraw from Guadalcanal.

CHAPTER 16

1943
The Tide Turns

WAR IN EUROPE 1943

Soviets begin offensive against Germany at Stalingrad: Germans surrender. Allies are victorious in North Africa. Invasion of Sicily/Italy begins. Italy changes sides in the war. Mussolini is sacked and later rescued by Germany. Conferences at Casablanca in January, and in Cairo (Pacific War) and Tehran, both in November.

NORTH AFRICA 1943

The Allies needed North Africa as a base from which to launch their fightback into Europe. Hitler and his Axis forces wanted control of it to prevent this happening. It was important enough in Hitler's plans for him to keep one of his best generals, Erwin Rommel, there for two years, when he could have been a major asset to Germany on the Russian front.

After the American and British forces invaded Morocco and Algeria towards the end of 1942, they were slow to organise themselves. For many of them, this was their first taste of desert warfare.

It was February 1943 before they were ready to move on Tunisia. In the meantime, Hitler had dispatched three divisions to join up with Rommel's forces, who had arrived in Tunisia from Tripoli at the end of January in remarkably good condition. The additional troops enabled Rommel to inflict a sharp defeat on the Americans at the Kasserine Pass in February. The Kasserine Pass was a gap in the Atlas Mountains in western Tunisia. This was Rommel's final battle in North Africa. The newly-arrived Americans suffered heavy casualties. Most of her troops were experiencing warfare for the first time. General George Patton was brought in by Eisenhower to take control of all American troops in North Africa. Patton requested that General Omar Bradley be appointed as his assistant.

Generals Patton and Bradley

Generals Patton and Bradley were two of America's top generals in World War II. The two were as different as chalk and cheese. Bradley was courteous, considerate and soft-spoken. Patton was flamboyant, outspoken and the ultimate loose cannon.

In one incident in Sicily on 22 July 1943, Patton shot two mules which were pulling a cart across a bridge that the Americans wanted to use. When the Sicilian owner objected, Patton attacked him with a walking stick. On another occasion in a field hospital in Nicosia on 3 August, Patton slapped two American soldiers who were suffering from battle fatigue and ordered them back to the war front. When Eisenhower became aware of the incident, he was furious and demoted Patton under Bradley. Both men were first-class army generals; Patton (nicknamed 'Old Blood and Guts'), in particular, liked to lead from the front. When Bradley was asked to serve under Patton in North Africa, he accepted but pointed out that his first loyalty was to Eisenhower.

Over the next few months in North Africa, the battle ebbed and flowed as Patton and Rommel sounded each other out. Tunis was rapidly becoming the 'meat in the sandwich' between American forces under Patton advancing from the west and British forces under Montgomery closing in from the east. Hitler, realising that all hope was lost in North Africa, recalled Rommel home to Germany in March. Axis forces began to withdraw in April. On 7 May 1943 Allied forces took the port city of Tunis and on 13 May the Germans surrendered. The war in North Africa, which had commenced in June 1940, was finally over. Hitler had suffered his first major defeat!

Casablanca Conference

Churchill and Roosevelt met in Casablanca in January 1943 to discuss strategy and plans to progress the war. Roosevelt (encouraged by Stalin) wanted to invade France across the English Channel: he believed that this would be the quickest way to Berlin. Churchill advised caution and reminded the American President of the ill-fated attempt at a Channel crossing to Dieppe the previous year. He pointed out that the Allied forces were nowhere near ready for a cross-channel invasion just yet.

A compromise agreement was reached. The Allies would invade Sicily, followed by Italy, and in this way attack the *"soft underbelly of Europe,"* as Churchill so delicately put it. If the Allies could take Italy, they would have direct access through Austria into Germany. Stalin did not attend the conference: he was too preoccupied with events in Stalingrad.

The main statement to emanate from the conference was the Casablanca Declaration, which stated that nothing short of *"unconditional surrender"* would be accepted from Germany and her allies at the end of the war.

ITALIAN CAMPAIGN 1943

At this stage in the war, it was obvious to most Italians that Mussolini's dream of a new Roman Empire around the Mediterranean was simply that: a dream! It was this dream that had tied up Rommel and German/Italian troops and armaments in North Africa for more than two years. Hitler must have reflected on many an occasion whether having Mussolini as an ally was a hindrance or a help!

Sicily

The invasion of Sicily (Operation Husky) began on 13 July when huge numbers of American and British troops invaded the island from North Africa. American forces under the command of General George Patton advanced up along the western side of the island, meeting stiff German resistance under Hermann Göring at Gela. Patton didn't dally — he simply skirted around the German defences. He was more interested in getting to the port of Messina (the gateway to Italy) before Montgomery. The city of Palermo was taken on 22 July, and from there the US troops headed for Messina and the Italian mainland. The Axis forces defending Sicily outnumbered the British and American Allies, but a large number of their troops were Italians, who at this stage had completely lost their appetite for war.

Meanwhile, Montgomery and his British forces had drawn the short straw. His brief was to advance up the much more difficult eastern coast of the island. He encountered a strong German defence led by Field Marshal Albert Kesselring along very mountainous terrain (including the volcanic Mount Etna). Tenacious German defences at Syracuse and Catania delayed Monty by several weeks and he did not reach Messina until 17 August, where the Americans had been patiently awaiting his arrival since the end of July. Operation Husky, which took place under a scorching summer sun, cost the lives of over 5,000 troops.

In early August, it was obvious to Kesselring that the island of Sicily was lost and, with Hitler's rare approval, the Germans evacuated Sicily on 11 and 12 August. For some reason, the Allies let them go unhindered even though they were retreating onto mainland Italy to set up defences to fight the Allies. German presence on the Italian mainland would continue until the end of the war in 1945.

War in Italy

Hitler, anticipating Italy's surrender, sent Rommel into northern Italy to organise the German defence of the region — in particular, to seal off the various Alpine mountain passes, including the Brenner Pass. The passes would have given the Allies access into Austria and then Germany.

Rommel was not left kicking his heels at Lake Garda for long. On 21 November 1943 Hitler moved Rommel to Normandy in France to supervise the preparation of defences against the long-anticipated Allied invasion. Kesselring was left in command of all German forces in Italy.

Mussolini's future was now in serious jeopardy. The Italian people had had enough of the war and Italian military officers had had enough of their arrogant Duce.

A meeting of the Fascist Grand Council was held on 24 July 1943 and Mussolini was voted out of office. King Victor Emmanuel III ordered his arrest. Marshal Pietro Badoglio was appointed head of a new Italian government. The Fascist regime that ruled Italy for twenty years was ended with the stroke of a pen!

Mussolini, now under arrest, was moved to an isolated mountain retreat at Gran Sasso in northern Italy. His location was an open secret, and on 8 September, on Hitler's instructions, he was rescued by a team of crack German paratroopers under Otto Skorzeny. With Mussolini gone, Italy surrendered to the Allies on 8 September in the hope of minimising war damage to her country, particularly Rome. Germany was left to defend Italy on her own!

Mussolini, now only a shadow of his former self, was moved by Hitler to Lake Garda in Lombardy, where he remained for two years. He was now merely a puppet of Hitler and spent most of his time with his mistress, Clara Petacci. While there, Hitler put pressure on him to execute some of the fascist leaders who had betrayed him at the last Fascist Grand Council meeting. One of those Mussolini executed was his son-in-law Galeazzo Ciano!

Bombing of Rome

In preparation for the arrival of her ground troops, the Allies bombed Rome on 19 July 1943 and again on 13 August. The following day, Rome was declared an open city by the Italians to prevent further bomb damage.

Italy surrendered to the Allies on 8 September. It was Germany who occupied Rome three days later and the occupation of Rome continued until June 1944. Vatican City, the headquarters of the Catholic Church,

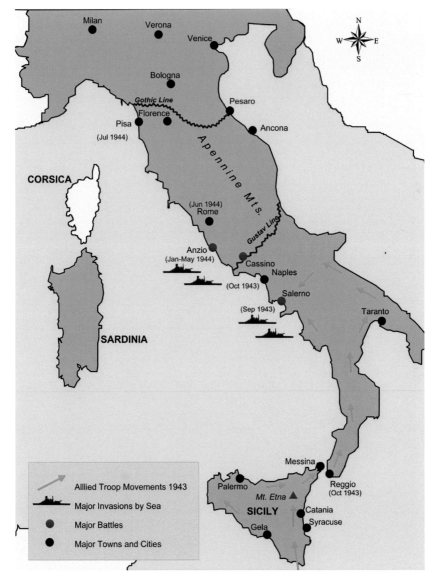

Map 22: Italian Campaign 1943–44

Suppression of Warsaw Ghetto Uprising — captured Jews are led by German Waffen-SS soldiers to the assembly point for deportation (Umschlagplatz), 1943.

is a small independent state located in Rome itself. Earlier in the year, Pope Pius XII had pleaded with President Roosevelt to avoid bombing the beautiful buildings of Vatican City and, probably as a result, little damage was done to the Vatican by the Allies.

Invasion of Italy

There was an inexplicable delay by the Allies invading Italy. The Germans had evacuated Sicily on 11 and 12 August without any intervention from the Allies. Montgomery's British forces did not reach Reggio (across the straits of Messina) until 3 September. Montgomery, whose brief was to take over the 'boot of Italy', then proceeded to lead his forces across the 'foot' of Italy and up along the east coast, taking control of the naval base at Taranto on the way.

This advance up the east coast took most of September, even though there was literally no opposition. Historians suggest that Montgomery's inability to get on with the American generals (Patton in Sicily and now Clark at Salerno) meant he did not give them the cooperation and support they expected and indeed were entitled to. Arrogance was not in short supply on either side!

The main invasion of Italy (Operation Avalanche) commenced on 9 September when American forces under US General Mark W. Clark landed at Salerno, south of Naples. The objective was to take the city of Naples. A huge Allied fleet comprising 700 ships of all sizes deposited 170,000 troops onto the beaches at Salerno. They encountered massive German resistance. Hitler was intent on preventing the Allied forces advancing northwards and, in particular, keeping airports controlled by the Allies as far from Germany as possible.

Such was the ferocity of the German resistance that Clark considered withdrawing his forces back out to sea again, but he was persuaded to persist. The Allies eventually succeeded in landing with major assistance from aircraft and battleships anchored offshore. The Americans suffered 12,000 casualties during the Avalanche campaign. They had expected to be in Naples by 12 September, but they did not reach the city until 1 October despite Montgomery's troops eventually coming to Clark's assistance. In anticipation of the arrival of the ground troops, Naples had been subjected to a major bombing raid on 4 August. Naples would become the most heavily-bombed Italian city in the war.

The Italian campaign over the next eighteen months was one of the toughest in the war. Kesserling was now in charge of the entire Italian operation and it was obvious at this stage that the Germans were going to resist all the way to the Austrian border. The Apennine Mountains are the spine of Italy and were a major obstacle for attacking forces.

The Germans built a series of strong mountain defensive systems from west coast to east coast across the Apennines similar to the Hindenburg Line in World War I. The most southerly of these was the Gustav Line, adjacent to the small monastery town of Cassino. The oncoming winter (which was very severe) and the Gustav Line put paid to any further advance by the Allies in Italy in 1943.

EASTERN FRONT 1943

The surrender of the Germans at Stalingrad was a grievous blow to Hitler. His 6th Army had been successful in the invasions of Belgium, France, Yugoslavia, Greece, Crete, and then in Operation Barbarossa up to the attack on Stalingrad. Now his 6th Army no longer existed.

Up until the surrender of the German forces at Stalingrad in January, the Russians had been fighting a defensive war. Now the tide had turned and they were in a position to attack westwards. To do so, they needed men and they needed arms. Manpower, and consequently soldier power, was never a problem in Russia. Now, after defeating the German army at Stalingrad, their confidence was high.

The factories that Stalin had moved behind the Ural Mountains in 1941 were now churning out armaments in unbelievable numbers. By the summer of 1943 Russia was producing 500 tanks and 750 aircraft every week! She quickly achieved superiority in quantities of arms and numbers of troops, which enabled her to drive the Germans back westwards. Soviet troops retook Kursk on 8 February, followed by Kharkov on 16 February.

Hitler had learned a lesson at Stalingrad. Until then, he had never allowed his troops to retreat. General Paulus had to disobey him to try to save the lives of his men by surrendering at Stalingrad. In March 1943, however, Hitler gave Manstein permission to retreat his forces from the Caucasus to avoid being trapped by the advancing Russians. He also permitted Manstein to lead the German troops in the Battle of Kharkov without any interference.

The outcome was startling and showed that the Germans were far from beaten. While they were outnumbered in terms of men and arms, their training and tactical leadership were far superior to that of the Russians. Manstein, supposedly in retreat, turned his troops around, attacked the Russians and retook Kharkov. With considerable help from a revitalised Luftwaffe, Manstein's German troops annihilated four Russian tank corps. Stalin was taken aback. He assumed he had the German army on the run, but now he had to think again!

As the spring thaw made roads impassable, there was a resulting lull in the war, which gave both sides the opportunity to regroup.

Yugoslavia

Throughout 1942 and 1943 Tito's Partisan forces resisted the Nazi invaders and Tito was given the title President of the National Committee of Liberation. At the Tehran conference in November 1943, Roosevelt, Stalin and Churchill — together with King Peter II of Yugoslavia and his government in exile — officially recognised Tito and his Partisans.

Warsaw Ghetto

The remainder of the Polish Jews living in Warsaw lived in the Warsaw Ghetto.

Warsaw Ghetto

A Ghetto was a small, confined, fenced-off area where Jews were forced to live. The areas were completely overcrowded; lacked cover and sanitation; and the food rations meted out by the Germans were totally inadequate to keep a person alive. In 1942, 300,000 Jews living in the Warsaw Ghetto were moved with great brutality to the concentration camp at Treblinka and by January 1943 only 60,000 remained in the Ghetto. Himmler ordered the liquidation of the Ghetto. Polish resistance fighters within the Ghetto decided they were going to resist further movement by whatever means they could. When German troops arrived to evacuate the Ghetto on 19 April, they were met with machine gun fire, grenades and Molotov cocktails (smuggled in to them by comrades outside). Small groups of fighters, both men and women, fought the Nazis bitterly. They knew they were going to die, but to die fighting for your country was infinitely more acceptable than starving to death in Treblinka. Just as in Stalingrad, the Germans had to search out the fighters building-by-building. By mid-May, they had all been found and sent to Treblinka for immediate extermination. 14,000 Jews were murdered in the operation!

WAR IN THE AIR 1943

At the Casablanca Conference in January 1943, Churchill and Roosevelt agreed to increase the bombing campaign on Germany. The RAF and the American air force planned to attack Germany's military bases by day and her major industrial cities at night. This had a hugely demoralising effect on the German people, who were now becoming aware that things were not as rosy as Hitler led them to believe. It also meant that Hitler had to divert forces from the war fronts to defend the homeland. As happened in Britain during the Blitz, children in Germany were evacuated to safer rural areas.

A series of bombing campaigns by the Allies commenced with the bombing of dams in the Ruhr Valley (17 May) *[more details in the box below]*, Dortmund (24 May) and Cologne (28 June) 1943.

However, these paled into insignificance when compared with the firebombing of Hamburg which commenced on 24 July and lasted a week. The bombing resulted in the deaths of 45,000 people (mostly civilians) and the devastation of ten square miles of the city.

Firestorm

A firestorm is a fire that attains such intensity that it creates its own wind system. In war, it is initiated by a bomb filled with incendiary jelly. An updraft fed by strong perimeter winds makes it a deadly weapon. Major firebombings occurred later in the war at Dresden (25,000 dead), Tokyo (100,000 dead), and Hiroshima, where it was not possible to separate the deaths from those caused by the atomic bomb.

During the second half of 1943 the German air defences were considerably improved, resulting in greater losses of Allied aircraft, and daylight bombing was temporarily suspended.

The Dambusters

The Dambusters was the name given to the RAF bombers, led by Guy Gibson, who attacked dams in the Ruhr Valley using 'bouncing bombs' that skimmed across the surface of the water before hitting the dam and exploding. Apart from the operation being a propaganda coup, the bouncing bombs were only moderately successful. Some dams were breached with consequential flooding, but only nine out of nineteen bombers returned to base. The remainder either crashed or were shot down.

WAR AT SEA 1943

The war at sea is generally referred to as the Battle of the Atlantic. After losing the *Bismarck* in 1941, the Germans confined their war at sea to attacking Allied shipping using their U-boats only. Between 1941 and 1943 the U-boats were so successful at sinking Allied merchant shipping that they came close to winning the Battle of the Atlantic.

Allied merchant shipping at this stage travelled in convoys escorted by warships. The U-boats also traveled in convoys, known as Wolf Packs. The Wolf Packs attacked mainly at night!

There were big developments in the technology of detecting and destroying submarines during this period. ASDIC was a detection device that located U-boats by bouncing sound waves off their hulls. When a U-boat was detected, warships dropped depth charges to bomb them under water! The ASDIC technology hugely increased the danger to submarines.

Crewmen on both warships and submarines lived in constant fear for their lives. More than 30,000 British seamen lost their lives in the Battle of the Atlantic!

Code Breakers
It is a big advantage in any war to know what your enemy is doing. Bletchley Park in England was the base for Allied code-breaking during World War II. Thousands of people were employed there. German forces used a code called the Enigma code to communicate with one another. Those employed at Bletchley Park had the job of cracking the German code and, as a result, keeping the Allies informed of German movements throughout the war. They were hugely successful. During the latter half of the war, the Allies were fully aware of all German plans and movements, which was a major help in winning the war.

In the Pacific the Americans were successful in cracking Japanese naval codes. In 1943 knowledge of Japanese movements enabled American aircraft fighters to shoot down Admiral Yamamoto, architect of Pearl Harbor and head of the Japanese navy. This was a major coup for the Allies!

EASTERN FRONT 1943 (CONT.)

Battle of Kursk
Hitler still believed he could smash the Soviets before he would be faced with war on his Western Front, where the expected attack would come either through France or Italy. In consultation with his generals, he decided that the next big battle would be in the Kursk salient.

Centred on the town of Kursk, the salient (bulge) was about 200 kilometres wide at the base and projected 150 kilometres into German lines. The idea was to attack at the pincer points, gradually closing up the pincer, trapping the Russians inside! Kursk was to be the location for the greatest tank battle in history, with the sides being led by two of the most successful generals in the war: Zhukov for the Red Army and Manstein for the Nazis.

Stalin was aware of Hitler's battle plans. Some historians suggest that the information might have come from members of the German High Command, who wished to see the end of the war.

Neither Hitler nor Stalin was in a hurry. Every month that Stalin waited meant a large increase in the number of tanks and aircraft at his disposal. He set about building a deep ground defensive system similar to the German Siegfried Line in World War I. To do this, he brought in 30,000 civilians (men and women) to dig trenches and ditches by hand.

Hitler, meanwhile, was awaiting the delivery of his new Panther tank to supplement his Tiger tanks (German tanks were now named after beasts of prey). However, the Russian T-34 tank was emerging as the finest tank in the war. A rugged tank, it was highly mobile with wide tracks; it could travel on snow or soft ground; and shells bounced off the sloping front armour.

On paper, the Germans had no chance: they were outnumbered 1.9 to 0.9 million men, 5,000 to 3,000 tanks, 2,800 to 2,100 aircraft, and 25,000 to 10,000 guns and mortars.

Zhukov's strategy for the battle was to soak up the German assault for a number of days before launching the Soviet counter-attack.

The battle began when Germany attacked on 5 July, quickly falling foul of the intricate Russian trench defensive system. Much of the fighting was concentrated around the town of Prokhorovka. Little advance had been made by Manstein during the first week and on 12 July Zhukov began his counter-attack. For three days from 12 to 15 July the extraordinary Battle of Kursk raged, involving up to 7,000 tanks between both sides. The tanks moved around the battle site like an army of ants, destroying any enemy tank they could get their sights on.

Sheer weight of numbers won the day for the Russians, even though their casualty list was far greater than the Germans'. When the smoke cleared, the casualties on both sides were huge: Russia suffered 850,000 casualties to Germany's 200,000, they lost 4,000 tanks to 750 German tanks and 1,600 aircraft to 750 German aircraft. However, the tactical ability, discipline and training of the German army simply could not match the Russian numbers. When the battle was over on 15 July, the battle site was like a desert, littered with the remains of tanks and aircraft. The sorry sight was reminiscent of Passchendaele in World War I.

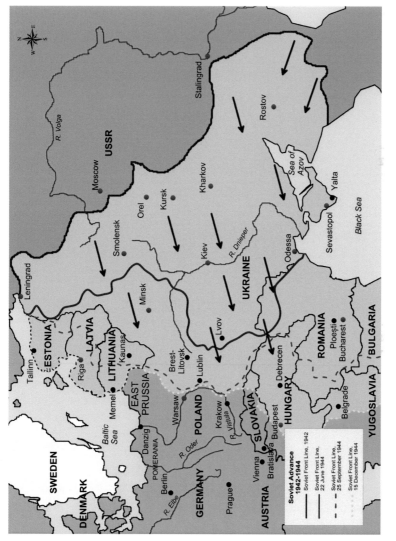

Map 23: Soviet Advance on Germany 1942–44

Crash landing of F6F on flight deck of USS *Enterprise* while en route to attack Makin Island. Lt. Walter Chewning, catapult officer, is clambering up the side of the plane to assist pilot Ens. Byron Johnson from the flaming cockpit, November 1943.

The Russians were now on a roll, heading westwards through Ukraine. Before the end of 1943, they had retaken Orel, Kharkov, Smolensk and finally Kiev.

At the end of 1943, the outlook for Hitler and his Nazi army was grim. Germany had been driven out of North Africa, Sicily and southern Italy. Hitler had lost Italy as an ally; the latter was now an ally of the Allied forces.

The Battle of the Atlantic was over and Germany had lost eighty per cent of her submarine fleet. Germany and the German people had suffered severe bombing. On the Eastern Front, Ukraine and vast tracts of Russian territory had been lost, back to the Russians.

On the Western Front, the Allies were making preparations to invade northern France. Apart from continuing to build the Atlantic Wall, there was nothing Hitler could do to prevent such an invasion.

CONFERENCES 1943

Tehran Conference
The last major event of 1943 was the meeting at Tehran between the Big Three: Roosevelt, Churchill and Stalin.

Any time a conference was planned, Stalin insisted it be held on or near Russian territory. His bully-boy tactics took no account of the travel difficulties experienced by wheelchair-bound Roosevelt, whose health was now deteriorating. Stalin also refused to travel by air, fearing sabotage. Stalin finally agreed to compromise with a meeting in Tehran at the Soviet Embassy.

The conference commenced on 28 November. Stalin arrived in good time to welcome Roosevelt — the first time the two had met face-to-face.

The main decisions at the conference were:
1. Agreement on Operation Overlord: the cross-channel invasion of northern France which would take place in May 1944.
2. Agreement on new boundaries for Poland: her eastern boundary with Russia to be pushed back to the Curzon Line. This meant ceding a large chunk of east Poland to Russia. Poland could be compensated with German territories on her western flank.

The **Cairo Conference** (22–26 November) to discuss the war in the Pacific was held a few days before the Tehran conference.

The Cairo Declaration stated that the three great powers (America, Britain and China) were fighting the war to restrain and punish the aggression of Japan; that they coveted no gain for themselves! A resolution was passed that, when the war was over, Japan would be compelled to return all territories seized by them in Asia and the Pacific since the beginning of World War I in 1914.

The Big Three
The various conferences held in 1943 — Casablanca in January, and both Cairo and Tehran in November — established the strategies of the Allied forces to end the war. The Cairo Conference was to deal specifically with the war in the Pacific and, since Russia was not as yet involved in the Pacific, Stalin did not attend. Nor did he consider it worthwhile to attend at Casablanca.

At Tehran, however, he was forthright in his opinion. He wanted a 'second front' opened up in Europe against the Nazis, and he wanted it without further delay. He also wanted Roosevelt and Churchill to acknowledge that the new boundaries Russia had established (particularly in Poland) since the commencement of the war would be accepted when the war was over. He was in a very strong position to argue, having just won a major victory at the Battle of Kursk. This position of strength now meant that neither Roosevelt nor Churchill dared criticise him, even as the horrors of the Katyn Forest massacre (perpetrated by Stalin at the start of the war) began to unfold. They needed him and he knew it!

Roosevelt's home was not in Europe, so he was not too worried about European boundaries. He was, however, very worried about Stalin's communism, but there was nothing he could do about that at the time. Roosevelt's one big aim in 1943 was to bring both wars (Europe and the Pacific) to a successful conclusion so that he could return home to a peaceful retirement. Unfortunately, this did not happen as he died in early 1945, just before the war ended. He did, however, build a working relationship with Stalin to bring both wars to a close.

Churchill at this stage had become the junior partner of the Big Three. He had more than played his part in the Battle of Britain in 1940, when his extraordinary courage and leadership were instrumental in denying Hitler the island of Britain. Now, however, the Americans had arrived in numbers and Churchill was forced to take a back seat. He kept trying to defer the Normandy Invasion, but both Roosevelt and, particularly, Stalin kept the pressure on. Churchill's salutary experience of maritime invasions at Dieppe and in Italy left him with a distinct lack of confidence regarding the planned invasion of Normandy.

Roosevelt did not have a great regard for Britain. Down through the centuries, Britain had built up an empire around the world, which was the very thing the Allies were now trying to prevent Hitler doing. One had to question whether the real reason Britain got involved in the war was the preservation of the British Empire. Regardless of his personal relationship with Churchill, it was clear to Roosevelt where his priorities lay.

1943 TIMELINE — EUROPE

02 Jan	Germans begin a withdrawal from the Caucasus.
10 Jan	Soviets begin an offensive against the Germans in Stalingrad.
14 Jan	Casablanca Conference begins between Churchill and Roosevelt.
23 Jan	Montgomery's Eighth Army takes Tripoli.
27 Jan	US bombing raid on Wilhelmshaven in Germany.
02 Feb	Germans surrender to Soviets at Stalingrad.
08 Feb	Soviet troops take Kursk.
14–25 Feb	Battle of Kasserine Pass between American troops and German panzers in North Africa.
16 Feb	Soviets retake Kharkov, a big industrial base in Ukraine.
18 Feb	Nazis arrest White Rose resistance leaders in Munich.
02 Mar	Germans begin to withdraw from Tunisia.
15 Mar	Germans recapture Kharkov.
16–20 Mar	German U-boats sink twenty-seven merchant ships in Battle of Atlantic.
06 Apr	Axis forces in Tunisia begin to withdraw.
19 Apr	Nazi SS attack Jewish resistance in the Warsaw Ghetto.
07 May	Allies take the port city of Tunis.
13 May	German and Italian troops surrender to end war in North Africa.
16 May	Jewish resistance in the Warsaw Ghetto ends.
16/17 May	British Dambusters air raid on the Ruhr.
22 May	Dönitz suspends German U-boat operations in North Atlantic.
11 Jun	Himmler orders liquidation of all Jewish ghettos in Poland.
05 Jul	Germany begins final offensive against Kursk.
09/10 Jul	Allies land in Sicily beginning the Invasion of Italy.
19 Jul	Allies bomb Rome.
22 Jul	Americans capture Palermo in Sicily.
24 Jul	British bombing raid on Hamburg.
24/25 Jul	Mussolini sacked and Italian Fascist government falls.
28 Jul	Allied air raid causes firestorm in Hamburg.
12–17 Aug	Germans evacuate Sicily.
17 Aug	US air raids in Germany.
	Montgomery's troops reach Messina.

23 Aug	Soviet troops recapture Kharkov.
08 Sep	Italy surrenders to the Allies.
09 Sep	Allied landings in Salerno and Taranto in Italy.
11 Sep	Germans occupy Rome.
12 Sep	Germans rescue Mussolini.
01 Oct	Allies enter Naples.
13 Oct	Italy declares war on Germany.
06 Nov	Soviets recapture Kiev.
18 Nov	Major British air raid on Berlin.
21 Nov	Hitler moves Rommel to Normandy.
22–26 Nov	Cairo Conference (Pacific War).
28 Nov	Roosevelt, Churchill and Stalin meet at Tehran Conference.
24–26 Dec	Soviets launch offensives on the Ukrainian front.

WAR IN THE PACIFIC 1943

Japanese evacuate Guadalcanal. Admiral Yamamoto is shot down. US troops under MacArthur head for Philippines, taking New Guinea and remainder of Solomon Islands en route. US Navy under Nimitz head for Japan via the Gilbert Islands. Mountbatten is appointed Supreme Commander of Southeast Asia with command of British, American, Indian and Chinese troops.

The Americans finally brought an end to the fighting on Guadalcanal when they drove the Japanese off the island in February 1943 after several months of the most intense fighting. Losses were severe, particularly on the Japanese side, not only from the fighting but also from the tropical diseases of dysentery and malaria. The Japanese withdrew to the nearby island of Bougainville.

The Japanese suffered a further setback in April when they lost Admiral Yamamoto, architect of Pearl Harbor and head of the Japanese navy.

US code breakers were tracking Yamomoto's movements when they established that he was flying from Rabaul to Bougainville. The Admiral's plane was shot down and Yamamoto was killed. His death was a big boost for the Americans and a huge setback for the Japanese navy!

The lull in fighting up to the summer months gave the US a welcome opportunity to regroup. Over a two-year period, they concentrated their huge industrial potential at home on the manufacture of ships, tanks and planes. They increased their forces immeasurably in strength and in numbers, similar to the Russians on the Eastern Front. One lesson they had learned from Pearl Harbor was that Japanese torpedoes were more efficient than their own, and this was one of the problems they addressed during the lull period.

In mid-summer, they proceeded to advance towards Japan by different routes. The army, under General MacArthur, headed for the Philippines (MacArthur particularly wanted to keep his idealistic *"I shall return"* promise!) On their way, they planned to take New Guinea and the remainder of the Solomon Islands.

The marines, under Admiral Nimitz, set their sights on faraway Japan, directly to the north across the vast mid-Pacific. They agreed in advance a policy of leapfrogging or 'island hopping'. Instead of getting tied down by every centre of resistance, they would isolate and bypass many islands, which could be dealt with later by air and sea assault. Directly in their path lay the Gilbert Islands, Marshall Islands, Caroline Islands and Mariana Islands. However, before they moved in on these islands, they chose to isolate the main Japanese base at Rabaul in the Solomon Islands. To achieve this, they blocked all supplies and communication to the base. Truk and Formosa were similarly placed under siege at a later stage.

The marines attacked the Gilbert Islands in November 1943. The American navy had now been built into a formidable fighting force, with its Fifth Fleet commanding twelve battleships and nineteen aircraft carriers (she started the war with three carriers). Japan was not in any position to fight such an overpowering navy. However, once troops landed, they were met with the usual suicidal Japanese fighting force. An example of this was the island of Tarawa in the Gilbert Islands in November. Here the marines suffered 3,500 casualties overcoming the 4,500-strong Japanese garrison. Only a handful of Japanese survived 'Bloody Tarawa'. The heavy losses by the US were partly due to landing craft getting stuck on a reef and the marines having to wade ashore. They were easy targets. After this, they took particular note of the tides when planning an island invasion.

Burma
British/Indian forces attempted limited counter-attacks against the Japanese in Burma in early 1943, during which a raid mounted by Chindits under Brigadier Orde Wingate suffered heavy losses. The Chindits were a British/Indian special force set up by Wingate to operate behind enemy lines in Burma and India in 1943 and 1944 using guerrilla tactics.

In August 1943 the Allies formed a new Southeast Asia Command, consisting of British, American, Chinese and Indian troops to take over strategic responsibilities for Burma and India. In October Churchill appointed Admiral Lord Louis Mountbatten as its Supreme Commander. Under British General Bill Slim, training and morale greatly improved. American General Joseph Stilwell, who was deputy commander to Mountbatten, commanded the US forces in the Burma-India-China zone.

1943 TIMELINE — PACIFIC

02 Jan	Allies take Buna in New Guinea.
22 Jan	Allies defeat Japanese at Sanananda on New Guinea.
01 Feb	Japanese begin evacuation of Guadalcanal.
08 Feb	British/Indian forces begin guerrilla operations against Japanese in Burma.
09 Feb	Japanese resistance on Guadalcanal ends.
02–04 Mar	US defeats Japan in the Battle of the Bismarck Sea.
18 Apr	Japanese Admiral Yamamoto shot down and killed.
10 May	US troops invade Attu in the Aleutian Islands.
31 May	Japanese end their occupation of the Aleutian Islands.
01 Jun	US begins submarine warfare against Japanese shipping.
21 Jun	Allies advance to New Georgia, Solomon Islands.
08 Jul	Allied bombers bomb Japanese on Wake Island.
01 Aug	Group of US PT-boats block Japanese convoy in the Solomon Islands. PT-109, commanded by Lieutenant John F. Kennedy rammed and sunk.
06/07 Aug	Battle of Vella Gulf in the Solomon Islands.
25 Aug	Allies complete occupation of New Georgia.
04 Sep	Allies recapture Salamaua-Lae, New Guinea.
07 Oct	Japanese execute 100 POWs on Wake Island.
26 Oct	Emperor Hirohito admits his country's situation is *very grave*.
01 Nov	US marines invade Bougainville in the Solomon Islands.
20 Nov	US troops invade Tarawa in the Gilbert Islands.
22 Nov	Cairo conference between Roosevelt, Churchill and Chiang Kai-shek.
15 Dec	US troops land in New Britain on the Solomon Islands.
26 Dec	Full Allied assault on New Britain by US marines.

CHAPTER 17

1944
D-Day and A Critical Victory in Normandy; Japan Suffers Naval Setbacks in the Pacific

WAR IN EUROPE 1944

Italian campaign continues. Allies land at Anzio. Rome is taken. Monte Cassino is bombed. Successful invasion of Normandy on D-Day. Paris is liberated. Russia continues to drive westward. Unsuccessful attempt on Hitler's life. Rommel dies at the behest of Hitler.

ITALIAN CAMPAIGN 1944

At the beginning of 1944, Montgomery was withdrawn from Italy to prepare for the Normandy landings. General Alexander was placed in charge of the reduced British forces in Italy with General Mark W. Clark controlling the American and Canadian forces.

Clark was tasked with breaking through the Gustav Line at Monte Cassino. The Allies' plan was to leapfrog the Gustav Line and get behind the Germans by attacking Anzio from the sea. Kesselring had anticipated the attack, and when it came on 22 January the Germans were waiting. The clever field marshal reported the attack as *"the expected Allied invasion of western Europe"*. Hitler immediately diverted reinforcements from France, which was exactly what Kesselring had hoped. This left Kesselring in a very strong position at both Anzio and Cassino.

The landing at Anzio took place on 22 January 1944. The Allies established a beachhead, but no breakout occurred until 23 May, four months later. There were two reasons for the delay: firstly the reluctance of American General John P. Lucas to attempt a breakout (his troops were gradually being weakened by Allied forces being moved to Normandy), and secondly the strength of Kesselring's German forces. When the Americans hit the beaches at Anzio, instead of advancing, they dug in — shades of Gallipoli in World War I. It took four major offensives between January and May for the Allied forces to achieve a breakout, which was eventually secured with the help of 'freedom fighters' from both Poland and French Morocco, plus a huge barrage from American battleships.

With the American forces pinned down at Anzio, the Canadian forces endured the toughest German opposition in the war and suffered major losses. They were due to be rewarded by capturing Rome, which was vacated by the Germans on 3 June 1944 and declared an open city. However, American General Mark W. Clark, whose orders were to continue driving the Germans northward, stole their thunder. Against orders, he advanced into Rome on 4 June after the breakout from Anzio. Instead of being sent home for insubordination, Clark was feted back in the US as the 'Liberator of the Eternal City'! The Germans were not defeated: Clark simply allowed them to retreat northwards to fight another day, while he basked in the glory of Rome.

Surprisingly, Hitler did not order the destruction of Rome, as he subsequently did with Paris two months later.

Massacre at the Ardeatine Caves

Postwar history disclosed the massacre at the Ardeatine Caves in Rome on 24 March when 335 Italian civilians were killed in retaliation for a Partisan attack that killed thirty-three German soldiers. Hitler ordered that ten Partisans be killed for every German. The SS officer in charge of the operation, Erich Priebke, fled to Argentina after the war where he lived for fifty years. He was extradited in 1994 and sentenced to life imprisonment. He spent the rest of his life under house arrest, dying in 2013 at the age of 100.

Monte Cassino

The mountaintop Benedictine monastery was a key observation point on the Gustav Line near the town of Cassino. In the belief that the Germans had occupied the monastery, British and American bombers dropped 1,400 tons of bombs on the monastery on 15 February 1944, reducing it to a heap of rubble. Several hundred civilians who had sought refuge in the monastery were killed. The bombing can only be described as wanton destruction and it was not an event that the Allies could be proud of. Many years later it was acknowledged that the Germans had not, in fact, occupied the monastery before it was bombed. Immediately after the bombing, the Germans occupied the cellars of the monastery, which had suffered little damage and served as a base for guerrilla warfare by the Germans until they were dislodged in mid-May. The monastery at Monte Cassino was rebuilt after the war.

During July and August 1944, the Germans retreated back to the Gothic Line, which ran north of Pisa and Florence to Pesaro on the Adriatic Sea and was almost impregnable. The Italian campaign was losing its momentum due to the demands for both Allied and Axis troops in Normandy. Kesselring successfully halted the dwindling Allied forces at the Gothic Line in the autumn of 1944. One of the casualties was Kesselring himself, who suffered serious head injuries when his car crashed into an artillery vehicle. He did not return to his command until January 1945, at which stage Hitler's forces were in dire need of assistance.

The Italian campaign stagnated at this stage, but did not finally come to an end until the war ended in May 1945.

D-DAY AND THE INVASION OF NORMANDY

Overview of Situation
Army chiefs on both sides were aware as early as 1941 that an invasion into northern France would occur sooner or later. Stalin wanted it to be sooner to take pressure off Russia on the Eastern Front. Roosevelt agreed with him, but Churchill preached caution. Churchill had good reason to be cautious. He had vivid memories of Gallipoli in World War I and knew how difficult an amphibious landing could be against a well dug-in defence. And the Germans were indeed well dug in!

Ever since his hugely-successful invasion of France and other countries in 1940, Hitler had the Todt Organisation (which built the Siegfried Line between Germany and France) design and build the Atlantic Wall, which stretched from Norway down to Spain. It consisted of a series of concrete bunkers, pillboxes, trenches and minefields along the Atlantic coast, mostly built by forced labour from occupied countries, which would make an invasion by sea very difficult indeed. (Some fine examples of pillboxes can still be seen in Denmark, Belgium, the Channel Islands and, of course, in France.)

When Rommel arrived in Normandy early in 1944, he concluded that the coastal defences were inadequate and he immediately set about strengthening them. Under his direction, a string of additional reinforced-concrete constructions were built along the beaches to house machine guns, anti-tank guns and light artillery. He built a series of obstructions on the beaches themselves, which resulted in the invasion plans being changed from high tide to low tide. He also planted minefields and barbed-wire defences both on the beaches and inland. The Atlantic Wall at this stage was formidable.

A further reason for Churchill's caution was the defeat the Allies had experienced at Dieppe in 1942, when a small invasion was attempted, but which was quickly put down by the Germans, with the loss of 5,000 Canadian soldiers and ninety aircraft! The Allies had also had more recent experiences at Salerno and Anzio, neither of which did anything to inspire confidence!

The message from Churchill was clear: an invasion should only be attempted when they were one hundred and ten per cent ready to do so! However, Churchill could not stall forever, and the invasion (Operation Overlord) was finally set for June 1944.

In the meantime, the Allies kept the Germans occupied by carrying out a substantial daylight bombing raid on Berlin on 4 March.

Options for Landings
The Allies had a major decision to make. Where would the landing take place? There were two options: Calais, where the English Channel was at its narrowest, or Normandy, where there was much more room at sea for the 7,000 ships the invading forces planned to use. There was one major problem with Normandy apart from the width of the Channel crossing: there were no harbours.

However, necessity is the mother of invention and nowhere is this more true than in wartime. The Allies designed the Mulberry Harbours, a series of interlocking reinforced concrete tanks cast in Britain, floated across the Channel and sunk into their final position on the Normandy coast.

With this problem solved, the decision was made: the landing would be in Normandy, but the preparations would include Calais, where additional intense activity might deceive the Germans into thinking that Calais was to be the landing point. A huge fleet of camouflaged tanks was assembled near Dover facing Calais. The Germans were not aware that the tanks were dummy inflatables! The deception worked so well that Hitler believed the Allies plan was an invasion across the Strait of Dover by a fictitious First United States Army Group commanded by General George Patton (back in favour once more). The presence of Patton (the Germans had experience of him in North Africa and Sicily) in Dover gave added credence to the belief that the Normandy landings were a diversionary tactic. Hitler was so convinced that he refused to move his forces from Calais to Normandy for two weeks after the actual landing had occurred.

Allied Command Structure
The American General Dwight D. Eisenhower was to be overall commander with British General Bernard Montgomery as commander of all ground forces. The American troops would be commanded by

General Omar Bradley. Eisenhower was chosen as much for his diplomatic skills as his decisiveness. Previous experience of American and British forces working together in World War I and in North Africa in World War II was not good, and Roosevelt and Churchill agreed that Eisenhower was the man to marry the two forces. Montgomery was renowned for his meticulous attention to detail and his popularity. He had extensive experience in North Africa where, at El Alamein, he had inflicted a rare defeat on Rommel.

German Command Structure

Field Marshal Gerd von Rundstedt was called back from his retirement (he was 69 years of age) to take overall command of the German forces in Normandy, much to Rommel's displeasure. Rommel and Rundstedt did not agree on strategy. Rommel wanted to attack the Allies on the beaches as they came ashore, whereas Rundstedt believed that they should gather their panzer formations back at his headquarters near Paris and attack on land they were familiar with. The disagreement was referred to Hitler. As usual, Hitler would not make a definitive decision.

Hitler's total army at this stage was 285 divisions, but — with 165 of these engaged on the Eastern Front against Russia and a huge number engaged on coastal defence duties (the entire Atlantic Wall) on the Western Front — only ten of the panzer divisions were available to defend Normandy. Three of the panzer units were allocated to Rommel in Normandy: only a fraction of the number he requested. The other seven were divided between Calais and as reserve units at Rundstedt's headquarters near Paris. Hitler made life difficult for Rommel and Rundstedt by insisting that none of these reserve divisions be moved or reallocated without his permission.

In the meantime across the Channel, the Allies were preparing fifty divisions to invade Normandy.

Preparations for D-Day

Throughout the spring a ten-mile strip along the south coast of England resembled a holiday camp, such was the huge level of activity. Trucks, tanks and artillery units were assembling in huge numbers and camouflage was used where possible.

Luck was on the Allies' side in that the renowned German Luftwaffe air force was now only a shadow of the Luftwaffe of 1939/40. They were not in a position to keep an eye on the huge assembly of forces in the south of England while at the same time fighting Russia on the Eastern Front. Reconnaissance flights were few and far between. Of greater importance, they were not in a position to oppose the Allied air forces. Germany had only 300 aircraft available to oppose the Allies' 11,000!

3.5 million troops assembled in the south of England to embark on the greatest seaborne invasion in history.

The numbers and the logistics were simply mind-boggling. Almost 7,000 ships were needed: 4,000 of them troop carriers and the remainder either battleships or supply ships. Most of the shipping was British; the US was engaged in a simultaneous naval war against the Japanese in the Pacific. Every port and harbour along the English Channel was roped into the action, with Portsmouth being the main harbour of embarkation. Admiral Bertram Ramsay — who had previous experience on the beaches at Dunkirk, North Africa and Sicily — was in overall command of the crossing.

The Royal Navy's brief was to ensure that no vessel from Germany's Kriegsmarine got within striking distance of the invasion fleet.

For several weeks before the invasion, Allied bomber aircraft, with support from French Resistance fighters on the ground, did major damage to the French rail system in Normandy. This made it difficult for German reinforcements to come to the aid of their front-line troops.

It was agreed in advance with Stalin that the Soviets would keep the Germans fully occupied on the Eastern Front while the Normandy Invasion was taking place.

The targets in Normandy were the five beaches of Utah, Omaha, Gold, Juno and Sword. The Americans were assigned Utah and Omaha; the British Gold and Sword; and the Canadians Juno.

Ready To Go
From May onwards, the Allied forces were ready to go. However, they were only one hundred per cent ready — not the one hundred and ten per cent that both Churchill and Montgomery insisted on. No detail was overlooked. Two Mulberry Harbours were ready to go within a few days of D-Day, it was planned to have the Harbours floated across the Channel and sunk into their targeted locations at Omaha and Gold beaches. An underwater fuel line (Operation Pluto) was being laid across the English Channel. This was completed four days after D-Day ensuring that the Allies would no longer be dependent on fuel tankers. Other innovations that proved of major assistance included amphibious tanks and landing vessels (DUKWs); tanks fitted with flails for exploding mines; tanks fitted with ploughs to assist in the excavation of entrances in the bocage territory in western Brittany; and Crocodile flamethrowers.

One detail, however, was outside of the Allies control: the weather! The invasion was planned for 4, 5 or 6 of June to coincide with a full moon and a high tide. The former would enable the Allied paratroopers

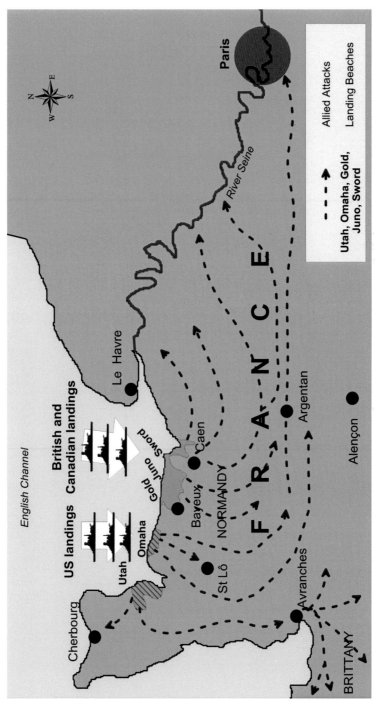

Map 24: Normandy Invasion 1944

Landing ships putting cargo ashore on a D-Day invasion beach at low tide during the first days of the operation, June 1944. Barrage balloons overhead. Army half-track convoy forming up on the beach. US coast guard photograph painted by Olive Eustace (cover image).

American soldiers wade ashore Omaha Beach during the
D-Day landings, Normandy, France, 6 June 1944.
Photograph by Robert F. Sargent.

to see where they were going (as it turned out, it was a cloudy night) and the latter would carry them over many of the Germans' beach defences.

However, Rommel increased the obstructions on the beach to such an extent that the invasion had to be changed from high tide to low tide. At low tide, the Allies would be able to see the obstacles they were trying to pass, but it increased the depth of beaches to be crossed under fire.

On Sunday, 4 June the weather was stormy and completely unsuitable. Monday, 5 June was not much better. Eisenhower received information from the meteorological service at Blacksod Bay in the west of Ireland that there would be a brief window of opportunity on Tuesday, 6 June. To defer the invasion at this stage would cause major logistical problems. Eisenhower decided to go for it. Tuesday, 6 June 1944 would be D–Day!

In Rommel's words, it was to be *"The Longest Day"*.

The D-Day Landings
During the night, paratroopers were dropped inland in Normandy to attack the German defenders from the rear. The paratroopers were dropped from gliders, many of which went astray in the dark. One of the more successful drops was at Pegasus Bridge on the canal at Caen, a key access point for the Allies (the bridge is a major tourist attraction today).

At dawn, landings commenced on the five beaches. Troop carriers of all shapes and description were queuing up to disgorge hundreds of thousands of troops as quickly as possible. The landings were preceded by heavy naval bombardment. The Germans were caught totally unaware. Rommel was at home in Germany celebrating his wife's birthday. Rundstedt still believed that the main invasion would be at Calais and he continued to wait. Hitler was asleep and nobody had the courage to awaken him to tell him the invasion had started and that it was not at Calais. The outcome was that none of the panzer divisions under Rundstedt moved until 6:00 p.m. on the day of the invasion. By this time, more than 150,000 Allied troops had landed and it was too late for the Germans to stop the invasion.

The invasion itself was an outstanding success. Churchill, settling down to sleep the night before, said to his wife, Clementine, *"Before we awake in the morning, 20,000 young men will have lost their lives."* He was very relieved twenty-four hours later to learn that less than 2,500 soldiers died, out of total casualties of 10,000. These were mainly US soldiers at Omaha Beach, who had to contend with strong defence by Rommel's panzers.

Breakout

While the Germans were caught unaware by the invasion, they almost made up for it by making an Allied breakout from Normandy extremely difficult. Rommel used the few panzer divisions he had to their maximum efficiency, but incessant air attacks by Allied aircraft made the fightback very difficult for the Germans.

The Allied invasion plans had called for the capture of Saint-Lô, Caen and Bayeux on the first day. None of these objectives was achieved. The German defence of Normandy was vigorous. It was a full month later before British and Canadian troops took Caen after a saturation bombing campaign on the town on 9 July.

Meanwhile, the American troops under General Omar Bradley, who landed (almost unopposed) on Utah beach, headed for the port of Cherbourg, knocking out any pillboxes they could on the way. They took over the entire Cotentin peninsula and Cherbourg was liberated on 27 June. The harbour at Cherbourg was badly needed since a severe storm had wrecked the Mulberry Harbour at Omaha Beach on 19 June. In the meantime, Allied troops continued to pour into Normandy. A month after D-Day, there were a million Allied troops in France!

Germany suffered a further setback on 17 July. Rommel's car was strafed by a British fighter plane. The car crashed and Rommel was hospitalised with serious head injuries. He took no further part in the war.

Once the Americans took Cherbourg, they headed south under General Bradley. Their target was Avranches on the edge of the Mont Saint-Michel Bay. Their route took them through well-defended bocage territory with fields divided by high dense hedgerows, sunken roads and steep earth banks. A single tank broken down on one of these roads caused a major traffic jam. The Allied tanks were fitted with ploughs, which proved very useful in creating openings from the narrow sunken roadways up into the adjoining fields.

This was easy territory for the Germans to defend, and difficult terrain for the Americans to advance on. Saint-Lô, due to be taken on the first day, was eventually taken on 24 July, followed by Avranches on 31 July. There were substantial casualties on both battle sites.

The Americans then headed eastwards to join up with the British and Canadian troops. Between them, the Allies surrounded the Germans in the Falaise Pocket, south of Caen. The 'pocket' became known as the 'killing fields of Normandy'. The Germans suffered major casualties before they eventually surrendered on 20 August. The Battle of Normandy was over and the Allied forces were ready to head for Germany.

The Normandy campaign cost the Germans 200,000 casualties, 1,500 tanks and 3,000 artillery pieces.

Between D-Day and the entry into Paris, 37,000 Allied soldiers died.

THE PLAN TO KILL HITLER

Problems were mounting for Hitler. He had failed to stop the Normandy Invasion and was now threatened by the Allied forces advancing on Germany from the west. Meanwhile, Stalin's Russian troops were advancing inexorably on Germany's Eastern Front.

Hitler's Health

Hitler's health was never good. In 1936 Dr. Theodore Morell was appointed as his physician. Morell was not a conventional doctor (several of Hitler's generals described him as a quack), but Hitler had great faith in him. As the tide began to turn, drug doses prescribed by Morell became increasingly stronger and gradually Hitler became totally drug-dependent. In 1944 he began to suffer blockages in his arteries and at the beginning of 1945 he showed signs of Parkinson's disease: his left hand shook constantly. In January 1945 he moved his entourage into an underground bunker in Berlin.

On 20 July 1944 a group of officers planned to kill Hitler at his office in the forest at Rastenburg in East Prussia. They were concerned for some time that Hitler was going to destroy Germany completely.

Colonel Claus von Stauffenberg had a bomb in an attaché case at a meeting in Hitler's headquarters in Prussia, and Hitler walked away from it just as it exploded. The officer standing next to Hitler was killed and Hitler's trousers were shredded by the blast. Revenge was swift! All officers who were involved in any way were rounded up and executed.

Some months later it was brought to Hitler's attention that Rommel was aware of the plot even though he took no active part in the attempted assassination.

Rommel's dislike of Hitler began in North Africa when Hitler did not provide him with the backup he requested. He then refused Rommel permission to retreat when he was greatly outnumbered by Allied forces.

Rommel had a humanitarian consideration for his soldiers that Hitler simply did not understand or did not wish to understand. The final indignity for Rommel was to be passed over in favour of Rundstedt as overall commander of the German forces in Normandy.

When Hitler learned that Rommel was aware of the plot to kill him but did not tell him, he summoned Rommel to his presence. He gave Rommel two options: trial by the People's Court, which would result in disgrace and execution, or suicide. Hitler assured Rommel that if he chose suicide, he would receive a state funeral, and his wife and family would receive his pension rights (this information was disclosed by Rommel's wife after the war ended). Rommel opted for suicide after explaining the situation to his family. Hitler gave him a cyanide capsule, which he took on 14 October. An ignoble end to a highly-respected general!

After the bomb plot, Hitler replaced Rundstedt with Field Marshal Günther von Kluge. On 6 August Kluge organised a counter-attack at Mortain in Normandy, but the attack was quickly broken up by the Allies' aerial power. The Allies at this stage were in total control in Normandy.

Kluge did not survive for long. He had also been aware of the bomb plot to kill Hitler. He committed suicide before Hitler had him executed. He was replaced by Field Marshal Walter Model, known as the 'Führer's Fireman', a reference to his ability to tackle emergency situations. Model would be Hitler's foremost general in the months to follow.

The Allies carried out a second invasion of France (**Operation Dragoon**) on 15 August. Several divisions of American and Free French troops landed on the south coast of France. The success of this operation enabled the Allies to liberate most of Vichy France in just four weeks. Hitler made it easy for the Allies by withdrawing his troops from the area. At this stage, his focus was on defending Germany and northern Italy. One of the main benefits of Operation Dragoon for the Allied forces was the liberation of the French port of Marseille, which became a vital supply port for the Allies in the year ahead.

PARIS 1944

On 7 August Hitler sent General Dietrich von Choltitz to Paris with orders either to defend the city or to destroy it. Hitler had seen the beauty of Paris when he visited the city with his architect, Albert Speer, in 1940. His decision to destroy the city was one of pure childish spite.

Choltitz could see from the huge Allied force advancing from Normandy that there was no way he could defend the city. However, he considered the alternative of destroying the beautiful city of Paris pointless and he was dissuaded from carrying out Hitler's order.

By agreement, a Franco-American force led by Charles de Gaulle liberated the city on 25 August. There were emotional scenes as Parisians took control of their virtually-undamaged capital after four years absence!

V-1 AND V-2 ROCKETS

One week after the Normandy landings, the first German rocket missile landed in England. Churchill got a major shock: rocket technology was unknown to the Allies but obviously not to Germany's Wernher von Braun and his team of engineers.

The V-1 rocket was a small, pilotless flying bomb powered by a pulse jet engine. It could be fired either from the ground or from an aircraft. The rocket fuel cut out at a distance of 250 miles and the one-ton bomb exploded when it hit the ground. Between June 1944 and March 1945, a total of 10,000 V-1 bombs were launched against England with seventy-five per cent of them successfully crossing the Channel. They resulted in the deaths of 6,000 people, mainly civilians. They made a noise like an aircraft and became known to the British as 'buzz bombs'.

The V-2 rocket was a ballistic missile powered by a rocket motor, the predecessor of today's intercontinental missiles. It was silent but very expensive. A total of 1,100 V-2 missiles hit Britain, resulting in the deaths of 2,700 civilians. They did not affect the outcome of the war, but they did major damage during the last year of the war.

The German Wernher von Braun was the technical director of the rocket programme. In March 1945 — along with 100 of his team — he escaped ahead of the Red Army from Germany to the United States, where they became a vital part of the American space programme.

WESTERN FRONT 1944

Eisenhower now had a problem. He did not know whether to place Bradley or Patton or Montgomery in overall charge of the assault on Germany. Realising that to place any one of the three over the other two would result in a major headache for himself, he decided to continue the role of Commander in Chief. He planned a three-pronged attack on Germany with Montgomery in charge of the northern flank, Bradley assisted by General Hodges in charge of the middle flank, and Patton in command of the southern flank.

After the Allies' success in Normandy, they proceeded to drive the Germans eastwards back to the boundaries of their homeland. The biggest problem the Allies faced was blown bridges. The Germans — wherever possible — blew up river, canal and rail bridges as they retreated, making life very difficult for the advancing Allies. The busiest Allies were the engineers ('sappers') — 50,000 of whom were responsible for repairing or replacing bridges, erecting temporary 'bailey bridges', and at times simply supplying boats to enable their armies to cross.

The British and Canadians under Montgomery advanced into Belgium, and a number of French and Belgian towns — including Antwerp, Brussels, Dieppe and Rouen — were liberated early in September. The liberation of Dieppe was particularly satisfying for the Canadians, who had lost 5,000 men in the failed cross-channel raid on Dieppe two years earlier.

Montgomery had dreams of ending the war by Christmas. The Allies had similar dreams in 1914 in World War I. Neither dream was fulfilled.

Hitler did not make it easy for the Allies. One of the major problems the Allies faced was lack of supplies. Because they had neglected to seize any of the Channel ports, their supplies had to come from Normandy — and supplies meant everything from foodstuffs to fuel for tanks to armaments.

Hitler had foreseen this weakness and, as the Germans retreated under the command of Field Marshal Model, Hitler instructed that German garrisons be left in the ports of Le Havre, Calais and Dunkirk. Even though Antwerp was seized on 4 September 1944, the Germans retained control over the Scheldt Estuary, preventing the Allies' use of the port of Antwerp. This showed poor decision-making by the Allies, and resulted in the need to form the Red Ball Express — a 6,000-strong truck convoy system hauling food, ammunition and fuel from Normandy to the Western Front. This situation continued until the end of November, when the Scheldt Estuary leading into Antwerp was finally taken.

Luxembourg was liberated on 15 September while Aachen, the first German city to fall to the Allies, was taken on 21 October. Further south in Alsace, American and French troops under General George Patton advanced slowly eastwards, driving the remnants of the defeated

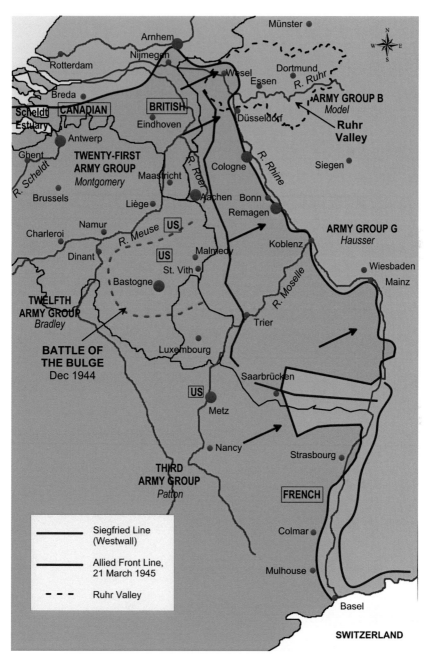

Map 25: Allied Advance on Germany 1944–45

Allied soldiers fight in fresh snowfall near Amonines, Belgium, towards the end of Battle of the Bulge, 4 January 1945.

German army before them. They continued through Lorraine and in mid-December they reached the River Rhine, ready for the final assault on Germany.

Operation Market Garden was Montgomery's plan to seize vital river bridges on their way through Belgium and Holland heading for Germany north of the Siegfried Line. The plan was to use their air superiority to drop paratroopers at the various bridges before ground assault forces arrived. The plan worked at Eindhoven and Nijmegen. These bridges were seized on 17 and 20 September with difficulty — the German defences under General Karl Student (who commanded the German paratroopers in 1940) and Field Marshal Walter Model being much stronger than anticipated. Montgomery's ambitious target was the bridge at **Arnhem,** located further north. Here, the British paratroopers were dropped too far from their target in an area where German panzer troops had recently regrouped. The British paratroopers never managed to link up with the ground forces and the Allied attempt to seize the bridge failed. The bridge at Arnhem became known as a 'A Bridge Too Far' and Montgomery's failure to take it meant the Allies would not cross the Rhine into Germany until 1945. Montgomery's failure at Arnhem did not upset American Generals Patton and Bradley too much since they felt that the arrogant Monty needed to be taken down a peg or two! They also felt that Eisenhower erred by letting Monty go ahead with Operation Market Garden before the supply problem into Antwerp was resolved.

Their criticism was justified. The Americans christened the road between Eindhoven and Arnhem Hells Highway. This key roadway was on an elevated bank running through low-lying, waterlogged ground, unsuitable for armoured vehicles. The one notable exception was the newly-designed American Buffalo. This was a complete amphibious carrier similar to the DUKWs at Normandy but was propelled by its own tracks.

Buffaloes proved very useful clearing the Scheldt Estuary, which was the key entrance to Antwerp from the North Sea. Opening up the Estuary to sea traffic proved a difficult task. The Germans had to be driven from both banks of the estuary and the waterway cleared of mines. This took from the end of September until the beginning of November. The port of Antwerp was eventually opened on 26 November, completely transforming the supply situation for the Allies. The battle for the Scheldt Estuary had taken eighty-five days. So much for Monty's dream of finishing the war before Christmas!

Hürtgen Forest
A very costly series of battles took place in the Hürtgen Forest near Aachen between 19 September and 16 December. Located just inside

the Belgian-German border, this was a low-lying forested area adjacent to the River Roer, which had to be crossed to reach the Rhine.

However, the Americans feared the Roer River Dams, which the Germans controlled and which, if opened, could flood low-lying areas and prevent any crossing of the River Roer. Also, the Germans were using the area to assemble their troops in preparation for the coming Battle of the Bulge.

Field Marshal Walter Model ensured that the Americans would not forget the Hürtgen Forest. Intense fighting took place throughout October and November and, when the smoke cleared, it was clear that the Americans under General Bradley had suffered 33,000 casualties, considerably more than the Germans. The most galling aspect of the battle was that nothing had been achieved. Not only had they not reached the Rhine, they were still bogged down at the River Roer. This was not America's finest hour. One thing the Allies learned from Hürtgen Forest was that the German army was far from being beaten.

Aachen
Aachen was the first German city to fall to the Allies. It was taken by the US First Army commanded by General Courtney Hodges. The Germans, not wishing to lose their first city fought bitterly. Fighting continued from mid-September until 21 October, when the city finally succumbed. Meanwhile, Patton had liberated Luxembourg on 15 September before advancing into Lorraine. US and French troops under Patton advanced slowly eastwards, driving the remnants of the defeated German army before them.

Metz
General Patton's troops arrived in Lorraine at the end of August. From there, their targets were Nancy and Metz. Nancy was taken without great difficulty, but Metz was a different proposition. A ring of forts defended the city and the Germans made good use of them. The Americans were commanded by General Walton Walker, who was taking his orders from Patton. Walker was unable to make any impression on the German defences for many weeks and suffered many casualties trying. Patton should have circumvented Metz but saw the ring of forts (particularly Fort Driant) as a trophy he could present to General George C. Marshall, the US Army Chief of Staff. Metz eventually fell on 22 November, after a huge loss of men and time. Getting sidetracked at Metz delayed Patton's troops by several months.

Ardennes Offensive — Battle of the Bulge
Hitler had one more ace up his sleeve. Not only did he surprise the Allies, he surprised his own generals as well. With memories of his very successful invasion of France through the Ardennes Forest in 1940 still fresh in his mind, Hitler decided to repeat the assault through

the forest. On 12 December Hitler instructed his generals that the German army was to turn and attack the Allies through the Ardennes and drive them back to the North Sea. Even though they had major misgivings (they had far fewer forces than they had in 1940), neither Rundstedt nor Model was able to persuade Hitler to abandon his plan.

The plan worked well initially for the Germans since the Allies' air force was grounded by bad weather. The Allies were taken by surprise: ever since Normandy they had been the hunters, now they were the hunted. Their conceit meant that they had totally underestimated the strength of Hitler's forces. A second factor was the weather. The winter of 1944/45 was very severe and both sides had to contend with heavy rain and snow, which made ground conditions very difficult. The Germans drove the Allies back westwards almost as far as Dinant in Belgium creating a substantial bulge in the war front: hence the offensive became known as the **Battle of the Bulge**. A key location in the battle was the Belgian town of **Bastogne**. Since all main roads in the Ardennes converged on Bastogne, it was essential that the Germans capture the town to facilitate troop movement if they were to progress. The Siege of Bastogne lasted until 26 December, when additional American forces under General Patton arrived from Lorraine to lift it.

By mid-December, the skies had cleared and the Germans felt the power of the Allied air force. The Germans were slowly driven back in wintry conditions and by mid-January the western war front had been restored. Casualties were very heavy on both sides, but the German losses were disastrous. They suffered 92,000 casualties, lost 700 tanks and almost 1,000 aircraft. These were losses that the Germans simply could not sustain at this stage in the war. The only recruits available to Hitler now were the **Volkssturm** — an auxiliary force of males between 16 and 60 years old conscripted in October 1944. They had no uniforms, no training, few weapons and were a poor imitation of the original German army.

A major war scandal occurred on 17 December when a German formation under Joachim Peiper killed seventy-one American POWs in the Belgian town of Malmedy. Atrocities like this were rare on the Western Front. The effect on the Allies was to stiffen their resolve to end the war as soon as possible. Peiper was later sentenced to twelve years imprisonment by a war crimes commission.

EASTERN FRONT 1944

Before Hitler attacked Russia in 1941, he had taken the precaution of seizing control in the Baltic states of Latvia, Estonia and Lithuania beforehand. He did likewise in the Balkans; and he also took Romania,

Hungary, Bulgaria and Greece. Hitler was ensuring that he would not be attacked from either side.

At the beginning of 1944 the positions were reversed. Stalin's Russian troops were advancing on Germany, but before doing so Stalin took the precaution of winning back the Balkans and the Baltic states. He was also thinking in advance of a postwar settlement.

In January the Russians finally lifted the Siege of Leningrad. The siege had lasted 920 days and cost the lives of almost a million civilians. Some had resorted to cannibalism in an attempt to stay alive.

Finland had entered the war on Hitler's side back in 1941 because of her historical hatred of Russia. Now, however, she could see what the future might bring and in February 1944 she entered peace talks with the Russians. Finland eventually sued for an armistice on 19 September.

Romania and Hungary, who had actively fought on Germany's side, watched with interest. At this stage, it was every country for herself!

In April Russia advanced into Crimea and, after a battle that lasted several weeks, the Germans in Crimea surrendered. Odessa was taken in April and Sevastopol in May. This was a different Russian army than that which tried to defend Russia in the early stages of Operation Barbarossa. Stalin now had limitless numbers of soldiers, tanks and aircraft. He set about retaking every country and every city that Russia had lost. During the summer and autumn of 1944, the Soviets retook Estonia, Latvia and Lithuania.

The Soviets planned a major summer offensive — code-named **Operation Bagration** (Bagration was a general in Napoleon's time) — to attack Hitler's old Army Group Centre, the main obstacle between themselves and their ultimate target: Berlin. The attack began on 22 June. Germany had thirty-five divisions to defend against an overwhelming Russian army consisting of 150 divisions supported by almost 4,000 aircraft.

Germany's Army Group Centre was annihilated. The Germans were driven out of Belorussia and eastern Poland, after losing control of major cities: Minsk (3 July), Lublin (23 July), Brest-Litovsk (28 July) and Lvov (29 July). During that month alone, the Germans suffered 500,000 casualties.

In August the Soviets advanced into the Balkans. Romania immediately changed allegiance and declared war on Germany, thereby depriving the Germans of the valuable source of oil in the Ploeşti oil fields. The Russians entered the Romanian capital Bucharest on 30 August. In September Bulgaria, who had been watching developments keenly, changed sides and declared her support for Stalin.

Before he invaded Russia in 1941, Hitler had taken both Greece and Yugoslavia by force. He now had no option but to withdraw his occupying forces from both countries, which he did in October 1944. This resulted in civil war breaking out in Greece between pro- and anti-communist factions.

In Yugoslavia Tito granted the advancing Russian army temporary access into his country to drive the occupying German forces out.

When the Soviets entered the Serbian capital Belgrade on 20 October, they found that the Germans had left.

Hungary was now the last Eastern European country still fighting on Germany's side. If Stalin could take Hungary, he would have a clear run into Austria and from there into Germany.

45,000 Hungarians stood shoulder-to-shoulder with 50,000 Germans in Budapest to face an overwhelming army of Russians, Romanians and Bulgarians. The Hungarians stoically accepted that this was their fate. They fought bravely but in vain. Between the beginning of December 1944 and mid-February 1945, a devastating battle took place in Buda and Pest on both sides of the Danube. The fighting — street by street, house by house — was reminiscent of Stalingrad!

The Russians perpetrated brutality after brutality. Rape, murder and pillage were the order of the day. When Stalin was asked to restrain his troops, he replied that rape and pillage were the rightful rewards of his soldiers for their sacrifices. When the guns in Hungary fell silent in mid-February 1945, the Hungarian/German forces had suffered 100,000 casualties, including 40,000 deaths. 35,000 Hungarian civilians also died. The Russians and their new allies suffered 200,000 casualties, including 80,000 deaths.

The Battle of Budapest did not get the worldwide attention it warranted. At this stage, the eyes of the world were focused on one place only: Berlin.

Warsaw Uprising

An uprising by the Polish resistance Home Army began on 1 August 1944. It was an attempt to liberate Warsaw from Nazi Germany. This turned out to be a case of 'out of the frying pan and into the fire'. The Poles timed it to coincide with the Soviet advance to the River Vistula on the east side of the city and the expected German retreat. The Polish Home Army attacked the occupying Germans on 1 August, fully expecting the Russians to assist them. Considering how badly the Russians treated the Poles at the start of the war in 1939, this was naïve. In one of the most cynical operations in the war, Stalin ordered his troops to halt. This allowed the Germans to regroup, which they did before launching a fierce attack on the Poles. The Poles, basically just a large resistance group, were no match for the Germans, and by the time the uprising was put down, 200,000 Poles had been killed and Warsaw devastated once more.

The treatment meted out to the Poles by the Germans during the uprising was as horrific as the treatment of defeated forces in any war. The Poles were raped, murdered and subjected to the most appalling brutalities.

Only when the Poles were defeated did the Russian army enter Warsaw. Once Warsaw was under Stalin's control, the Russians were in a position to resume driving the Germans westward.

Anne Frank

On 4 August 1944 Anne Frank, along with various family members and friends all of whom were Jews, were arrested by the Gestapo in Amsterdam and taken to various concentration camps. A neighbour had betrayed them. Anne and her sister Margot were taken to Bergen-Belsen concentration camp where they both died of typhus in early 1945; just months before the camp was liberated by the advancing Allied forces. The only family member to survive the camps was Anne's father Otto. He had been interned in Auschwitz, which was liberated by Russian troops in 1945. He returned to Amsterdam in June 1945. He was instrumental in publishing *The Diary of Anne Frank* at the behest of many of his friends. It became an international bestseller.

1944 TIMELINE — EUROPE

06 Jan	Soviet troops advance westwards into Poland.
17 Jan	First Allied attack on Cassino, Italy.
22 Jan	Allies land at Anzio in Italy.
27 Jan	Leningrad relieved after 900-day siege.
15–18 Feb	Allies bomb the monastery at Monte Cassino.
16 Feb	Germans counter-attack against the Anzio beachhead.
04 Mar	Soviet troops begin offensive on Belorussian front.
	Allies carry out major daylight bombing raid on Berlin.
15 Mar	Second Allied attempt to capture Cassino begins.
18 Mar	British drop 3,000 tons of bombs on Hamburg.
08 Apr	Soviet troops begin offensive to liberate Crimea.

09 May	Soviet troops recapture Sevastopol.
11 May	Allies attack Gustav Line south of Rome.
12 May	Germans surrender in Crimea.
25 May	Germans retreat from Anzio.
05 Jun	Americans enter Rome, after Germans declare it an open city.
06 Jun	D-Day invasion on the northern coast of France.
09 Jun	Soviet offensive against Finland begins.
13 Jun	First German V-1 rocket attack on Britain. Battle of Villers-Bocage in Normandy, France.
22 Jun	Soviets drive Germans out of Belorussia and eastern Poland.
27 Jun	American troops liberate Cherbourg, France. On the Eastern Front, Soviets capture Minsk.
09 Jul	British and Canadian troops capture Caen, France, after massive bombing campaign on the town.
18 Jul	American troops reach Saint-Lô, France
20 Jul	German officers led by Colonel Claus von Stauffenberg unsuccessfully attempt to assassinate Hitler.
24 Jul	Soviet troops liberate first concentration camp at Majdanek.
25 Jul	Americans begin break-out of Saint-Lô.
28 Jul	Soviet troops take Brest-Litovsk. US troops take Coutances.
01 Aug	US troops reach Avranches. Polish Home Army uprising against Nazis in Warsaw begins.
04 Aug	Anne Frank and family arrested by Gestapo in Amsterdam.
07 Aug	Germans begin major counter-attack toward Avranches.
15 Aug	Allies invade southern France (Operation Dragoon).
19 Aug	Resistance uprising in Paris. Soviet offensive in Balkans begins with attack on Romania.
20 Aug	Allies encircle Germans in Falaise Pocket.
25 Aug	Liberation of Paris.
29 Aug	Slovak uprising begins.
31 Aug	Soviets take Bucharest.
01–04 Sep	Multiple French and Belgian towns liberated including Verdun, Dieppe, Rouen, Antwerp and Brussels.
04 Sep	Finland and Soviet Union agree a ceasefire.
13 Sep	Allies advance to the Siegfried Line in western Germany.
15 Sep	Luxembourg liberated.
17 Sep	Air assault by Allies on the Netherlands (Operation Market Garden).
26 Sep	Soviet troops occupy Estonia.
02 Oct	Warsaw uprising ends. Polish Home Army forced to surrender to Germans after expected Russian help does not arrive.
10 Oct	Soviet troops capture Riga.
14 Oct	Allies liberate Athens. Rommel commits suicide at the behest of Hitler.

21 Oct	Massive German surrender at Aachen, Germany.
30 Oct	Last use of gas chambers at Auschwitz.
20 Nov	Allied troops reach the Rhine.
22 Nov	Metz finally falls to the Allies.
24 Nov	Strasbourg liberated.
26 Nov	Port of Antwerp taken by Allies.
04 Dec	Civil war in Greece; Athens placed under martial law.
16 Dec	Battle of the Bulge begins in the Ardennes.
17 Dec	The SS murders seventy-one American POWs at Malmedy.
26 Dec	General Patton relieves Bastogne.
Dec–Feb	Soviet troops besiege Budapest.

WAR IN THE PACIFIC 1944

MacArthur heads for the Philippines. Nimitz takes Marshall Islands, Caroline Islands (Truk) and the Mariana Islands (Saipan and Guam) — all on a direct flight path to Japan. Major naval battle at Leyte Gulf in the Philippines. By the end of 1944, Americans are in control of the Pacific. Mountbatten's forces, British under General Slim and American under General Stilwell, invade Burma.

Submarine Warfare
It was not until 1944 that the US Navy began to use its new submarine capability to maximum effect. New submarines with onboard radar were built, torpedoes were redesigned and submarine commanders retrained.

The number of Japanese ships sunk by American submarines increased from 180 in 1942 to 335 in 1943 to 600 in 1944. By 1945 sinkings had actually decreased because there were so few targets left on the high seas. During those three years, Allied submarines destroyed 1,200 Japanese merchant ships. Most were small cargo ships, but 125 were tankers carrying desperately-needed oil from the East Indies. Another 320 were passenger ships or troop carriers. At critical stages of the Guadalcanal, Saipan and Leyte campaigns, thousands of Japanese troops were killed before they reached the battlefield. More than 200 warships were sunk, including eight extremely valuable aircraft carriers. An auxiliary function of the submarines was the rescue of hundreds of downed pilots, one of whom was George H. W. Bush, who went on to become President of the United States.

Burma and India
In the early months of 1944 the British/Indian Allies were intent on driving the Japanese out of Burma and reoccupying the country. The

Japanese response was to launch their own offensive through central Burma on Imphal and Kohima in India. The Japanese knew that if they could take both of these locations, there was little to prevent them advancing on Delhi in India. However, this was not the all-conquering Japan of 1942, and they were up against much tougher resistance. Between March and June, fighting was intense. Japanese forces entered Assam in an attempt to take both Imphal and Kohima. The area was densely-wooded, mountainous territory, and the arrival of monsoon weather made fighting conditions even more intolerable.

The Japanese had an additional problem: lack of supplies — the British/Indian air forces ensured that Japanese supplies were not getting through. In addition, the intense training of troops by General Slim was now paying dividends. His men fought with courage and confidence, and there was no question of retreating. Also, the Americans launched their own version of Wingate's Chindits and called them Merrill's Marauders, after their commander Brigadier General Frank Merrill. They harassed the Japanese throughout 1944.

The Japanese cracked first! In June they began to retreat. In Slim's words, the British and Indian troops had mastered, man for man, the best that the Japanese could throw at them. Imphal was relieved after an eighty-day siege. So long a defensive stronghold, Imphal now became an attacking launch pad. The Japanese troops, decimated by continuous fighting and starvation, retreated towards the Chindwin River. By the end of 1944, the Japanese assault on India had collapsed into a retreat towards Rangoon. This was a major success for General Slim. Burma, including the Arakan coastal area, was now back in Allied hands.

The Pacific 1944
Once the Normandy landings in France were completed successfully, the Americans divided their forces between Europe and the Pacific. They returned to the Pacific numerically- and logistically-superior, and they meant business!

MacArthur's forces, aided by some Australian divisions, advanced through New Guinea en route to the Philippines. Further north Nimitz took the Marshall Islands. Carrier-borne aircraft devastated the Japanese base at Truk in the Caroline Islands. The Mariana Islands were next.

On 15 June 500 ships began landing 130,000 US army and marine personnel on the island of Saipan in the Marianas.

A gigantic but one-sided air battle began. Dubbed by the Americans as the 'Great Marianas Turkey Shoot' (turkeys being easy targets), the Japanese were destroyed. In just two days, they lost three aircraft carriers and 450 planes. The Japanese carrier force was effectively destroyed. The Americans had two new weapons at their disposal. One was their much-improved radar guidance for aircraft, and the second was a new proximity fuse for use on anti-aircraft guns, which meant that the shells would not explode until targets came within a pre-set range.

While there was a huge increase in American air and sea forces, the Japanese forces had regressed. They were unable to replace aircraft and men as quickly as required. They resorted to kamikaze warfare. Bomb-carrying aircraft were intentionally crashed into American warships and, while this was very effective, it meant writing off a plane and a pilot each time. While kamikaze pilots were volunteers in the early part of the Pacific war, the willingness to die soon dissipated and, as the war progressed, pilots had to be ordered to fly kamikaze missions.

Having control of the Marianas was a big advantage to the Americans. They immediately set about building an airfield, from where their new giant B-29 Superfortress bombers could reach the Japanese homeland. The first B-29 Superfortress bomber was launched by the Americans in the Pacific in July 1944.

The island of Guam was also taken in July.

In the Pacific, the Philippines was one of the territories prized most by both the Americans and the Japanese. After the Americans had vacated the islands in mid-1942, the Japanese occupation was harsh, was accompanied by widespread atrocities and resulted in large numbers of Filipinos being pushed into slave labour. This gave rise to a strong Filipino guerrilla movement on the islands, which looked forward to MacArthur's return. The assault on the Philippines was initially planned for the south island of Mindanao, but resistance in Mindanao had ceased in June. MacArthur decided that a naval attack on the centre island of Leyte was a better option.

The **Battle of Leyte Gulf** that followed was one of the greatest naval battles ever, involving 280 warships. The battle started on 20 October and for five days both sides tried to outmanoeuvre and outgun one another. The Japanese resorted to kamikaze suicide attacks crashing into American battleships. The outcome was a disastrous defeat for the Japanese. They lost four aircraft carriers, three battleships, nine cruisers and ten destroyers. The US Navy lost three carriers and three destroyers. The Japanese suffered 70,000 casualties against the US total of 15,000. By the end of the year the Philippines was back under American control with the exception of the island of Luzon. The Japanese air force was reduced to 4,500 aircraft against a US force of 18,000. Apart from the battleships, many of the ships sunk by the Americans were oil tankers carrying oil from the Dutch East Indies to

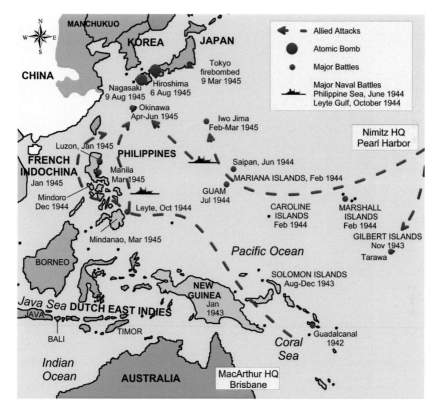

Map 26: War in the Pacific 1943–45

A Japanese kamikaze fighter swoops down on a US warship in the Battle of Leyte Gulf, October 1944.

Japan. This battle virtually marked the end of the Imperial Japanese Navy. However, Japan had one thing in common with Germany: neither would admit defeat and neither would surrender. This policy cost both countries dearly.

1944 TIMELINE — PACIFIC

09 Jan	British and Indian troops recapture Maungdaw in Burma.
01–07 Feb	US troops capture Kwajalein and Majuro atolls in the Marshall Islands.
17 Feb	US carrier-based planes destroy the Japanese naval base at Truk in the Caroline Islands.
20 Feb	US planes destroy the Japanese base at Rabaul.
23 Feb	US carrier-based planes attack the Mariana Islands.
24 Feb	Merrill's Marauders begin a ground campaign in northern Burma.
05 Mar	General Wingate's groups begin operations behind Japanese lines in Burma.
15 Mar	Japanese begin offensive towards Imphal and Kohima.
17 Apr	Japanese begin their final offensive in China.
27 May	Allies invade Biak Island, New Guinea.
05 Jun	US planes bomb Japanese railway facilities at Bangkok, Thailand.
15 Jun	US marines invade Saipan in the Mariana Islands.
16 Jun	US planes based in Bengal, India, carry out bombing raid on steel works at Yawata in Japan.
19 Jun	In what became known as the Great Marianas Turkey Shoot, US carrier-based fighters shoot down 220 Japanese fighters with the loss of only twenty of their own fighters.
08 Jul	Japanese withdraw from Imphal.
19 Jul	US marines invade the island of Guam in the Marianas.
24 Jul	US marines invade Tinian.
27 Jul	US troops complete the liberation of Guam.
08 Aug	American troops complete the capture of the Mariana Islands.
11 Oct	US air raids against Okinawa.
18 Oct	US planes based on the Marianas attack the Japanese base at Truk.
20 Oct	US Sixth Army invades Leyte in the Philippines.
23 Oct	Battle of Leyte Gulf results in decisive US naval victory.
25 Oct	In Leyte Gulf, the first kamikaze (suicide) attacks occur against US warships.
11 Nov	Iwo Jima bombarded by the US Navy.
24 Nov	American planes bomb the Nakajima aircraft factory near Tokyo.

15 Dec   US troops invade Mindoro in the Philippines.

17 Dec   American air force establishes the technology to drop an atomic bomb.

CHAPTER 18

1945
Atomic Bombs Dropped;
World War II Ends

WAR IN EUROPE 1945

Yalta Conference is attended by Roosevelt, Churchill and Stalin. Allies on Western Front and Russia on Eastern Front begin their assault on Germany. Fighting in Italy comes to an end. Hitler commits suicide, and throughout Europe World War II comes to an end.

Canada

Some historians minimise the contribution that Canada made during both World War I and World War II, but she made a major contribution to both wars. In World War I she first came to prominence in the Second Battle of Ypres, while she was the major ally in the Battle of Vimy Ridge in 1917. In 1942 the Allies were under pressure from Stalin to invade France, and a decision was taken to proceed with a cross-channel invasion of the French coastal town of Dieppe. The majority of the 6,000 Allied troops were Canadian and there were 3,600 casualties. The lesson learned was that the Allies were far from ready for a major cross-channel invasion. When the Normandy Invasion did occur two years later, the Canadians were given responsibility for Juno beach. Between the two wars, Canada lost more than 100,000 men. Her troops would have had the honour of being first to enter Rome at a later stage but for the egotistical US General Clark snatching it from them.

ITALIAN FRONT 1945

From early in World War II, both sides were aware that the war would not be decided on the Italian Front. For this reason, the commanders on both sides tended to view the Italian campaign as a supply basin for other fronts. This was particularly true in Normandy and in the invasion of southern France.

During February 1945, some Canadian troops were moved from Italy to supplement Montgomery's forces in Belgium.

But the campaign in Italy was not finished. For two long years, Allied troops from America, Britain and Canada had fought long and hard through all weathers on battlefields as varied as the Italian Riviera and the Apennine Mountains. The war in Italy was destined to continue until Hitler was dead.

The Allied offensive in Italy resumed in April 1945, preceded by a huge bombing campaign — the Allied air force completely outnumbered the Luftwaffe at this stage. On 14 April the Allies finally broke clear of the Apennine mountain range into northern Italy and on 21 April they took Bologna. This was followed in quick succession by Verona on 26 April and Venice on 29 April, with major assistance from New Zealand troops. It was obvious at this stage to Hitler's generals that the end was near and, although most of them were afraid to mention the word 'surrender' while Hitler was still alive, a few were already making overtures to the Allies. German SS General Karl Wolff met an American diplomat Allen Dulles in Switzerland in March for secret talks to try to end the war.

As the war drew to a close, Mussolini and his mistress Clara Petacci, who had spent the previous two years at Lake Garda in Lombardy, feared for their lives. They were headed for the airport to fly to neutral Spain when they were captured by communist Partisans and shot dead. Along with several other fascists, their bodies were hung upside down at a petrol station in Milan. Mussolini died his ignominious death on 28 April.

450,000 German troops in Italy surrendered on 2 May, bringing the long drawn-out war in Italy to an end.

There was one final operation on Italian territory before the end of the war. While the port of **Trieste** was in Italy, it was located in a key position on the Adriatic Sea between Italy and the Balkans. It had come under German control after the Italian armistice in September 1943.

Many Jews were murdered by the Germans while they were under occupation. However, on 1 May 1945 the German occupiers of Trieste were ousted by Tito's Partisans. The occupiers were taken prisoner and many were murdered, despite Tito's orders to the contrary. At the end of the war Tito's forces refused to vacate the area when asked to do so. The Allies did not wish to fall out with one another and a crisis ensued. Tito was finally persuaded by Stalin to back down, and on 9 June — a month after the war was over — Yugoslavia withdrew. In a short space of time, control of Trieste had passed from the Germans to the Yugoslavs to the Allies.

When the war was over Yugoslavia became a republic with Tito as Prime Minister until his death in 1980. He was one of very few who stood up to Stalin and lived to tell the tale.

The **Yalta Conference** was held in Crimea from 4–11 February and was attended by Roosevelt, Churchill and Stalin.

This would be their final meeting together. President Roosevelt was very ill and had just two months to live. The stresses of World War II had taken their toll. However, he had never let his infirmity (he had contracted polio in 1921 and subsequently needed to use a wheelchair) affect his duties, and he is considered one of the finest American Presidents ever. Both Roosevelt and Churchill feared Stalin and the power of the Russian army, and in the months preceding the conference, they both sought to humour their Russian ally. All parties were aware, however, that the Russians would be a major factor in bringing an end to the war in Europe. Both Roosevelt and Churchill knew that Stalin would be very demanding in peace negotiations.

Each of the three had cards to play, but some had higher cards than others. Roosevelt knew he might need Stalin's assistance to finish off the war in the Pacific against Japan and accordingly tended to yield to Stalin's demands. Stalin, adopting the attitude that *"possession is nine-tenths of the law"* was not going to give up his newly-possessed Eastern Europe countries without a fight. Stalin wanted a barrier between east and west — the innovative Churchill christened the barrier 'The Iron Curtain'.

Churchill had the weakest hand to play. Britain wanted the Commonwealth restored to what it was in 1939. She also wanted France involved in the settlement, believing that a strong France was an essential constituent in a stable Europe. While both Britain and the US wanted to see Nazism crushed, they did not want it replaced by communism! They had much to discuss, but first they had to end the war.

One of the main agreements at the Yalta Conference was that Berlin would be divided into four sections after the war: the US, Britain, the USSR, and France occupying one zone each. However, Roosevelt and Stalin had at least one private meeting at Yalta without Churchill being present. This was to discuss the war in the Pacific, where Roosevelt wanted Russia's help to bring the war to an end. But the question of who would take Berlin was high on the agenda. Stalin was adamant that his army would be first to enter Berlin. Roosevelt did not oppose the demand — after all, he had the Pacific war to contend with and he knew that the American people would not thank him for the loss of American soldiers taking Berlin. History books suggest that Stalin and Roosevelt reached a verbal agreement that the Russians would take Berlin.

WESTERN FRONT 1945

At the beginning of 1945, the Western Front was basically located on the common boundary that Germany shared with France, Belgium, Luxembourg and the Netherlands. This boundary was the location of the German Siegfried Line, which had been originally built opposite the French Maginot Line in World War I. Hitler rebuilt the 630-kilometre Siegfried Line between 1938 and 1940 and rechristened it the **Westwall.** It consisted of a line of 18,000 defensive bunkers, tunnels and tank traps (dragon's teeth), but it was nowhere near as effective as the Atlantic Wall at Normandy. The Allies found the River Rhine a much more formidable obstacle.

The Allied forces, which had been set back by the unexpected attack by Hitler's forces in The Battle of the Bulge in the Ardennes in December, had now regrouped and were ready to move forward again.

Eisenhower assembled his powerful Allied army in three sectors:
1. The Northern Sector: British and Canadian troops under General Montgomery.
2. The Central Sector: the main American forces under Generals Bradley and Hodges.
3. The Southern Sector: American and Free French troops under Patton.

The plan was to advance the Western Front eastwards to the German border. The weather in January and February was particularly bad, delivering ground conditions reminiscent of Passchendaele in World War I. Regardless, the main attack started on 8 February. Eisenhower's eighty-five divisions advanced against twenty-six German divisions. Much of the ground was heavily mined and the Allies made good use of the 'flail' tanks designed for blowing mines at Normandy. They also found good use for their Crocodile flamethrowers to clear out German pillboxes along the Siegfried Line.

Remagen Bridge
Hitler had instructed his engineers that all bridges over the Rhine were to be blown up, thus making the Allies advance very difficult. However, the Germans slipped up at the Ludendorff railway bridge at Remagen (near Bonn) on 7 March. Insufficient explosives or a wiring problem resulted in the bridge 'jumping' but not collapsing when the

explosives went off. The US engineers immediately sheeted the railway tracks with timbers. Allied tanks, trucks and soldiers in huge numbers travelled across the bridge establishing a major bridgehead on the eastern bank of the Rhine. Eight thousand troops crossed the bridge in the first twenty-four hours. Eisenhower declared that the bridge was *"worth its weight in gold"*.

Two weeks later the bridge collapsed suddenly into the river, causing the deaths of eighteen army engineers. However, at this stage the bridgehead was established and US engineers had additional pontoon bridges in place. The Allies then took Cologne, which they had heavily bombed on 2 March, miraculously sparing the Cathedral. Three different bridges over the Rhine near Cologne were blown up by the Germans, but the Allies still managed to cross.

Hitler was furious when he heard the news of Remagen Bridge: he reacted by sacking his Commander in Chief Field Marshal Rundstedt and replacing him with Field Marshal Kesselring from the Italian Front. However, no command change was going to change the situation at this stage.

Bombing
An intense bombing campaign by the Allies took place all along the east side of the Rhine during the months of February and March 1945. Cologne, Berlin and Dresden were specifically targeted.

The bombing of Berlin was relentless. 68,000 tons of bombs were dropped on Berlin in this period killing 35,000 people. But Hitler would not surrender. On 13 February Dresden suffered major bomb damage as a result of attacks by the Allies instigated by Russia. Dresden was on their path to Berlin. There has been much discussion since about the morality of bombing Dresden. The city was destroyed and more than 30,000 of its civilians killed both by the bombing and the subsequent firestorm. Dresden had to be completely rebuilt after the war, as indeed did Berlin.

Hitler, for his part, continued to launch V-1 and V-2 rockets into the south of England right up to the end, in the belief that they would influence the outcome of the war. They were certainly very effective: during the last two years of the war, the rockets killed almost 10,000 British civilians. They did not, however, influence the outcome of the war.

During the winter of 1944/45, the Germans flooded the lowlands of the Netherlands as a defensive measure by opening the dykes. This resulted in major food shortages: 15,000 Dutch people died from starvation. Allied bomber aircraft had to be diverted to drop hundreds of tons of food to the beleaguered Dutch, an operation which saved many lives.

With considerable help from Remagen Bridge and US bridge-building engineers, American forces under Patton crossed the southern Rhine in early March; British and Canadian troops under Montgomery did likewise in the north on 23 March. In the centre, American armies under Bradley and Hodges crossed the Rhine into the industrial heartland of the Ruhr Valley. During the last two weeks in March, four million Allied soldiers rolled forward into Germany. The roll was unstoppable and would continue until they met up with Stalin's Russian troops at the River Elbe in central Germany.

On 4 April American armies surrounded **the Ruhr**, Germany's industrial heartland. German Army Group B was trapped within the pocket and they finally surrendered on 18 April, yielding 325,000 prisoners. Hitler's 'fireman', Walter Model, was unable to tackle this fire and on 21 April he walked into a nearby forest and shot himself.

The Germans defended the 'fatherland' to the bitter end, but they were heavily outnumbered. More than one million German soldiers were killed in the spring of 1945. Hitler was now pitifully short of troops on both the Western and Eastern fronts.

Not even the death of President Roosevelt on 12 April 1945 could interrupt the Allied advance. When Goebbels informed Hitler of Roosevelt's death, Goebbels suggested that this was a sign from above that God was on their side. However, it would take more than divine intervention to reverse the course of the war at that stage!

Harry Truman replaced Roosevelt as US President. The contribution of Franklin Delano Roosevelt to America during the Great Depression in the 1930s and in World War II can never be forgotten. He served as President from 1933 to 1945 (no other President served for more than eight years) and is consistently rated as one of the top three US Presidents, along with Abraham Lincoln and George Washington.

The British general Bernard Montgomery had his sights set on Berlin but was ordered by Eisenhower to concentrate on Hamburg and northern Germany. In the south Patton swept forward into Bavaria and on into Austria and Czechoslovakia. Patton was chomping at the bit to attack Berlin and had a major row with Eisenhower when prevented from doing so. American forces in the centre under Bradley and Hodges were in a better position than either Patton or Montgomery to advance on Berlin but were ordered by Eisenhower to mark time (neither advance nor retreat).

THE HOLOCAUST

As the pace of the Allied advance slowed, they had time to look around and what they came across made grim viewing. On 12 April American and British forces liberated the concentration camps at Buchenwald and Bergen-Belsen. There were 10,000 unburied Jewish bodies there and starvation so advanced that a further 15,000 died during the following weeks. Many hardened soldiers were physically sick at the sight before them. Eisenhower was sent for and, having taken time to digest the scene before him, his reaction was to march all local residents through the camps to view what went on under their noses. They were then forced to assist in the burial of the dead. He instructed his own generals to record everything on camera. He had the foresight to realise that, *"in years to come, people will try to deny that this ever happened."* Buchenwald and Bergen-Belsen were only two of the many concentration camps uncovered. Auschwitz and Treblinka in Poland were two of the most infamous.

EASTERN FRONT 1945

The situation on the Eastern Front in January 1945 was similar to Operation Barbarossa in 1941 except that the attack was now in a westerly direction and the aggressors were Russian not German. The German army at this stage was completely outnumbered by Stalin's forces. Hitler could muster three million soldiers between the Wehrmacht, the Volkssturm and the Hungarians. They were supported by 4,000 tanks and 2,000 aircraft with little or no fuel. Ominously advancing on them from the east were five million Russians backed up by 11,000 tanks and 14,000 aircraft.

The Russian advance began on 13 January, spearheaded by Russia's two foremost field marshals in the war: Zhukov and Konev. Zhukov made his name in the defence of Moscow and in the Battles of Stalingrad and Kursk; he later went on to become Stalin's military deputy. Ivan Konev made his name at Kursk and in Ukraine. Zhukov commanded the First Belorussian Front fighting alongside the First Ukrainian Front commanded by Konev. To Zhukov's north, the Second Belorussian Front commanded by Konstantin Rokossovsky was directed at the Baltic Area and northern Germany. Rokossovsky was tall and of much more impressive military bearing than either Zhukov or Konev. He also had a fine war record, having successfully directed Soviet operations in Operation Bagration earlier in the war. He was, however, of Polish origin and for this reason Stalin decided to keep him out of the limelight.

The attack from all sides was methodical and relentless. By the end of February the Russians had reached the Rivers Oder and Neisse, and were now well advanced into Germany. The Russians on the Eastern Front and the Allies on the Western Front between them were now squeezing the life out of Germany's defence.

By the beginning of March Russian troops led by Zhukov and Konev had advanced to the Oder River and were now only forty miles from Berlin. Rokossovsky's troops advanced north of Berlin, meeting up with Montgomery's Allied army. In the south, Russian troops advanced through Hungary, Poland and Austria. As the Russian troops advanced through Poland, they came across the concentration camps at Auschwitz and Treblinka, where the scenes were — if possible — more stomach-churning than at Buchenwald and at Bergen-Belsen.

During the advances on the Eastern Front, the Red Army carried out mass rapes and murders on thousands of German women. This was in revenge for similar atrocities carried out by German soldiers during Operation Barbarossa four years previously. Throughout the spring there was a mass exodus of German women and soldiers to the west. Nobody wanted to be left at the mercy of the Russians!

Stalin was not confident that any agreement he had with Roosevelt would be honoured now that Roosevelt was dead. He decided to give his generals a pep talk. On April 1 Stalin summoned Zhukov and Konev to Moscow. He suggested to his generals that the Americans were intent on taking Berlin first and that they would need to move faster.

He gave them lines of demarcation as far as Lubben. After that, whichever commander drove his army into Berlin first would be honoured. Stalin's pep talk had the necessary effect: the two field marshals were now competing for the ultimate prize of Berlin.

In March the Russians took Danzig, and occupied Poland and most of Czechoslovakia. In April they advanced into Austria, taking Vienna on 13 April. On the same day the American army took Nuremberg, the spiritual home of the Nazi Party in Germany. US troops reached Magdeburg on the River Elbe on 12 April.

American troops shook hands with Konev's Russian forces at the village of Torgau on the Elbe on 26 April. All that remained now was to take Berlin.

Slave labourers in the Buchenwald concentration camp
near Jena. Many had died from malnutrition before
US troops of the 80th Division entered the camp.
Germany, 16 April 1945. Photograph by Harry Miller.

USS *Santa Fe* lays alongside USS *Franklin* rendering
assistance after the carrier had been hit and set on fire
by a Japanese dive bomber, March 1945.

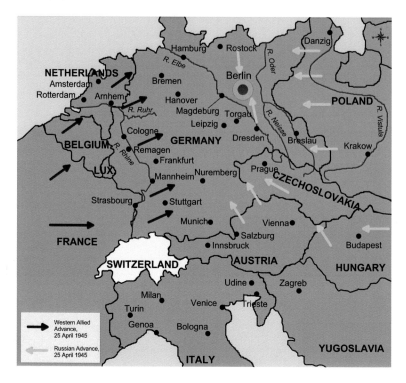

Map 27: Berlin Surrounded 1945

Japan formally surrenders on board USS *Missouri*, 2 September 1945.

BERLIN

At this stage, the German army consisted of boys, old men and the remaining Nazi fanatics who had retreated to make a last ditch stand in Berlin. They faced up to 6.5 million Russians under Zhukov, Konev and Rokossovsky, stretching from the Baltic to the Adriatic.

The Allies on the Western Front were now — in theatre parlance — waiting in the wings. During the month of March they consolidated breakouts on the east side of the Rhine at Wesel (Montgomery), Remagen (Hodges), Oppenheim (Patton) and in the Ruhr Valley (Bradley). They were in an ideal standby position if required. Early in April Eisenhower confirmed to Stalin that he had abandoned his plans to invade Berlin.

At 5:00 a.m. on 16 April, Zhukov launched an artillery attack against the Seelow Heights on the outskirts of Berlin. Later in the day Konev's forces joined in. At this stage there was literally a traffic jam between the two forces, which together comprised a vast Russian army. But the Germans weren't finished. They had withdrawn from their initial trench positions and the original Russian bombardment — which went on for two days — fell on empty trenches. The Germans responded with their own attack, but the vast numbers of Russians eventually triumphed. The **Battle of Seelow Heights** lasted for four days and resulted in the deaths of 30,000 Russians and 12,000 Germans. This was Hitler's dying kick!

By 25 April the Russians had completely encircled Berlin with a twofold objective: to keep the Germans in and to keep the Americans out. They then proceeded to destroy everything within the circle, street by street, building by building. It wasn't long before Berlin was reduced to a sea of rubble. This was a reminder to the remaining Germans of what they had done to Stalingrad in 1942. On 30 April 1945 the Russian flag was flying on the roof of the German Reichstag — an iconic photograph!

Hitler's Final Days
Hitler had moved his headquarters to an underground bunker under the Chancellery in Berlin. He was becoming increasingly deranged. He spent his time moving pieces around a map table planning offensives for armies he no longer had. One of his last orders to the SS was to execute all deserters. Party fanatics spent the early days of April seeking out those they considered to be deserters and hanging them from the nearest lamppost: a humiliating end to their war efforts.

Hitler was joined in the bunker by his mistress Eva Braun, his faithful dog Blondi, Goebbels (later to be joined by his family) and his

Secretary Martin Bormann. Bormann remained loyal to Hitler to the end. He spent his last days writing Hitler's version of the war, and updating the Führer's diary.

Hitler, surprisingly, had given Speer, Himmler and Göring permission to leave. Himmler was quickly captured by Allied troops, at which point he took his own life. On 9 May Göring was captured by US troops.

Meanwhile, back in the bunker, Hitler was preparing for his own death. He requested a priest to marry himself and Eva Braun. They were married early on the morning of 29 April. The following day, after taking leave of his staff, they withdrew to his study. She took a cyanide tablet. Hitler shot himself in the head. The two bodies were taken outside to the Chancellery garden, where they were doused with petrol and set alight as per Hitler's instructions.

Blondi was given a cyanide tablet. Goebbels had earlier been joined in the bunker by his wife Magda and their six children. Magda was besotted by Hitler. All their children had Christian names beginning with the letter 'H'. She could see no future without Hitler. In one of the saddest events of the war, she took the lives of Helga, Hildegard, Helmut, Holdine, Hedwig and Heidrun with cyanide tablets before she herself and her husband ended their lives in similar fashion. Magda Goebbels believed that the children's lives would have been intolerable once Hitler was dead and the war was over.

Once the death of Hitler became known, the commander of the Berlin garrison, General Helmuth Weidling surrendered Berlin to avoid further casualties. He read the following statement: *"On 30 April 1945 the Führer took his own life, abandoning those who had sworn loyalty to him. For every hour you keep fighting, the terrible suffering of the civilian population of Berlin and our injured soldiers will be prolonged. Therefore, in agreement with the high command of the Soviet forces, I call on you to stop fighting immediately."*

Before Hitler died he appointed Admiral Karl Dönitz as President. On 5 May Dönitz sent Hitler's Chief of Operations, General Alfred Jodl, to meet up with Eisenhower to sign a ceasefire. The unconditional surrender was signed on 7 May in the French city of Rheims.

Stalin was furious when he heard the news that Germany had surrendered to the Americans and not to the Russians. On his insistence, a second surrender document was signed in Berlin by Field Marshal Wilhelm Keitel. After several re-drafts, this second surrender was signed in the early hours of 9 May. This was followed by a number of ceasefires being signed throughout Europe. The Channel Islands, Dunkirk, Brest and Lorient, all of which had been garrisoned by the Germans at various stages in the war, were vacated by the Germans once they heard of the surrenders.

Throughout Europe, World War II was finally over!

1945 TIMELINE — EUROPE

01–17 Jan	Germans withdraw from the Ardennes.
16 Jan	US First and Third Armies link up after a month long separation during the Battle of the Bulge.
17 Jan	Soviet troops take Warsaw in Poland.
26 Jan	Soviet troops liberate Auschwitz concentration camp.
04–11 Feb	Yalta conference attended by Roosevelt, Churchill and Stalin.
13/14 Feb	Dresden destroyed by firestorm after Allied bombing raid.
06 Mar	Last German offensive of the war begins to defend oil fields in Hungary.
07 Mar	Allies take Cologne and establish a bridge across the Rhine at Remagen.
30 Mar	Soviet troops capture Danzig.
Apr	Allies discover stolen Nazi art and wealth hidden in German salt mines.
04 Apr	US troops encircle Germans in the Ruhr Valley. Allied offensive in northern Italy.
12 Apr	President Roosevelt dies. Succeeded by Harry Truman. Allies liberate Buchenwald and Bergen-Belsen concentration camps.
13 Apr	Vienna liberated.
16 Apr	Soviet troops begin their final attack on Berlin. Americans enter Nuremberg.
18 Apr	German forces in the Ruhr Valley surrender.
21 Apr	Soviets enter Berlin. Bologna liberated.
26 Apr	Allies free Verona.
28 Apr	Mussolini captured and hanged by Italian Partisans. Allies take Venice.
29 Apr	US Seventh Army liberates Dachau. Allies free Venice. Hitler and Eva Braun get married.
30 Apr	Hitler and Eva Braun commit suicide.
02 May	German troops in Italy surrender.
07 May	Unconditional surrender of all German forces to Allies.
08 May	Official V-E (Victory in Europe) Day.
09 May	Göring captured by members of the US Seventh Army.
23 May	Himmler commits suicide.

05 Jun	Allies divide up Berlin and Germany and take over government.
26 Jun	United Nations Charter signed in San Francisco.
01 Jul	American, British and French troops enter Berlin.
16 Jul	Potsdam Conference begins outside Berlin.
26 Jul	Clement Atlee succeeds Churchill as British Prime Minister.
24 Oct	United Nations is formed.
20 Nov	Nuremberg war crimes trials begin.

WAR IN THE PACIFIC 1945

Allies set about finishing the war by driving the Japanese out of Burma, taking Luzon in the Philippines, and taking the islands of Iwo Jima and Okinawa before finally forcing Japan to surrender by dropping atomic bombs on Hiroshima and Nagasaki.

Burma

At the beginning of 1945 Japanese troops in Burma were fighting a losing battle — a big change from their assault in 1942. They were short of arms and short of supplies. General Slim's army was now a much-improved fighting force and had been strengthened by the arrival of troops from India and from both East and West Africa. Chinese nationalist troops had also arrived into northern Burma to assist the Allies.

The Burma Road was reopened on 28 January and General Slim, intent on driving the Japanese out of Burma, crossed the Irrawaddy River at the end of February. Slim's troops took the important Japanese base at Meiktila and on 20 March British and Chinese troops took Mandalay. They then headed for Burma's capital Rangoon, which they intended to take before the monsoon weather arrived. Rangoon duly fell on 3 May. The Burma campaign, which started so disastrously in 1942, ended in triumph for the Allies. Almost 200,000 Japanese were killed.

The Pacific 1945

At the beginning of 1945 the target of the US forces was the Japanese homeland itself. On the way, they would have to deal with the major obstacles of Iwo Jima and Okinawa. However, first they had some unfinished business in the Philippines. The main island of **Luzon** was still occupied by some 250,000 Japanese under General Tomoyuki Yamashita. On 9 January a huge US force under General Walter Krueger landed on the west coast of Luzon and, with heavy air support, swept inland. They were well supported by Filipino resistance fighters who had remained active throughout the two years of invasion.

Clark Field, in north-west Manila, was taken in the last week of January. Additional troops arrived by parachute, making it possible to secure the inhospitable Bataan Peninsula in early February. Japanese resistance on Corregidor ended on 27 February leaving only the capital Manila. Fighting in Manila was harsh, with the Japanese, as usual, refusing to surrender. They fought doggedly until 13 April when the Americans blew up Fort Drum in Manila Bay. The massive explosion brought fighting in the Philippines to an end. Casualties were heavy on both sides.

The Philippines was back in US hands, fulfilling MacArthur's promise.

Iwo Jima

Iwo Jima is a small volcanic island located midway between Japan and Saipan. As distinct from all of the other islands the Japanese had seized in 1942, Iwo Jima had always been part of the Japanese empire. The Americans invaded the island on 19 February 1945, valuing its airfields as a major asset in their advance on Japan itself. 25,000 Japanese were well prepared for them and the fighting for the next five weeks included some of the fiercest and bloodiest in the Pacific. This was the first American assault on Japanese home territory and the Japanese simply did not consider surrender.

America suffered 25,000 casualties, 6,000 of whom were killed. Of the original Japanese defenders, only 1,000 survived out of a fighting force of 35,000! Fighting came to an end towards the end of March.

Iwo Jima will always be remembered by the photograph of American marines raising the US flag on top of Mount Suribachi on 26 March. This was one of the iconic photographs of the war.

Okinawa

Okinawa is an island seventy miles long by eight miles wide, located 350 miles south of the Japanese mainland. The Americans saw it as an ideal launch pad for an attack on Japan itself, but first they had to conquer it and that was not going to be easy. The Japanese attitude to surrender — which was *"no surrender"* — was a major concern to the Americans. Thinking ahead to the forthcoming assault on Japan itself, the Americans knew they had to capture Okinawa. The island was a key location as it was also within range of the Chinese coast and Formosa, therefore the Japanese were going to defend it to the death. They poured 100,000 troops into the island and conscripted many of the local population of 500,000 to assist them. Two thousand aircraft, many of them prepared for kamikaze action, were made available. In a change of tactic, they did not defend the beaches as strongly as before, instead they mounted powerful defences inland. The Japanese referred to the Battle of Okinawa as the 'Typhoon of Steel'. This referred to the ferocity of the fighting, the intensity of the kamikaze attacks and the huge numbers of casualties on both sides.

The Americans did not underestimate the enormity of the task. 300,000 troops transported by a fleet of 1,400 ships were prepared for the invasion. The invasion began on 1 April and fighting continued relentlessly until mid-June. The Japanese had spread their forces throughout the island. They fought savagely, but the Americans made steady progress.

Losses on the Japanese side were huge. 77,000 Japanese soldiers were killed or committed suicide. 150,000 of the local population also died. Kamikaze attacks reached a new intensity: an ominous sign for the battle ahead! Several Japanese commanders committed hara-kiri, a ritualised form of suicide.

In comparison, American losses were relatively light. 14,000 American soldiers died out of an overall casualty figure of 65,000.

Japanese resistance ceased on 21 June, bringing an end to the bloodiest battle in the Pacific war.

In May Australian troops landed on Borneo, overrunning the oilfields there. Now all that remained was the Japanese homeland itself.

THE END IN JAPAN

While air raids on Tokyo were intensified, it was obvious that the Japanese were not going to surrender. Their refusal to surrender meant they would have to be invaded. The Americans knew from Iwo Jima, Okinawa and the rest of the Pacific war that an invasion of the magnitude required would result in unimaginable slaughter on both sides. Hundreds of thousands of men would die — perhaps even a million!

There simply had to be an alternative solution!

Atomic Bomb: Hiroshima
For several years previously, several countries — including Germany and the US — had been experimenting with the possibility of splitting the atom and thereby creating an atomic bomb. In 1939 Albert Einstein, who ironically had emigrated from Germany to the US, warned President Roosevelt that Germany was experimenting with the development of an atomic bomb, which would have the power of 1,000 tons of TNT. It would later be revealed to have a much greater power!

Panoramic view of Hiroshima showing the devastation after an atomic bomb – the first ever used in warfare – was dropped on 6 August 1945.

A dense column of smoke rises more than 60,000 feet into the air over the Japanese port of Nagasaki, the result of an atomic bomb dropped from a US B-29 Superfortress on 9 August 1945.

From that moment on, American scientists had been working on the development of an atomic bomb: an initiative called The Manhattan Project.

When Truman succeeded President Roosevelt in April, there were many who wondered how he would measure up to his highly-regarded predecessor. He turned out to be firm and decisive, and he was certainly no shrinking violet! Despite the extreme repercussions of using the bomb, he gave the order to proceed with the project.

The bomb was first tested in the desert of New Mexico in mid-July. It was frighteningly successful. The blast it generated was equal to 20,000 tons of TNT. Observers saw a huge light brighter than the midday sun. All of the colours of the rainbow lit up the sky.

News of the successful test was passed on to President Truman, who was attending the Potsdam Conference. He decided to inform the Japanese of the successful test. He informed them that a similar atomic bomb would be dropped on Japan if they did not surrender. The message was ignored.

On 6 August the B-29 Superfortress *Enola Gay* departed the island of Tinian in the Marianas carrying the atomic bomb. The bomb was released over Hiroshima, where it exploded at a height of 2,000 feet. It was a devastating explosion: killing 118,000 people, injuring 79,000, and leaving a completely devastated landscape. Most of the injured died later from radiation. Still the Japanese refused to surrender!

Russia Joins Pacific War
At that time, out of the blue, Stalin and his Russian army arrived to join the Pacific war. He had promised President Roosevelt that he would come to his assistance three months after the war in Europe had ended, and he showed up supposedly to keep his promise. In fact, he appeared on the scene to see what he could gain territorially. On 8 August Russia declared war on Japan. She launched an attack on the Japanese in Manchukuo and, with the advantage of huge superiority in tanks and aircraft, she quickly defeated the Japanese Kwantung Army. The Americans were disappointed to see Stalin arriving on the scene. They had fought long and hard to achieve a victory, which was now just around the corner, and they were appalled at the thought of Stalin stealing their thunder.

Atomic Bomb: Nagasaki
Since there had been no response from the Japanese to the bombing of Hiroshima, on 9 August the Americans dropped a second atomic bomb, this time on Nagasaki. 73,000 people were killed and 75,000 injured. While some of the Japanese officers continued to be as belligerent as ever, asking that the war continue until death, the Japanese Emperor

Hirohito — who held a god-like position in Japan — decided that his country must surrender.

In his first and only radio broadcast to his people, he said: "*Should we continue to fight, not only would it result in an ultimate collapse and obliteration of the Japanese nation, but also it would lead to the total extinction of human civilisation.*" Such was his position that nobody would go against his wishes. The surprise was that he didn't intervene earlier.

Japan Surrenders

On 15 August Japan surrendered. The war in the Pacific was over after forty-four months of fighting. This date would be commemorated evermore as V-J Day (Victory in Japan Day).

On 2 September a document of surrender was signed by General Douglas MacArthur and representatives of the Japanese government on board the American battleship USS *Missouri*. MacArthur took control of the Pacific.

World War II — which had lasted for six years and cost the lives of more than fifty million people — was finally over!

1945 TIMELINE — PACIFIC

03 Jan	General MacArthur placed in command of all US ground forces. Admiral Nimitz in command of all naval forces in preparation for planned assaults against Iwo Jima, Okinawa and Japan itself.
04 Jan	British occupy Akyab in Burma.
09 Jan	US Sixth Army invades Lingayen Gulf on Luzon in the Philippines.
11 Jan	Air raid against Japanese base in Indochina by US carrier-based planes.
28 Jan	Burma Road reopened.
03 Feb	US Sixth Army attacks Japanese in Manila.
16 Feb	US troops recapture Bataan in the Philippines.
19 Feb	US troops invade Iwo Jima.
01 Mar	US submarine sinks Japanese merchant ship carrying supplies for Allied POWs.
02 Mar	US air troops capture Corregidor in the Philippines.
03 Mar	US and Filipino troops invade Manila.
09 Mar	Part of Tokyo erupts in flames after being firebombed by B-29 planes.
10 Mar	US Eighth Army invades Zamboanga Peninsula on Mindanao in the Philippines.

20 Mar	British troops liberate Mandalay in Burma.
27 Mar	B-29s lay mines in Japan's Shimonoseki Strait to disrupt shipping.
01 Apr	US Tenth Army invades Okinawa — last amphibious landing of the war.
07 Apr	US carrier-based fighters sink the Japanese super battleship *Yamato.*
12 Apr	President Roosevelt dies, succeeded by Harry Truman.
03 May	Rangoon falls.
20 May	Japanese begin withdrawal from China.
25 May	US Joint Chiefs of Staff approve Operation Olympic, the Invasion of Japan.
09 Jun	Japanese Premier Suzuki announces that Japan will fight to the bitter end — that there will be no unconditional surrender!
18 Jun	Japanese resistance ends in Mindanao.
22 Jun	Japanese resistance ends in Okinawa.
28 Jun	MacArthur's headquarters announces the end of all Japanese resistance in the Philippines.
05 Jul	Liberation of Philippines declared.
10 Jul	1,000 bomber raids against Japan begin.
14 Jul	The first US naval bombardment of Japanese home islands.
16 Jul	Atomic bomb successfully tested in the US.
26 Jul	Components of the first atomic bomb unloaded at Tinian island in the South Pacific.
29 Jul	Japanese submarine sinks the cruiser USS *Indianapolis*, resulting in the loss of 880 crewman.
06 Aug	First atomic bomb dropped on Hiroshima, Japan, from a B-29 flown by Colonel Paul Tibbets.
08 Aug	Russia declares war on Japan exactly three months after war in Europe ends. Russia invades Manchukuo.
09 Aug	Second atomic bomb is dropped on Nagasaki from a B-29 flown by Major Charles Sweeney. Japan seeks immediate peace.
15 Aug	Japan accepts unconditional surrender. General MacArthur appointed to head the occupation forces in Japan.
27 Aug	B-29s drop supplies to Allied POWs in China.
29 Aug	US troops land near Tokyo to begin occupation of Japan. Russia shoots down a B-29 dropping supplies to POWs in Korea.
30 Aug	The British reoccupy Hong Kong.
02 Sep	Formal Japanese surrender ceremony on board the USS *Missouri.* President Truman declares official V-J (Victory in Japan) Day.
04 Sep	Japanese troops on Wake Island surrender.
05 Sep	British troops land in Singapore.
08 Sep	MacArthur enters Tokyo.
09 Sep	Japanese in Korea surrender.
13 Sep	Japanese in Burma surrender.

WORLD WAR II — ESTIMATED DEATH TOLL

[Note: figures do not include deaths from famine or disease]

Allied Forces		Axis Powers	
Soviet Union	18,668,000	Germany	6,501,000
China	10,357,000	Japan	2,650,000
Poland	5,860,000	Hungary	564,000
Yugoslavia	1,027,000	Romania	500,000
France	600,000	Italy	492,400
Great Britain	450,900	Austria	370,000
United States	419,400	Finland	85,000
Czechoslovakia	340,000	Bulgaria	21,500
Dutch East Indies	311,500		11,183,900
Burma	252,600		
Greece	206,900		
Netherlands	194,000		
Philippines	191,000		
Malaya and Singapore	100,000		
Ethiopia	100,000		
Belgium	88,000		
India	87,000		
Canada	43,600		
Australia	40,400		
Portuguese Timor	40,000		
Albania	30,000		

Papua New Guinea	15,000
South Africa	11,900
New Zealand	11,700
Norway	10,200
Thailand	7,600
Denmark	6,000
Egypt	1,100
Guam	1,000
	39,471,800

Allied	**Forces**	**39,471,800**
Axis	**Powers**	**11,183,900**
	TOTAL	**50,655,700**

CHAPTER 19

The Aftermath of World War II

It was obvious for some time that major differences in outlook between the Allied forces the United States, Britain and Russia would have to be reconciled when the war ended. The first major conference to discuss the postwar world took place at Yalta in Crimea in February 1945, several months before the war ended. It was attended by Roosevelt, Churchill and Stalin. A further meeting took place at Potsdam in Germany in July. In the short intervening period, much had changed. The war had ended. President Roosevelt had died and been replaced by Harry Truman, who saw communism as the major threat in the world. Clement Attlee replaced Churchill as Prime Minister in a democratic voting process in Britain. Stalin was the only one of the Big Three still in command and he wasn't shy about calling the shots! He was arguing from a very strong position: the Nazis might not have been defeated for decades without the enormous input from the Soviet Union.

It was agreed at the various conferences that when the war ended, Berlin would be divided into four sectors, each controlled by a separate country (the USSR, the US, Britain and France). Stalin ensured that the division heavily favoured the Soviet Union. Germany itself would be divided into West Germany and East Germany, and the latter would be controlled by the Soviet Union.

Stalin helped himself to a large chunk of eastern Poland, suggesting that the Poles could compensate themselves by taking a slice of Germany on their western side. The Soviet Union took control of the Baltic states of Latvia, Estonia and Lithuania. Stalin proceeded to install communist governments in each of the Eastern Bloc countries that he had taken towards the end of the war. By 1948 East Prussia, Poland, East Germany, Czechoslovakia, Hungary, Romania and Bulgaria were under Soviet control. The Iron Curtain had descended over Europe. Yugoslavia and Albania, although outside the Iron Curtain, were under separate communist control. The Cold War between the US-led NATO countries and the Soviet-led Warsaw Pact countries had begun!

OTHER PACIFIC COUNTRIES

Several Pacific countries were in turmoil during and after World War II.

The French Vichy Government ceded control of **French Indochina** to the Japanese in 1941. When the war was over in August 1945, the Allies took back control of the country from the Japanese, and returned it to France the following year. The French eventually withdrew from Indochina in 1954 and the Geneva conference of that year paved the way for the modern-day countries of Vietnam, Laos and Cambodia to establish independence. Later the same year, however, they were all dragged into the war in Vietnam.

Korea was a Japanese colony for 35 years. This rule ended with the victory of the Allies in 1945. The Allies could not agree on Korea's future and, as a temporary arrangement, Soviet troops occupied the area north of the 38th parallel while US troops occupied the area to the south. In 1950 the South declared independence, which sparked an invasion by North Korea. In 1953 an armistice ended the Korean War, which cost more than two million lives. The problems between North and South Korea continue to this day.

Between 1895 and 1945, the island of **Taiwan** (Formosa) was a dependency of the Empire of Japan. When World War II ended in 1945, Taiwan was placed under the control of the Chinese Nationalist Party. In 1952 Japan formally renounced all territorial rights to Taiwan in the San Francisco Peace Treaty.

Indonesia (formerly Dutch East Indies)
When World War II began, Indonesia — as the name 'Dutch East Indies' indicates — was a colony of the Netherlands. It was a wealthy country with major deposits of oil and minerals. The Japanese, who desperately required the oil, attacked the East Indies in December 1941. The Allies, who had major commitments in the war in Europe, were unable to offer the Dutch much assistance and by March 1942 Indonesia had fallen to the Japanese. Japan remained in control until the war in the Pacific ended in September 1945.

Whereas the Dutch expected to retake control at this stage, the Indonesians — led by their founding father Sukarno — had other ideas. They wanted independence and they were willing to fight for it. The struggle between them lasted from 1945 until 1949, when the Dutch finally conceded the territory. President Sukarno became first president in 1945 and continued in office until 1967.

THE NUREMBERG TRIALS

The Nuremberg Trials were a series of military tribunals held by the Allied forces after World War II to prosecute prominent members of the political, military and economic leadership of Nazi Germany for

Churchill waves to crowds in Whitehall on the day he broadcast to the nation that the war with Germany had been won, 8 May 1945.

Jubilant crowds in New York's Times Square on V-J Day in 1945 after Japan surrendered.

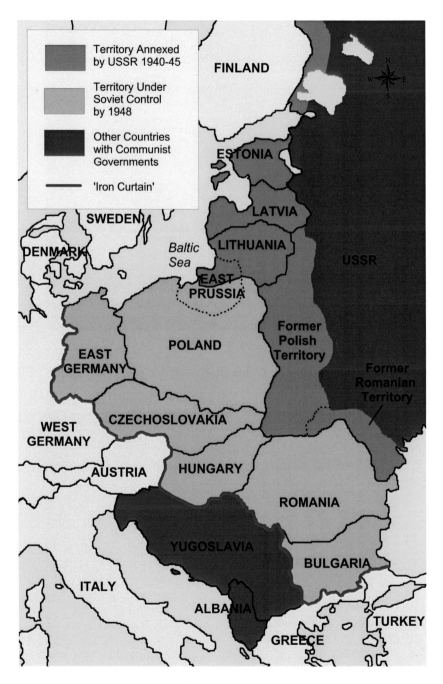

Map 28: Postwar Europe

crimes against humanity committed during the war. The trials, which took place from 20 November 1945 to 1 October 1946 were held in the Palace of Justice in Nuremberg, Germany. Nuremberg was considered the birthplace of Nazism and it had emerged from the war virtually unscathed by bomb damage. In the main trial, twenty-three top Germans were charged with crimes against humanity. Hitler, Himmler and Goebbels were not included since they had already committed suicide. Twelve of the defendants were sentenced to death by hanging. Three were found not guilty; the others, including Rudolf Hess, were sentenced to life imprisonment.

There were mixed feelings about the Nuremberg Trials. Only Germans were tried. Many felt that Russia and Japan should be on trial also: Russia for the Katyn Forest Massacre and Japan for the Nanking Massacre.

The Marshall Plan

By the end of World War II, much of Europe and Asia was devastated.

Massive territorial damage had occurred, mainly in Germany, Russia, Poland, France, Britain, Italy, Japan and China. The only countries that prospered as a result of the war were the United States and Canada. They suffered no territorial damage while their industries were working flat out to meet the needs of the other Allied countries.

Britain and the US pursued a policy of industrial disarmament in western Germany in the years 1945–48. This resulted in European economic stagnation and delayed European recovery for several years.

After they arrived home, the Americans realised that they would have to come to the aid of the Allied countries financially. The Allies were broke and, as long as that situation remained, American order books would remain empty!

On the question of whether Germany should be assisted financially or not, former President Herbert Clark Hoover reported back from Europe in 1947: *"The whole economy of Europe is interlinked with the German economy through the exchange of raw materials and manufactured goods. The productivity of Europe cannot be restored without the restoration of Germany as a contributor to that productivity."*

Furthermore, the disastrous impact of the Treaty of Versailles had not been forgotten: it humiliated and economically crippled Germany, which created the opportunity for Hitler and the Nazi Party to gain popularity.

General George C. Marshall had moved from his position of Commander in Chief of the Allied forces in Europe during the war to the political position of US Secretary of State when the war ended. Marshall initiated the European Recovery Program (commonly referred to as the Marshall Plan), in which the United States provided economic support to help build European economies, including Germany's. The Soviet Union was also offered aid, but Stalin declined it and — under instruction from Stalin — the Eastern Bloc countries reluctantly followed suit. By controlling the economies of the Eastern Bloc countries, Stalin could effectively dictate the other aspects of communist policy and life.

All of the European countries, including the neutral countries Sweden, Ireland and Switzerland, were offered aid in the form of grants or loans, but not all of them accepted. The one country not offered aid was Spain which, since the end of the Spanish Civil War in 1939, had remained a dictatorship under Franco.

The Marshall Plan was initiated in 1948, and the period 1948 to 1952 saw the fastest period of growth in European history. Industrial production increased by thirty-five per cent while agricultural production surpassed pre-war levels. The amount of construction work, much of it rebuilding towns and cities destroyed in the war, rose to unprecedented levels. Western Europe embarked on an unparalleled two decades of growth that saw standards of living increase dramatically.

Separately to the Marshall Plan, the US provided financial assistance to the Asian countries of China, Japan, India, Pakistan, Indonesia, South Korea and the Philippines. Financial help was also provided to Israel and to some of the Middle East countries.

The total of American grants and loans to the rest of the world from 1945 to 1953 came to $44.3 billion: a vast sum of money at that time!

There are some who argue that America did not have to embark on the Marshall Plan. This may be true, but from a financial perspective it was a very enlightened viewpoint since she had benefited enormously from the war and depended hugely on the European economy as a market for US trade.

The last of these loans was finally cleared in recent decades!

Bibliography

A Woman in Berlin, Anonymous. Virago Press, 2005.

A Coward If I Return, A Hero If I Fall: Stories of Irishmen in World War I, Neil Richardson. O'Brien Press, Dublin, 2010.

All Hell Let Loose: The World At War 1939–45, Max Hastings. Harper Collins, London, 2011.

Behind the Green Curtain: Ireland's Phoney Neutrality During World War II, T. Ryle Dwyer, Gill & Macmillan, Dublin, 2009.

Berlin At War, Life and Death in Hitler's Capital, 1939-45, Roger Moorehouse. Vintage Books, London, 2010.

Berlin, The Downfall 1945, Antony Beevor. Penguin Books, London, 2003.

Battles of World War II, Documenting World War II, Neil Tonge. Wayland, London, 2007.

World War II Behind Closed Doors: Stalin, the Nazis, and the West, Laurence Rees. BBC Books, London, 2008.

Bloodlands: Europe Between Hitler and Stalin, Timothy Snyder. Vintage Books, London, 2010.

Borrowed Time: The Story of Britain Between The Wars, Roy Hattersley. Little Brown Book Group, London, 2007.

Churchill, Roy Jenkins. Pan McMillan, London, 2001.

D-Day: The Battle for Normandy, Antony Beevor. Viking/Penguin, London, 2009.

Exorcising Hitler: The Occupation and Denazification of Germany, Frederick Taylor. Bloomsbury Publishing, London, 2011.

German Campaigns of World War II, Chris Bishop/Adam Warner. Grange Books, Kent, England, 2001.

Goodbye To All That, Robert Graves. Penguin Books, London, 1960.

HHhH, Laurent Binet, Harvill Secker. London, 2012.

Hitler: A Short Biography, A.N.Wilson. Harper Press, London, 2012.

Liberation: The Bitter Road to Freedom, Europe 1944–1945, William I. Hitchcock. Faber and Faber, London, 2009.

Military Effectiveness, Volume 2, The Interwar Period, Allan R. Millett/Williamson Murray. Cambridge University Press, New York, 2010.

Nazi Germany and the Jews, 1933–1945, Saul Friedländer. Orion Books, London, 2009.

Night, Elie Wiesel. Hill and Wang/Farrar, Straus and Giroux, New York, 2006.

Over The Top: Great Battles of the First World War, Martin Marix Evans. Acturus Publishing Ltd., London, 2002.

Paper Promises: Debt, Money and the New World Order, Philip Coggan. Allen Lane/Penguin, London, 2011.

Stalin: The Court of the Red Tsar, Simon Sebag Montefiore. Weidenfeld & Nicholson, London, 2003.

Stalin's General: The Life of Georgy Zhukov, Geoffrey Roberts. Icon Books, London, 2012.

Stalingrad, Antony Beevor. Penguin Books, London, 1999.

Storm of War: A New History of the Second World War, Andrew Roberts. Allen Lane/Penguin, 2009.

The Battle of Britain: Five Months that Changed History, May–October 1940, James Holland. Transworld Publishers, London, 2010.

The Bombing War, Europe 1939–1945, Richard Overy, Allen Lane/Penguin, London, 2013.

The Diary of a Young Girl, Anne Frank. Penguin Books, London, 1997.

The End: Germany 1944–45, Ian Kershaw, Penguin Books, London, 2012.

The Faces of World War I, Max Arthur. Octopus Publishing Group, London, 2007.

The First World War: An Illustrated History, A.J.P. Taylor. Penguin Books, London, 1963.

The First World War, A New Illustrated History, Hew Strachan. Pocket Books/Simon & Schuster, London, 2006.

The Illustrated History of WWII, John Ray. Weidenfeld & Nicolson, London, 2003.

The Long Road Home: The Aftermath of the Second World War, Ben Shephard. Vintage Books, London, 2012.

The Raj At War, A People's History of India's Second World War, Yasmin Khan. The Bodley Head, 2015.

The Second World War In Photographs, Richard Holmes in association with The Imperial War Museum. Carlton Books, London, 2000.

The Taste of War: World War Two and the Battle for Food, Lizzie Collingham. Allen Lane, London, 2011.

The Third Reich: A Chronicle, Richard Overy. Quercus, London, 2012.

The Victory in Europe Experience, Julian Thompson. Carlton Books, London, 2005.

The Years of Extermination: Nazi Germany and the Jews 1939–1945, Saul Friedländer. Orion Books Ltd., London, 2008.

The War of the World: History's Age of Hatred, Niall Ferguson. Allen Lane/Penguin, London, 2006.

The World War I Story, Chris McNab. The History Press, United Kingdom, 2011.

Turning The Tide: Decisive Battles of the Second World War, Nigel Cawthorne. Arcturus Publishing, London, 2002

Warlords: The Heart of Conflict 1939–1945, Simon Berthon and Joanna Potts. Methuen Publishing, London, 2005.

World At War 1914–1939, Duncan Hill (Editor). Welcome Rain Publishers/Transatlantic Press, Hertfordshire, 2011.

World War One: A Short History, Norman Stone. Penguin Books, London, 2008.

World War II, Reg Grant. Dorling Kindersley Ltd., London, 2008.

With Our Backs To The Wall: Victory and Defeat in 1918, David Stevenson. Allen Lane/Penguin, 2011.

Why The Allies Won, Richard Overy. Pimlico, London, 1995.

Index

31 YEARS OF HELL!

1914–1945

If you enjoyed this book, please post a review on
Amazon and Goodreads.

Thank you for your custom!

www.31YearsOfHell.com

www.facebook.com/31YearsOfHell

www.twitter.com/WorldWarBook